Acclaim for *The World's Most Dangerous Place*:

'Fergusson has a talent for shedding light in dark places. While most reporters have opted to stay away, Fergusson has risked his life to cover the ground and, an even greater achievement, succeeded in making the Somali mess understandable and relevant. It is this insight, alongside his harrowing account of life in the grief zone that gives Fergusson's book its power'
Anthony Sattin, *Observer*

'Essential reading for those who seek to counter the menace. With ingenuity and no little courage he has travelled far and wide, delving into the soul of a ravaged community'
The Economist

'An elegant writer, with a scholarly understanding of history, he brings to terrible light the catastrophe that is Somalia'
Caroline Moorehead, *Spectator*

'Coruscating reportage ... such truly brilliant investigative work offers the seeds, the suggestions of remedies for the contagion beneath the reporter's microscope'
Roger Hutchinson, *Scotsman*

'One of the best narratives of discovery I have read for years. The sense of place is acute, the characters and landscapes vivid ... rivals Ryszard Kapuscinski and Robert Byron at their best'
Robert Fox, *Evening Standard*

'Riveting ... Fergusson rounds out this invaluable work by noting the glimmers of hope appearing'
Publishers Weekly

Also by James Fergusson

Kandahar Cockney
The Vitamin Murders
A Million Bullets
Taliban

THE WORLD'S MOST DANGEROUS PLACE

James Fergusson

BLACK SWAN

TRANSWORLD PUBLISHERS
61–63 Uxbridge Road, London W5 5SA
A Random House Group Company
www.transworldbooks.co.uk

THE WORLD'S MOST DANGEROUS PLACE
A BLACK SWAN BOOK: 9780552777803

First published in Great Britain
in 2013 by Bantam Press
an imprint of Transworld Publishers
Black Swan edition published 2014

This book is a work of non-fiction. In some limited cases names have been changed
solely to protect the privacy and security of others. The author has stated to the
publishers that, except in such minor respects not affecting the substantial
accuracy of the work, the contents of this book are true.

A CIP catalogue record for this book
is available from the British Library.

Addresses for Random House Group Ltd companies outside the UK
can be found at: www.randomhouse.co.uk
The Random House Group Ltd Reg. No. 954009

The Random House Group Limited supports the Forest Stewardship Council®
(FSC®), the leading international forest-certification organisation. Our books
carrying the FSC label are printed on FSC®-certified paper. FSC is the only
forest-certification scheme supported by the leading environmental organisations,
including Greenpeace. Our paper procurement policy can be found at
www.randomhouse.co.uk/environment

Typeset in 11.5/14pt Granjon by Falcon Oast Graphic Art Ltd.
Printed and bound by CPI Group (UK) Ltd, Croydon, CR0 4YY.

2 4 6 8 10 9 7 5 3 1

For Fergus

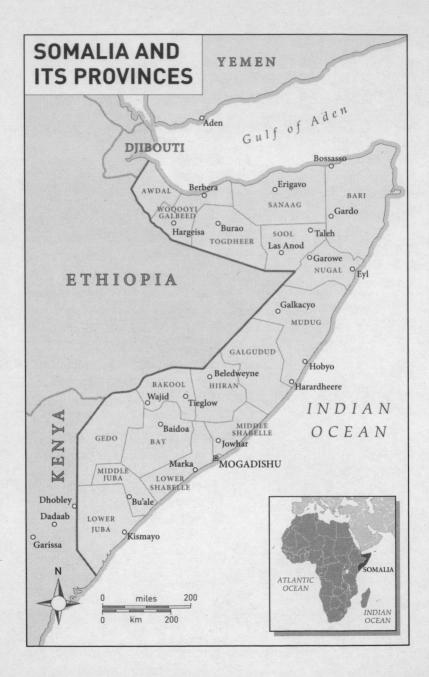

SOMALIA AND ITS PROVINCES

YEMEN

Gulf of Aden

Aden

DJIBOUTI

Bossasso

AWDAL

Berbera

Erigavo

BARI

WOQOOYI
GALBEED

SANAAG

Gardo

Hargeisa

Burao

SOOL

Taleh

TOGDHEER

Las Anod

Garowe

NUGAL

Eyl

ETHIOPIA

Galkacyo

MUDUG

GALGUDUD

Hobyo

BAKOOL

Beledweyne

HIIRAN

Wajid

Tieglow

Harardheere

INDIAN
OCEAN

Baidoa

MIDDLE
SHABELLE

GEDO

BAY

Jowhar

MIDDLE
JUBA

Marka

MOGADISHU

LOWER
SHABELLE

KENYA

Dhobley

Bu'ale

Dadaab

LOWER
JUBA

Garissa

Kismayo

N

miles

0   200

km

0   200

ATLANTIC
OCEAN

SOMALIA

INDIAN
OCEAN

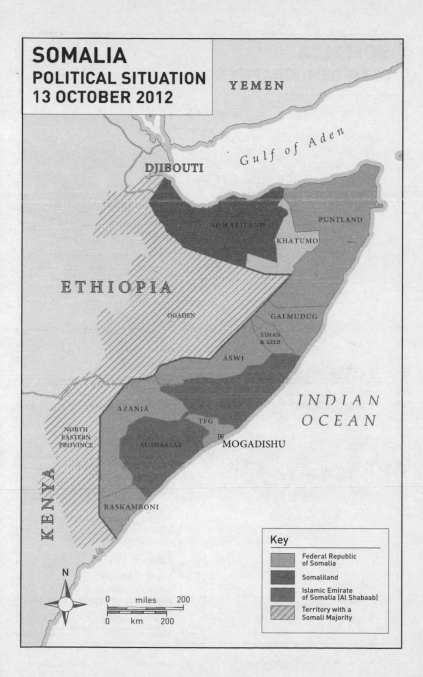

SOMALIA
POLITICAL SITUATION
13 OCTOBER 2012

YEMEN

Gulf of Aden

DJIBOUTI

SOMALILAND

PUNTLAND

KHATUMO

ETHIOPIA

OGADEN

GALMUDUG

XIMAN
& XEEB

ASWJ

INDIAN
OCEAN

AZANIA

TFG

NORTH
EASTERN
PROVINCE

AL-SHABAAB

MOGADISHU

KENYA

RASKAMBONI

N

0   miles   200
0   km   200

Key

Federal Republic
of Somalia

Somaliland

Islamic Emirate
of Somalia (Al Shabaab)

Territory with a
Somali Majority

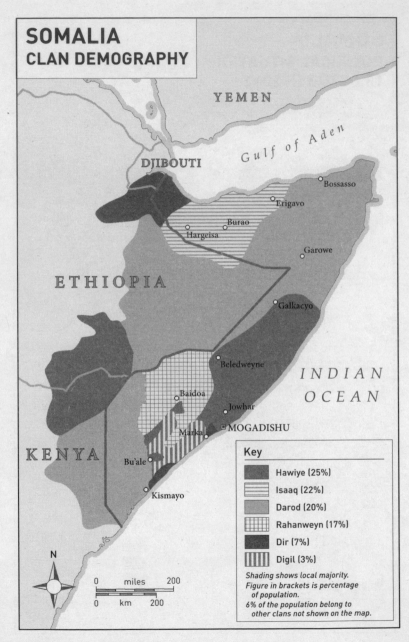

SOMALIA
CLAN DEMOGRAPHY

YEMEN

Gulf of Aden

DJIBOUTI

Bossasso

Erigavo

Burao

Hargeisa

ETHIOPIA

Garowe

Galkacyo

Beledweyne

INDIAN OCEAN

Baidoa

Jowhar

Marka

MOGADISHU

Bu'ale

KENYA

Kismayo

N

0 miles 200

0 km 200

Key

Hawiye (25%)

Isaaq (22%)

Darod (20%)

Rahanweyn (17%)

Dir (7%)

Digil (3%)

Shading shows local majority.
Figure in brackets is percentage
of population.
6% of the population belong to
other clans not shown on the map.

Source: CIA World Fact Book

Contents

Introduction

After sixteen years, off and on, of writing about Afghanistan and the Taliban, the Horn of Africa felt a natural destination to me. In 2008 when a populist, al-Qaida-linked Islamist movement called al-Shabaab took over the southern half of Somalia, including the country's capital, Mogadishu, the parallels with the Taliban were immediately obvious. It wasn't just that Mullah Omar's militants had also emerged from the poor, neglected south of their country to take over Kabul in 1996. Al-Shabaab explicitly modelled themselves on the Taliban. Indeed, many of the new movement's leaders had fought alongside them against US led forces in the early 2000s; and just as the Taliban had once sheltered Osama bin Laden, so al-Shabaab welcomed senior members of al-Qaida into their fold.

In early 2010, as America's drone war in the mountainous borderlands of north-west Pakistan began to heat up, al-Qaida fighters were reported to be 'streaming' out of that region towards Yemen and Somalia, which were said to offer the terrorists many more hiding places than 'Af-Pak' was now able to. It was these reports that finally prompted me to come to Somalia. The Horn of Africa was the battlefield in the War on Terror that mattered now – the next chapter in a story I have been following for a third of my life.

My interest in Somalia was not new. The first TV images of that country's terrible civil war in the early 1990s were not easily forgettable. The feral violence, and the astoundingly destroyed urban landscape against which it was set, were unlike anything that has occurred in my lifetime, with the possible exception of Grozny. That may be why Somalia, so often labelled 'the world's most failed state', still occupies a special, dark place in the imaginations of so many of my generation of Westerners. When I explained my new project to a journalist friend in London, who had spent many years covering the danger zones of South America, she replied: 'Mogadishu? That's one of those places that gives me nightmares, even though I've never been there.'

What has happened to Somalia since the civil war stands as a kind of cautionary tale for grown-ups, a vision of the anarchy that we too can expect should our own systems of governance ever be allowed to collapse. There has, famously, been no properly functioning central government in Mogadishu for over two decades. For the last several years, Afghanistan has come 179th in Transparency International's annual Corruption Perceptions Index, an international league table that measures the level of graft in the public life of each of the world's 180 nations; only one country has consistently ranked lower. An African Taliban, at war in a country more corrupt than Afghanistan! That was a place I was very curious to see.

Mogadishu lived up to expectations when I got there. It truly was the stuff of nightmares, particularly on my second visit in July 2011, when the southern half of the country was in the grip of a famine said to be the worst for sixty years. Refugees were pouring into the capital from the drought zones looking for help, even as trench warfare between al-Shabaab and the government's forces backed by AMISOM, the Ugandan-led African Union Mission in Somalia, was raging across the city's centre. A British photographer I met, an experienced Africa hand based in Kampala, observed that however often the four Horsemen of the Apocalypse rode out into the world, Somalia was where they always came back to, because this was where they were stabled; this was their home. War, famine, pestilence and death were indeed constants that summer, and Somalia really did seem to be the world's most dangerous place.

By the time this book went to press in late 2012, however, things looked a little different. So much had changed since I began my dizzying journey through the Somali nation, a research project that took me to nine different countries across four continents, and still only scratched the surface. In August 2011 al-Shabaab, to the amazement of most in the international community, suddenly withdrew from Mogadishu, and have been in retreat ever since. At the end of 2011, the armies of Somalia's southern and western neighbours, Kenya and Ethiopia, joined forces with AMISOM, forming an alliance that by September 2012 was poised to capture the economically vital port of Kismayo, al-Shabaab's most important stronghold.

A handful of hardliners were expected to mount a heroic last stand against the infidel invaders, as remnants of al-Qaida and the Taliban had done in Kandahar against US-led forces in 2001. But few Somalia-watchers thought Kismayo would hold out for long. In Mogadishu, crucially, the military endgame in the south coincided with the winding up of the Transitional Federal Government, the TFG, whose UN-backed mandate had expired after eight years in office. In September, a newly selected parliament voted to replace President Sheikh Sharif Sheikh Ahmed with Hassan Sheikh Mohamud, a little known university professor who used to work as a consultant for the UN. The newcomer, a moderate Islamist with links to the Muslim Brotherhood, is admired for his perceived lack of corruption as well as for the fact that, unlike most educated Somalis, he did not flee Mogadishu during the civil war. His election was against all expectations. The incumbent, President Sheikh Sharif, was rumoured to have many supporters in the Gulf who had reportedly spent $7m in bribes in a bid to secure his re-election.[1] It was the first genuine presidential poll in a generation, representing what the UN Special Envoy Augustine Mahiga called 'an unprecedented opportunity for peace'.

There are other reasons for cautious optimism. So many of Mogadishu's long-abandoned seafront villas are being rebuilt, in many cases by owners returning from twenty years of refugee exile, that the city is experiencing a minor property boom. Piracy in the Indian Ocean, although far from eradicated, appears to have peaked thanks to land-based efforts by the regional Puntland government and cleverer counter-piracy measures at sea. Even the threat of further famine receded thanks to unusually kind winter rains. By the end of 2012, in short, Somalia no longer looked quite as dangerous as it had done just a year previously – and I still worry that the title of my book will be seen by some (such as the taxi driver who took me to task over it in Minneapolis, home to America's largest Somali community) as unfairly negative.

I decided to let the title stand, however, for two reasons. First, the gains of 2011–12 are all perilously fragile, and could easily be reversed. The process of political reform was flawed from the start, with even the UN admitting that the clan elders had rigged the selection of the new parliament through bribery, intimidation and violence: a dispiriting case of *plus ça change*, in other words. Some two-thirds of MPs in the new parliament served in the previous one. Rivalry between the clans may be in abeyance but is hardly eliminated. The challenges facing the untried new president are huge, and the possibility of another cycle of communal blood-letting remains. Will Somalia's new dawn turn out to be yet another false one?

After all, al-Shabaab are far from defeated, despite their recent territorial losses, and seem unlikely to disappear as an insurgency. Indeed, they had already begun the tactical switch from conventional war-fighting towards a deadly, Taliban-style guerrilla campaign in the summer of 2011. In September 2012, a spokesman for al-Shabaab immediatcly dubbed the newly elected president a 'traitor'. Their determination to carry on their jihad was made abundantly clear less than thirty-six hours after Professor Mohamud had taken office, when two suicide bombers attacked the Mogadishu hotel where he was giving a press conference. The president survived, but at least five people, including an AMISOM soldier, died.

The second reason is that Somalia's underlying problems have still not been dealt with, and chief among these, I would argue, is the question of what to do with the country's millions of young men.

'The US does not have a robust and comprehensive strategy for targeting the connection between youth and conflict,' Professor Jennifer Sciubba, a demographer and adviser to the US Department of Defence, said recently. 'Victory, in whatever form, will remain elusive as long as this segment of the population is marginalized.'[2]

She was speaking about Afghanistan, but her observation was just as applicable to Somalia, a country with almost the same low median age of eighteen, well under half the median in America or Europe.

The challenge posed by exploding populations in the Muslim world is a global one, as the outbreak of the Arab Spring in 2011 perhaps proved. But the problem is particularly acute in the case of Somalia, where the state has conspicuously failed to provide any of the essentials for a decent life for over twenty years. For all the fanfare surrounding the election of the new president, it was far from clear what concrete steps he proposed to improve the lot of the young. While recognizing the challenge, the new speaker of parliament, Mohamed Osman Jawari, could do no more than put his faith in the divine.

'May God help us to elect a good leader in an atmosphere of tranquillity,' he told the new parliament. 'We must give the youth of Somalia a bright future.'

The children of the civil war want what everyone wants: education, jobs, security, a home. Without these things, young people anywhere, and particularly young men, may turn in desperation to violent rebellion; young Muslim men may also turn to extreme forms of Islam. In the course of my research I was constantly struck by the similarity of al-Shabaab foot soldiers, pirates and the members of Somali street gangs I interviewed in Britain and the US. They were all young men, and in some cases – such as Abdi-Osman, a 23-year-old ex-pirate, ex-al-Shabaab fighter whom I met in Mogadishu – literally interchangeable.

'Every man who has nothing will try something to get money,' Abdi-Osman explained.

The clue, perhaps, was in what the insurgents first called themselves: al-Shabaab in Arabic means 'the Youth'.

The regional dangers are obvious enough. Somalia's location, barely 150 miles from the Arabian Peninsula, has long made it Africa's natural gateway for Wahhabist ideas. With the recent rise of Boko Haram and other extremist Islamic groups in West Africa, it is no longer fanciful to worry that such groups could link up with al-Shabaab, spreading their violent brand of Islam across the entire continent. The threat posed by al-Shabaab, however, already extends far beyond Africa, for one, very twenty-first-century reason: the immense size and distribution of the Somali diaspora. In the view of the British ambassador Matt Baugh, the ease with which people can travel in our globalized era has introduced 'a kind of threat we haven't seen before ... [Somalia] is no longer a traditional, geographical country, but a diffuse, global entity – and that is not physically containable.'

An estimated two million Somalis have fled abroad during and since the civil war of the 1990s, putting down roots in almost every country in the world. But many young

Somalis, most of whom left when they were small children and are now typically in their early twenties, have failed to adapt as they should to life in the West, leading to all kinds of troubling social problems. Young Somalis everywhere, in Canada, America, Europe and Australia, are noted for their atrocious performance at school and high levels of un-employment. Somali street gangs have also become a byword for lawlessness and violence. One London com-munity leader spoke to me of a Somali crime 'time-bomb' in Britain. On a visit to the Youth Offenders' Institution at Feltham in west London, he was shocked to find it con-tained more inmates from Somalia than from any other foreign country – 'more, even, than the Jamaicans', as he put it. It seems that the cycle of social deprivation and alienation that so often leads to frustration and hostility is spinning almost as fast for the diaspora as it is in Somalia itself.

As I found in both London and Minneapolis, the West has proved fruitful territory for the radical recruiting sergeants of al-Shabaab. Dozens of young Somalis have abandoned their lives in the West in recent years in order to go and fight for the Islamists in the homeland, with direct consequences for the security of us all. Jonathan Evans, the head of MI5, warned in a speech in 2010 that it was 'only a matter of time before we see terrorism on our streets inspired by those who are today fighting alongside al-Shabaab'. The threat of Somali-linked, home-grown terrorism is in any case not new, as Ramzi Mohamed and Yassin Omar – both born in Somalia – amply demonstrated when their suicide bombs failed to detonate on the London Underground on 21 July 2005. In 2011, when Prime

Minister David Cameron described Somalia as 'a failed state that directly threatens British interests', the first threat he cited was that posed by the radicalization of young Somali Britons.

There is, happily, another side to the diaspora. The vast majority of young Somalis are of course not disgruntled future terrorists. In fact, the more I saw of them, the more convinced I became that it is the diaspora young, more than any other group, who have the power to steer Somalia and Somalis towards a better future. Not only do Somalis abroad bankroll the home country with millions of dollars of remittances to friends and family each year. The best of the young exile generation has also taken full advantage of the opportunity to better themselves through hard work and education, absorbing Western values and ideas along the way. This class of young Somali is out of patience with the traditions of their elders, most of all the old system of *qabyalad*, tribalism, which played such a central role in the destruction of their country. Some of them, such as Adam Matan, 25, and his impressive London-based organization, the Anti-Tribalism Movement, are actively campaigning for a real break with the past. And his kind are, very encouragingly, determined to export their ideas back to their troubled homeland.

Will they succeed? If so, they will need all the support they can get from the West, for the obstacles are certainly immense. There are some signs that Western leaders have understood the importance of engaging with Somalia's youth. For instance, the London conference on Somalia in early 2012, a major international event attended by senior representatives of forty governments and organizations, was notable for the inclusion of the young. International conferences come and go, however – Somalia has been the subject of twenty-one of them since 1991 – and the new spirit of engagement must be sustained if Somalia is ever to be turned around. This applies to the war against al-Shabaab, too. The time may fast be approaching when it will make more sense to talk to the movement's moderate elements rather than to go on trying to destroy or contain them militarily. Or as the Somali imam Sheikh Hassan Jaamici put it to me in Minnesota – on the day he learned of the death by missile of the celebrated American al-Qaida ideologue, Anwar Al-Awlaki – 'What is needed is fewer drones, more debate.'

In the summer of 2012 there was no better or more obvious illustration of the benefits of properly engaging with Somali youth than the inspiring story of Mo Farah, the British-Somali long-distance runner from Hounslow in west London who won two Olympic gold medals. When he first arrived in London in 1991, he was just another troublesome, traumatized refugee. He spoke poor English and struggled academically at his school, Feltham Community College, where he was constantly in trouble with the authorities.

Farah could easily have 'gone off the rails', as his agent Ricky Simms later said, and ended up like so many other displaced Somali boys in the Young Offenders' Institution down the road. Instead, his athletic talent was spotted by a PE teacher, Alan Watkinson, who took him under his wing and forced him to train and focus. The 'FlyMo' is now a Union Jack-draped national hero. He did a favour to immigrants in general with his achievement: in a poll following the Games, 32 per cent said they felt more positive – or less worried – about immigration.[3]

'Everyone is happy,' said Mahmoud Adan, a Somali shopkeeper in Whitechapel. 'It's something that makes us very proud. The stories you hear about Somalia are always bad.'[4]

In Western cities, as in the Horn of Africa, sustained engagement with Somalia's young men is the key to a better future for us all. Without it, as one London exile said to me in a slightly different context, Somalis will become 'the worst people in the world'; and Somalia itself could again unequivocally become *The World's Most Dangerous Place*.

Part I
LIVING ON THE LINE

1

An African Stalingrad: The war against al-Shabaab

Hawl Wadaag district, Mogadishu, March 2011

Of the West's many fronts against Islamic extremism around the world, I am thinking, this one has to be the most literal. I have the oddest feeling that I have stumbled on to a film set: a Hollywood producer's recreation of a front line, not the real thing.

I am sitting on a faux antique armchair, with sagging springs and the stuffing spilling out, in the living room of a wrecked townhouse in downtown Mogadishu. A colonel of the UPDF, the Ugandan People's Defence Force, who has requisitioned the house as his field headquarters, is waving a stick at a large wall map. His name, helpfully spelled out on his breast pocket, is John Mugarura. Both he and the map are interestingly spot-lit by sunshine from a jagged hole in the corrugated-iron roof where, I have just been told, a mortar shell exploded the previous night.

'In the last two weeks, my battalion has advanced here,

here and here,' the colonel booms, 'and we are ... *here*.'

He taps on the bottom edge of a red-inked 'U' that cuts across the heart of the city: the al-Qaida-linked militants of al-Shabaab on one side, us on the other. A cluster of yellow arrows surrounds our position, which is marked with the Uganda Battle Group acronym UGABAG.

Mugarura's diction is the same as all the other Ugandan officers I have met: clipped, confident and elision-free, almost more English-sounding than the English. It is fifty years since Ugandans fought for the British Empire's East African regiment, the long-disbanded King's African Rifles, yet the colonial legacy lives on. The colonel's rank is still denoted as it is in the British Army, by red flashes on the lapels of his jacket. Even the name of the man who sent him here, Uganda's President Yoweri Museveni, means 'Son of a man of the Seventh', a reference to the KAR's Seventh Battalion. Mugarura's blue-black cranium, shaved bald in the regulation way, shines with perspiration as though polished. He reminds me, as many of his colleagues do, of Idi Amin, as played by Forest Whitaker in the film *The Last King of Scotland*.

'We have now paused to allow our TFG allies to come up and protect our flanks,' he continues. 'There is no question that we are winning. The problem is the speed of our progress, which is too slow ... we give the enemy an opportunity to regroup every time we stop.'

The TFG is Somalia's Transitional Federal Government, whose forces are supposed to be leading this war. Mugarura and the 9,000 other mostly Ugandan 'peace enforcers' who make up AMISOM, the UN-mandated African Union Mission in Somalia, are officially only here in a supporting role. The truth, of course, is that the foreigners are running the offensive – AMISOM versus Islamisom, as the local joke goes – because the TFG's 'army' is actually an uncertain alliance of clan militias incapable of leading anything much. There have been stories of TFG troops deserting their posts, and of shooting at each other instead of at al-Shabaab. They are even suspected of selling the enemy their weapons and ammunition.

'So the TFG,' I ask, 'is now actively impeding the advance against al-Shabaab?'

Mugarura turns and blinks languidly at me. His face is expressionless but he pauses for longer than seems necessary before answering. This is another trait I have noticed among the Ugandan officers, although I have yet to get used to it and still find it mildly unnerving.

'There is room for . . . improvement among our TFG allies,' he says eventually. 'Of course there is. If this was not the case there would be no need for our presence here – because they would have no need for our help.'

I look over at Richard and Ngethe, the only other non-combatants here. They both work for the public relations department of AMISOM. Richard is the senior of the two, an ex-British soldier and a former Whitehall political advisor. His expression remains opaque. But Ngethe, an easy-going cameraman from Nairobi whom Richard is training up, rolls his eyes: confirmation that we are going to be spun the official line today. Mugarura is not the type of officer to risk saying anything controversial to a visiting foreign journalist.

It is midday, and a hot, salt-laden wind is picking up outside. The twisted strips of iron around the hole in the roof begin to flap, clanging like a gong, a noise that is answered from the roofs of all the neighbouring houses. Mugarura says the enemy have learned to manoeuvre at night using this noise as cover; it will be a relief when the harsh *Jilal* season gives way, in April, to what passes for a monsoon in Somalia. Desultory gunfire sounds in the distance. I feel, inappropriately, like sleeping: a reaction not so much to the sweltering heat as to the adrenalin expended on the short but much-anticipated journey here in one of AMISOM's armoured personnel vehicles. But then a solitary rifle round lands with a loud snap somewhere above our heads, the ricochet skittering away across the rooftops. 'Harassing fire,' says the colonel with a dismissive wave. 'They are try-ing to keep us pinned down.'

I had been thinking of removing my flak jacket for a few minutes in order to shake out my sodden shirt. I had thought, too, of taking off my borrowed helmet, which is so heavy it is making my head loll. The Ugandans in the room have removed theirs, after all; and because this is my first time at the front – indeed, it is my first time in Somalia, as well as the first time I have ever worn body armour – I am inclined to copy them minutely. This no longer seems a good idea. Through a smashed window I can see two soldiers slumped against the wall of a courtyard, playing cards. The incoming round causes one of them to glance up at the sky, as though wondering if it is going to rain. He decides that it isn't, and returns to his game. I touch the Velcro on my hips, and – nonchalantly, so as to avoid seem-ing frightened – tighten the chin-strap of my helmet to the last available notch.

Like much of Mogadishu, this part of Hawl Wadaag, a

sub-district known as El Hindi, is built on a grid pattern, with red sandy roadways defining each city block. The blocks are large but the houses within them are small and square and densely packed together behind high compound walls. The gaps between these walls are often so narrow that you can touch either side at once, forming a network of canyons easy to defend and exceptionally difficult to attack. During the civil war of the 1990s, long before the arrival of AMISOM, the district was notorious for inter-block warfare between rival clan militias, and so dangerous to enter that it was known locally as 'Bermuda'. Now, however, El Hindi is being contested by an army of jihadis whose religiously motivated stubbornness has become legendary.

'Cleaning out one small little house can take four days,' says the colonel. 'It is very costly.'

He is not exaggerating. AMISOM's casualty rates are proportionally worse than anything experienced by Nato in Afghanistan. Over eight hundred of their soldiers have been killed since they first deployed in 2007, the severest test ever faced by the nine-year-old, 54-nation African Union which, as the continent's answer to the EU, sanctioned the AMISOM mission. The AU's Burundian contingent, on the left of the line, suffered worst during the most recent short push, in which over forty of them died in a fight for a single building, the symbolically crucial Ministry of Defence. In the past six months AMISOM have advanced just two kilometres, and they are not even half way to their main objective yet, which is to control the Bakara Market, the geographical and financial centre of the city. The market is reckoned a vital source of income for al-Shabaab, who levy heavy taxes on the businesses there; they are said to police the area ruthlessly, including with brainwashed child soldiers armed with Kalashnikovs and whips. This truly is a forgotten campaign in the global war on terror.

The briefing ends and Mugarura, properly helmeted now and armed with a stout walking stick, leads us off in single file towards the front line proper, 300 yards to the north. Since every intersection between the houses is a potential ambush point, the Ugandans avoid them wherever possible by digging 'mouse holes' through the compound walls. The colonel plunges through one of these and we follow him into somebody's kitchen, left through a hole into a bedroom, down some steps, along a path between two high compound walls, right into the bathroom of another home, up some steps and across the courtyard of a third. It would be easy to get lost in this disorienting maze. It is like negotiating a real-life print by M. C. Escher.

Mugarura's men are not the only ones to use burrowing tactics. During an earlier offensive, AMISOM were astonished when they overran an elaborate network of concealed trenches. The colonel pauses briefly to show us one which snakes across somebody's backyard and beneath a garden wall. Its construction is business-like: deep enough to crawl along unseen, but no more. His men, he says, are still finding new branches of this network, which appears to cover half the city. Al-Shabaab have dug secret tunnels under AMISOM's lines, too. It is impossible not to think of the mine warfare of Flanders during World War One, although the deadly hidey-holes, the post-apocalyptic dereliction, and the constant threat of snipers, ambushes and booby-traps also bring to mind the horrors of

Germany's Eastern Front in World War Two. I did not expect Mogadishu to be an African version of Stalingrad.

Two decades of bullets and abandonment have wrought astounding transformations in the fabric of these buildings. The most exposed walls have been shot so often that their cratered surfaces appear to be dissolving, like the fragile interior of a half-sucked Malteser. At one point our route takes us through a corrugated iron shed which bullets have turned into a giant colander. The latticework of sunbeams it contains is unexpectedly beautiful.

In some of the houses we penetrate, I glimpse the forms of soldiers sleeping on camp-beds beneath grimy grey mosquito nets. A fortnight previously, al-Shabaab's fighters were resting in the very same places. Scrambling through rooms in dirty boots where shoes were once habitually removed, it suddenly strikes me how deeply violated these homes have been by the tide of twenty years of war. Floors once proudly swept by housewives seem permanently defiled by the accreted filth of fighting men. Alongside the flies and faeces there are tragic glimpses of family lives hastily abandoned: a child's rusting tricycle, a kitchen cupboard with an old kettle still in it, a pair of curtains in a glassless window frame, flapping in the salty breeze. El Hindi feels haunted by anguished, accusing ghosts.

In an essay written in 2008, Nuruddin Farah, Somalia's most famous novelist, described returning to his family home in El Hindi in 2002, eleven years after locking the front door for the last time.[1] He remembered a six-room home with a spacious courtyard and 'a kitchen where my mother and her friends used to sit talking as they sifted rice and cooked ... The city put on a sunny smile soon after siesta; the evenings were starry fun, and the city came alive. In those days, the city was innocent of the meanness of crime.'

In 2002, however, Farah struggled to find his home of many years. The civil war, an era sometimes known to Somalis simply as *Burburki*, 'the Destruction', had turned his old neighbourhood into 'a zone of total grief', where the roofless, windowless and doorless houses 'look like no houses at all'. The devastation called to mind 'wartime images of humans with their eye sockets emptied, their noses removed, heads bashed in until they were featureless and couldn't be recognized as humans anymore'. When at last he found his old home, he couldn't bear to go inside, 'fearful that I might do or say something stupid, or perhaps even faint from the shock of the destruction before my eyes ... This was judgement day, and I didn't like the thoughts that were crossing my mind.'

Out in the derelict gardens of El Hindi today, only thorn scrub thrives, sprouting rich crops of snagged plastic rubbish. The neighbourhood was once dotted with old *neem* trees, thick-leaved Indian lilacs, whose carpets of shade formed a natural place for locals to meet and sit and chat. But the neems are mostly gone now, reduced to angry jagged stumps by soldiers foraging for firewood on which to cook.

In a small clearing on the far side of the first block we traverse, Mugarura stops and indicates a long thin pit full of ashes. The lingering smell, and unburned coils of steel mesh, show that a heap of tyres have been burned here. Richard tells Ngethe to be sure to film everything. He says the fire pit is rare evidence of a crude but effective enemy propaganda trick. AMISOM's reputation has been damaged of late by allegations that they have accidentally killed civilians with their artillery barrages in and around the Bakara Market. Grainy mobile-phone footage of the aftermath of these attacks – a raging fire, choking black smoke, dead bodies lying about – has even appeared on al-Shabaab-controlled websites. AMISOM, while acknowledging that such 'mistakes' were sometimes made early on in the campaign, insist that they now never shell residential areas, and accuse al-Shabaab of faking the images, by setting fires such as this one, and dragging the bodies of people killed elsewhere into camera shot. It is a reminder that in this war, the virtual battlefield is as important as the physical one.

We emerge on to a wider patch of open ground which we are ordered to dash across to foil snipers, and then at last we arrive at the line of control. In two weeks, Mugarura's men have constructed a parapet with sandbags and Hesco containers that looks as though it has been here for months: nine feet high in places, complete with fire steps and built-in sniper points. We make our way along the line behind their colonel, who is clearly a regular and popular visitor. The soldiers are happy to be photographed. Several of them have slung belts of machinegun bullets across their chests, and strike moody martial poses with their weapons. One soldier mans a heavy machinegun from the comfort of a requisitioned armchair, the upholstery of which is incongruously covered in bright orange flowers. He studiedly ignores his mates laughing at him as I point and shoot my camera, and I am struck once again by a surreal film set feeling. Some of the men, in their aviator sunglasses and decorated helmets, look so astonishingly like extras in a

Vietnam war movie that I think they must consciously be emulating Hollywood. Yet there is no doubt what generation they actually belong to when one of them nods and grins and says in a near flawless American accent, 'How ya doin', man? Are you on Facebook? I'll catch you later on YouTube.'

The troops are thickly spread, with most of them up on the fire step with weapons trained and ready to shoot. Mugarura explains that *dhuhr*, the noon prayer, is almost over, and that although al-Shabaab's main sorties tend to be at night, they are also reliably aggressive after each of their five daily prayers. As if on cue, an AMISOM rifle starts firing rapidly a little way down to our left. The troops in our section all swing their weapons in the same direction, and the air suddenly explodes with gunfire. We crouch and wait. The shooting only lasts for a minute, and when it has died down we make our way along to the source.

The rifleman who started it is bristling like a pointer dog through his tiny gun slit. Mugarura scuttles forward and confers with him, their voices low. He peers briefly through the hole and then signals for me to crawl up and take his place.

'Green door, straight ahead,' he breathes. 'You want to look? Be quick.'

I inch my head into position and immediately locate a green, lean-to cellar door. It is scarily close: 50 yards at the most.

'He saw the door moving,' Mugarura murmurs, leaning back comfortably on some rubble. 'He has been watching it for hours. The enemy are dug into the basements all along this sector. We can hear them calling out to us at night,

"Amisom! Amisom!" They sometimes throw grenades over our parapet. That is our biggest problem here, but if you keep a good eye out you can get them first.'

The colonel grins and pats the helmet of the rifleman, who smiles crookedly but doesn't take his eye, or his weapon, off the door to his front. Mugarura says his snipers picked off two al-Shabaab fighters the night before. The night before that, however, a new arrival from Kampala failed to keep in cover while negotiating his way to a field toilet and was peremptorily shot through the head. The soldiers here are engaged in a giant game of whack-a-mole; the only difference is that, in this game, the moles can hit back.

As we loop back to our start point, the colonel leads us to the sandbagged rooftop of a three-storey building from where the medium-rise tower blocks and radio masts of the Bakara Market are just visible on the horizon about a mile ahead. The gently rising foreground is dominated by a badly damaged, ochre-tiled minaret. This is the famous Red Mosque, the burial place of an important Sufi saint, which Mugarura describes as his 'personal' objective, a place he hopes to overrun before summer's end. Richard persuades Mugarura to do a short interview to camera with the Red Mosque in the background. Halfway through, however, there is a thunderous bang as a small-calibre mortar round drops in, barely a hundred yards away up the street. We turn and watch the corner of a building crumble slowly to the ground.

'That was close,' says Richard. 'In fact, I'd say we've been spotted. In fact: Move!'

We all run from the roof into better cover – all except the

colonel, who walks at his usual dignified pace. We are back in Vietnam again: the scene in *Apocalypse Now* where the Stetson-wearing Lt-Col Bill Kilgore announces, while under heavy fire: 'If I say it's safe to surf this beach, captain, then it's safe to surf this beach!' For Colonel Mugarura, being mortared has become routine: an everyday event on this extraordinary, nightmarish front line.

2

At the Bancroft Hotel:
America's proxy war

By Aden Adde International Airport, March 2011

Until a few years ago, journalists visiting Mogadishu tended to stay at the Hotel Sahafi, a *pensione* near a major street junction prosaically known as Kilometre 4, or K4 for short. In February 2005, however, the BBC producer Kate Peyton, 39, was shot dead outside the Sahafi by gunmen loyal to Aden Hashi 'Eyrow', an al-Shabaab hardliner linked to al-Qaida. The Sahafi, and indeed every other city-centre hotel, has been shunned by sensible foreign visitors ever since.

During 2011, my home in Mogadishu was an air-conditioned Portakabin on the military base by the airport, which was protected by sandbags, barbed wire and several battalions of combat-ready African Union troops. Security had been tightened greatly since a spate of devastatingly successful suicide bomb attacks. In September 2008, the militants tricked their way past the checkpoints in a stolen

UN truck which blew up at the convoy point, a large open square where AMISOM's armoured vehicles and their crews formed up before going out on patrol in the city. Around fifty Ugandan soldiers were killed. I passed through K4 many times in the spring and summer of 2011, but only because it lies on the road to the airport; and I only ever did so in the back of a Casspir, an 11-ton, South African-built armoured vehicle with a V-shaped hull designed to deflect mine blast. As a guest of AMISOM, there was no other means of reaching town.

The narrow rectangular windows in the sides of the Casspirs were cracked and dirty and didn't afford much of a view of Mogadishu's street life. My first and many subsequent impressions of the city were gained in jolting cinemascope, as the vehicles lurched and bumped along the disastrously pot-holed roads. What I did see, however, was that something approaching normal civilian life had returned to the TFG-controlled areas. Spectacular ruination was everywhere, but shops had reopened between the ruins, and hawkers sold fruit, sweets or plastic kitchenware from rickety barrows. K4 had turned into a bustling street market, a sure sign of security and progress, as the AMISOM press officers were quick to point out. In places there were quite surprising numbers of private vans and cars moving about – enough, even, to form the occasional traffic jam, which had the security-conscious drivers revving their engines with nervous impatience.

Here and there one spotted an ancient Vespa, with spinning flywheels where the engine casing should have been, still splendidly serviceable after half a century of independence from the Italians. These rickety machines are not the only legacy of Somalia's colonial past. Older Mogadishans still routinely greet foreigners with a cheery *Buongiorno*. The taps in the city's bathrooms, where they have not been ripped out and looted, are still marked C and F for *Caldo* and *Freddo*. A strong flavour of Italy also remains in the city's white-painted buildings, even in their super-dilapidated state. The public buildings and shops along the city's main artery, the Makka al-Mukkarama, are still organized into shady colonnades, with balconies and decorative crenellations along their tops. The café culture thriving along the shattered pavements also retains a distinctly Italian feel, even if habits have evolved somewhat since colonial times. For instance, it was evident even from the back of a bouncing Casspir that many of the customers were animated by the chewing of *qat** rather than the drinking of espresso; while the shirts and suits that Somalis working in the colonial administration had once been obliged to wear had been replaced for the most part by the *macawiis*, a colourful, sarong-like wrap much better suited to Mogadishu's equatorial heat. The cafés looked especially inviting from the back of a sweltering Casspir, and I longed to jump out and go into one. To report properly on the war against al-Shabaab required an understanding of the society and culture from which the insurgents sprang – and that meant talking to ordinary Somalis. I, however, was

---

* *Qat*, the leaves of *Catha edulis*, a flowering shrub native to East Africa, have been chewed for centuries in the region for their stimulating effect. The plant contains cathinone, a naturally occurring alkaloid that acts like an amphetamine by triggering the release of dopamine to the brain.

surrounded almost exclusively by Ugandans and Burundians, and it wasn't immediately apparent to me how I was going to change that.

On the other hand, my arrangement with AMISOM had its compensations. The base was set among sand dunes and scrub-filled ravines along the western edge of the runway, with the Indian Ocean crashing up the beach to the east. It made a natural headquarters for AMISOM, and not only because it was relatively easy to defend. As they realized when their peace-keeping troops first deployed in March 2007, control of the airport was the key to political power in Mogadishu. It was a vital source of tax revenue without which the TFG could not even pretend to govern, as well as the principal gateway to the outside world through which flowed the arms, aid and personnel that kept the admin-istration alive.

Its strategic importance was not lost on al-Shabaab, whose suicide bombers had tried six months previously to force the heavily fortified gates leading to the terminal, killing several soldiers and civilian bystanders in the process.[1] In those days they were still able to infiltrate the buildings visible beyond the airport perimeter, and occasionally stationed a sniper there, but they couldn't do that now thanks to AMISOM's advances in the city, and the airport was the safest it had been in years. There was no doubting we were still in a warzone, though. While waiting for my lift when I first arrived, I turned to watch a Katyusha rocket battery in action, just past the end of the runway. There was a jet of flame and a belch of white smoke as each missile whooshed from its tube towards the enemy's territory beyond the city, making a distinctive moaning sound that gave the Katyusha its other nickname, 'Stalin's organ'.

AMISOM-accredited journalists had to stay in a compound set aside for foreign contractors. Guarded by Ugandan sentries, and surrounded by rubble-filled Hesco barriers, it was a spartan but not unpleasant place to stay. Rows of Portakabins, only some of which were sandbagged against the possibility of mortar attack, were arranged along neat sandy paths that led to an open-air recreation area equipped with an erratically stocked bar, a barbecue, a dartboard, two widescreen televisions, and wi-fi. Skeins of sacred ibis passed overhead each evening, rushing to their roosts before the plunge of the tropical sun. The tails of manoeuvring aircraft could often be seen above the tree-line to the east, gliding back and forth like the dorsal fins of patrolling sharks. At quiet times it was easy to stroll across the unfenced runway to the beach beyond, where shore-crabs danced on the surf-swamped rocks, waving their claws in the air like castanets. The air was permanently sticky with salt, the temperature a steady 32 degrees. The camp felt so much like a cheap holiday resort that it was easy to see why its longer-term residents nicknamed it the 'Bancroft Hotel', after the American security firm that built and ran it, Bancroft Global Development.

There were few better places from which to contemplate the successes and failures of twenty years of international intervention in Somalia. On 3 October 1993, this patch of sky was filled not with sacred ibis but formations of American attack helicopters, as the 160 soldiers of Task Force Ranger rode into the city to capture the militia commanders of the Habr Gidr warlord Mohamed Farah

Aidid. The task force was spectacularly ambushed. Two Black Hawk helicopters were shot down, and during the 24-hour effort to rescue the marooned crews, a battle ensued in which as many as seven hundred Somalis were killed, including a great many civilians. So too were eighteen US servicemen, some of whose bodies were dragged by enraged mobs through Mogadishu's streets, a spectacle that was also televised. A horrified President Clinton ordered a withdrawal from Somalia soon afterwards.

Although it happened almost twenty years ago, the 'Day of the Rangers', as Mogadishans still call the incident, goes on colouring Western perceptions of Somalia to an extraordinary degree. Made famous by Mark Bowden's bestselling book of 1999, *Black Hawk Down*, and then a blockbuster film of the same name by Ridley Scott in 2001, it remains a classic tale of American military hubris. Osama bin Laden also held it up as proof that the mighty US war machine could be defeated by lightly armed Muslims, even though the Habr Gidr's resistance had nothing to do with Islam. Indeed, few Somalis had even heard of al-Qaida in 1993. But it was too useful a narrative for the world's future arch-terrorist to ignore – and it undoubtedly inspired the next generation of jihadis in Iraq and Afghanistan.

Richard, the ex-British Army officer, grew exasperated when journalists asked him about *Black Hawk Down*, which of course they always did. It was his belief that Ridley Scott had more or less single-handedly set back Somalia's prospects for peace for an entire generation.

'The film gave the audience no context whatsoever to the events, and stereotyped Somalis as a bunch of bloodthirsty savages,' he said.

As a spokesman for AMISOM, he was professionally obliged to defend the doctrine of military intervention, and, as an ex-soldier, perhaps inclined to do so anyway. He was not alone in thinking that in Somalia's case, the doctrine had been given an unnecessarily bad name. *Black Hawk Down*, he argued, was just one, short, not particularly relevant episode in a wider UN mission in Somalia which ran between 1992 and 1995, and which included some quite notable military successes. For instance, by wresting control of the docks from the warlords in early 1993, the American military's Operation Restore Hope allowed food aid to get out from the city to the rural areas, thereby succeeding in its primary aim of alleviating Somalia's worst famine for twenty years. Some analysts estimate that as many as a quarter of a million lives were saved.[2]

Despite this, America remains almost pathologically afraid of 'another Black Hawk Down', a fear that has governed its thinking on the Horn of Africa ever since.

'The United States does not plan, does not direct, and does not coordinate the military operations of the TFG, and we have not and will not be providing direct support for any potential military offensives,' insisted Johnnie Carson, the State Department's secretary for African affairs, in a speech in March 2010. 'Further, we are not providing nor paying for military advisors for the TFG. There is no desire to Americanize the conflict in Somalia.'[3] Paying for military advisors to AMISOM, however, was apparently a different matter. *Black Hawk Down* was the reason the Bancroft Hotel existed in the semi-clandestine form that it did.

In its early days, Bancroft Global Development had specialized in land-mine clearance, although it quickly mutated into something much bigger. Somalis commonly suspected it of being a front for the CIA. This was an exaggeration, although I could see how they might have jumped to that conclusion, because the company, head-quartered in the heart of Washington DC's embassy district, undoubtedly was an instrument of US foreign policy. It employed about forty former soldiers from around the world, veterans of Iraq and Afghanistan as well as many smaller wars in Africa, whose job was to advise and train AMISOM in the art of urban warfare. The governments of Uganda and Burundi had reportedly paid them over $12m for this service since they began operations in 2008. It was the American taxpayer who picked up the final bill, how-ever, because Bancroft's fee was reimbursed by the US State Department. This opaque arrangement allowed the US to publicly distance itself from the conflict while keeping a hand in the game.[4]

The camp had expanded greatly since it was set up in 2008, and was now a base for all sorts of itinerant foreign consultants and contractors, most of whom had nothing to do with Bancroft. But the original tenants still formed the nucleus of the community: a tough, close-knit group with brusque manners and suntans developed over years in desert battle zones. Scandinavians were dominant among the Europeans, and Afrikaaners among the Africans. Wherever they came from, they all thrived on the adrenalin of war. They were wary of newcomers and – of course – highly suspicious of visiting journalists. Conversations would often stop abruptly as I moved about the canteen or recreation area. It wasn't hard to imagine that I was interrupting discussions about the teaching of darker military skills that Bancroft was sometimes accused of by suspicious Somalis or the left-wing press in the US.

Many of the Bancrofters were combat engineers who called themselves 'mentors' and were often to be found on the front line alongside their AMISOM protégés, working unarmed even during offensives. Some of the South Africans were involved in a curious subplot of the war involving armoured bulldozers. These vehicles weighed over 17 tons, and had emerged as a key piece of kit in the close urban warfare that AMISOM was engaged in. They were essential for clearing roadways of debris and ordnance, the only way of consolidating newly won territory. They were so feared by the enemy's field commanders that one of the al-Shabaab-controlled radio stations had announced that the bulldozers' newly trained drivers were to be targeted as particular enemies of Islam.

One of these drivers, a short, bespectacled private from Kampala called 'K', was the toast of the Bancroft Hotel for his fearlessness. The story went that Private K was clearing a road near the front one day when he and his supporting ground troops were ambushed by al-Shabaab. His comrades beat a retreat, but not Private K who raised the bucket of his bulldozer and slowly advanced on his attackers, the bullets pinging off the glass and metal of his armoured cab. His surprised opponents broke and fell back into the surrounding buildings. Private K roared on, demolishing the exterior wall of a house as he went. The South Africans hooted with laughter as they described how he caught up with a gunman and ran him down in slow motion, even methodically reversing back over him to make sure that he was dead.

The Bancrofters were far from the only interesting people in the camp. There was, for instance, a team of Frenchmen, po-faced DGSE intelligence officers and glowering special forces soldiers, who used to barricade themselves in a corner of the bar each evening behind a wall of open laptops and (I suspected) specialist tracking equipment that they kept in dustproof metal suitcases. They spoke to no one other than themselves, but were assumed to be focused on the rescue of a DGSE colleague, Denis Allex, who had made the fatal mistake of staying at the Sahafi Hotel in July 2009 while masquerading as a journalist. Kidnapped by al-Shabaab, he was still in their custody three years later, the longest-held foreign hostage in the country.[*]

Then there was a British military adviser, Roger Lane, a moustachioed former Royal Marines brigadier and another veteran of Afghanistan, who was trying to persuade AMISOM to deploy a radar system that would locate the launch point of shells and mortars, thus allowing them to prove they were not responsible for the civilian deaths that al-Shabaab accused them of.

Most colourful of all was another Frenchman, Richard Rouget, a former soldier of fortune of about fifty. He once fought for the presidential guard in the Comoros Islands, a former French colony almost synonymous with political coups and mercenary activity. Under the sobriquet 'Colonel Sanders', he had also commanded a force of South African-recruited mercenaries during the Ivory Coast's civil war in 2003 on behalf of President Laurent Gbagbo, an adventure

---

[*] Denis Allex was killed by his captors in January 2013, following a failed rescue by 50 French commandos.

that led to his conviction in a court in South Africa. He was a product of *Françafrique* straight from the pages of *Tintin*.

His knowledge of Somalia's clan structure was encyclopaedic, and he worked closely with the boss of Bancroft, Mike Stock, the 34-year-old scion of a wealthy Virginian banking family, who had used some of his private fortune to found the company soon after graduating from Princeton in 1999. Stock was a regular visitor to Mogadishu, and maintained an idealistic, almost preppy enthusiasm for his company's Somali project. In the summer of 2011, by when visits to Mogadishu's front line were no longer such a novelty to me, I came across Stock and Rouget at a forward operating base in the district of Bondhere, just north of the Bakara Market. They were wearing non-khaki flak jackets and helmets, and stood out in the open, discussing battle tactics with the hand-waving intensity of true enthusiasts.* I was travelling in a group of three other journalists then, with a Burundian press handler who insisted that on no account were we to photograph the 'foreign advisors'; which of course meant that we all did when he wasn't looking.

Stock, for his part, didn't seem particularly troubled by our presence, and certainly wasn't trying to conceal his – although, as it turned out, he might have been wiser to do

---

* Later that summer, on the advice of AMISOM's public relations department, Rouget broke cover when he gave an interview to the *New York Times* in which he gave a good flavour of the sort of advice he dispensed. 'Urban fighting is a war of attrition. You nibble, nibble, nibble,' he said.[5]

so. The following day an al-Shabaab spokesman, Sheikh Abdi-Aziz Abu Mus'ab, called a press conference specifically in order to announce – inaccurately – that 'a white man and an American military expert' had been shot and killed by an insurgency sniper.

'We are fully aware that more Westerners are fighting alongside our enemy which is also the enemy of Allah,' he said. 'We are calling all Muslims to come to Somalia and fight the enemy of Allah and the infidels whether they are black, red or white, because they are fighting together against us.'

Abu Mus'ab gave no names but could only have been referring to Stock and Rouget, who must have been spotted from an enemy position the day I was there. No wonder the US State Department were anxious not to 'Americanize' the conflict, if al-Shabaab were using even Mike Stock's lone presence on the front line as an international recruiting sergeant against the Islamist world's most hated infidels.

But that was in the future. Back in March 2011, I was stuck on the AMISOM base, fascinated and frustrated in equal measure. As an embedded journalist I was entirely reliant on AMISOM's Casspirs to reach the city where the story was. But securing a place on one of these vehicles proved a slower and more difficult process than I had anticipated. There were a great many false starts and long waits.

Access was controlled by a legendarily capricious Ugandan press officer, Major Bibi, who had been in Mogadishu for three years. This was a long front-line tour by any standards – the British Army, for instance, limited its tours in Iraq or Afghanistan for most personnel to six months – and he had perhaps inevitably grown cynical about the war. His posting was at last coming to an end, however, and now he could hardly wait to go home. His enthusiasm, not surprisingly, had been slipping for months. Nevertheless, the success of any journalist's Mogadishu visit could depend on whether or not he liked you. And so one evening, Richard and Will, another British ex-soldier resident at Bancroft, took me to meet him, bumping along the sand dunes in an armoured Land Cruiser with the hazard lights on, as camp regulations required.

They knew their mark well, and had brought a bottle of Monkey Shoulder Scotch whisky for me to give to him, along with a set of Perudo liar dice. Bibi turned out to be a droll and sophisticated 51-year-old, who had once spent seven years studying in Cuba – President Museveni had flirted with Marxism in the 1960s – and consequently spoke Spanish as well as English fluently.

'Ahhh, Espada de Mono!' he purred, when I presented the whisky. 'Welcome to my palace!'

His quarters amounted to an officer's Portakabin set down in the ruins of a once lovely seaside villa, and were palatial only in the sense that they were better than the tents that the UPDF's rank and file had to make do with. I asked him if he had managed to pick up any Somali during his time here.

'The only way to learn any language is socially – drinking with them, screwing their women,' he replied, his eyes glazing at the memory of his youth in Cuba. 'Unfortunately there has been no opportunity for me to do that here.'

The evening was balmy, as usual. Bibi sent his lanky batman, Mubarak, to fetch glasses while we sat down at a plastic table with the dice on what remained of a patio.

Somewhere off in the darkness to the north, a Dushka heavy machinegun opened up with a kettledrum flourish.

'Ladies and gentlemen,' Bibi announced, flipping out the whisky cork with practised thumbs, 'the music is playing and the nightclub is open.'

I had played Perudo often before, but Bibi's rules were new to me. Instead of the normal last-dice call of 'Palefico', we were instructed to use the phrase 'Al-Kabaab'. And instead of saying 'Dudo' on suspicion that the previous player was lying, we had to say, inexplicably, 'On the knob, John.'

The hilarity grew as the whisky flowed. Bibi was a mine of good stories. He recalled an incident, early on during his deployment, when the militants tried to attack AMISOM's heavily defended checkpoint at the K4 junction, but threw away any element of surprise by arriving in a minivan.

'A bus full of martyrs!' he laughed. 'Can you imagine? They got out one by one, all of them wearing white, with their hair nicely oiled and singing Muslim chants. We ordered them to move on but they just kept coming closer and closer . . . We had no choice in the end. The van was turned to ashes.'

It sounded a strangely wasteful sort of suicide attack, although Bibi said he'd seen such things before. Most of his military contemporaries had fought bush wars back home against Joseph Kony's eccentric Christian insurgency, the Lord's Resistance Army, or against his even more eccentric predecessor Alice Lakwena's Holy Spirit Movement. 'The possessed priestess', as Lakwena was known, notoriously sent her fighters into battle smeared in shea butter that she told them would ward off bullets, and armed with rocks that were supposed to explode on impact. She added her own insane injunctions to the Ten Commandments, including: 'Thou shalt not go into battle armed with a walking stick.' It was a reminder that Islam is not the only religion that harbours extremists, and that Christians in Africa are just as susceptible as Muslims to outlandish superstition.

A bottle of rum joined the Monkey Shoulder on the table, and before very long we were all uproariously drunk. Only Mubarak stayed sober, watching his master impassively from a daybed by the door. He sat cross-legged and with a Zen-like stillness, moving only to answer his mobile phone, the shrill and unnecessarily loud ringtone of which was a muezzin's call to prayer. I asked Bibi discreetly if his batman was a Muslim. 'Mubarak?' he roared. 'Is the Pope a Catholic? Of course he is!'

I had not appreciated until that evening how big a proportion of Ugandans were Muslim – as many as 30 per cent, according to Bibi.* What, I wondered, did Uganda's Muslims make of al-Shabaab?

'Ask Mubarak,' Bibi replied.

Mubarak smiled inscrutably and said nothing.

'There is a very small number of Muslims in Uganda who are extremists,' Bibi answered for him. '*Not* in the army ... political Islam is tightly controlled in the ranks.'

But, as Bibi pointed out, the world was changing. Radical Islam was on the rise in Uganda, just like

---

* The CIA *World Factbook* puts the proportion at 12 per cent, but that figure relies on the census of 2002, since when Uganda's overall population has grown from 24 million to 34 million.

everywhere else; and terrorist campaigns do not require large armies.

On 11 July 2010, three suicide bombers attacked Kampala, killing seventy-four people and injuring seventy more. Most of the victims were football fans who had gathered at a rugby club to watch an open-air screening of the World Cup Final. It was al-Shabaab's first-ever terrorist strike outside their homeland: a significant step towards the al-Qaida-style internationalization of their cause that the West had feared for so long.

'Uganda is a major infidel country supporting the so-called government of Somalia,' one of al-Shabaab's leaders, Sheikh Yusuf Sheikh Issa,* announced. 'Whatever makes them cry makes us happy. May Allah's anger be upon those who are against us.'[6] The suicide bombers did not act alone. Ugandan police made several arrests and eventually charged thirty-two people with murder. Somali nationals were naturally among the accused but so, alarmingly, were several Ugandans. There were also Kenyans among the suspects, and even Pakistanis.

Opponents of Museveni often questioned his motives for involving Uganda in AMISOM's battle, accusing him of strutting on the world stage at the expense of the lives of his people. None of the AU's other members had responded as fulsomely as Uganda when the appeal for troop

---

* The rules governing the use of the honorific 'Sheikh', a title used in many parts of the Muslim world, are particularly loosely applied in Somalia. Taken from the Arabic word for 'elder', the term denotes political authority and/or religious scholarship. Many al-Shabaab 'Sheikhs', however, are not recognized as anything of the sort by Somalis outside the movement.

contributions was launched in 2006. They argued that al-Shabaab was not Uganda's problem, and that Museveni had brought the Kampala bombings upon himself. Yet Uganda, it was easy to forget, is just one country away from Somalia, with only the increasingly lawless, Somali-dominated regions of northern Kenya to separate them.

It occurred to me that Museveni might understand, better than his critics, how much Uganda had to lose from the growth of Islamic extremism in the Horn. There are Muslim communities in every sub-Saharan country between Somalia and Mauritania, many of whom live as minorities with legitimate social grievances. AQIM, al-Qaida In the Maghreb, was active in Algeria, Mauritania and Niger. Ansar Dine, a militant Tuareg group thought to be linked to AQIM, was taking control of northern Mali. Another group, Boko Haram – 'Books Forbidden' or 'Western education is sinful'– was already terrorizing swathes of northern Nigeria. Did Museveni worry that such Islamist groups could link up in the future, and that Islamism, if left unchecked, could topple his country like a domino? He was not alone, if so.

The Ugandan military had encountered a contingent of Boko Haram operating from a former pasta factory in northern Mogadishu when they first arrived in 2007.[7] In 2012 General Carter Ham, the commander of Africom, the US Africa Command, told an audience in Washington that there were other more recent indications that extremist groups, particularly AQIM and Boko Haram, were attempting to coordinate their efforts through the sharing of funds, training and explosives; and he warned that others, including al-Shabaab, could do the same in the future.[8]

The westward creep of Islam, including its extremist elements, was hardly a new phenomenon in Africa. Gerald Hanley, a British officer who spent years among the northern Somali in the 1940s, theorized in 1971 that it was a reaction to a century or more of colonial racism. 'Christianity is right to worry about the spread of Islam in Africa, and must honestly face the question of why it has happened,' he wrote.[9] 'Islam does wonders for the self-respect of non-white people ... I have never been able to find any colour bar in Islam, and, dreary though the ignorant and fanatical portion of Islam can be – as dreary as Victorian Imperial Christianity was – it does start off from a firm base about colour. It does not *try* to show it has no colour bar; it has none.'*

Bibi's mobile phone rang almost constantly. He generally ignored the calls, although once when he did answer I was astonished to hear him launch into a protracted series of comedy farting noises, loud and impressively inventive. It turned out that the mobile phone company had sold or given his number to al-Shabaab, who then paid locals to plague him with nuisance calls, including death threats. I asked him why he didn't just change his number.

'I have,' he said. 'Dozens of times.'

'But – doesn't it drive you mad?'

---

* Even Hanley, however, might have been surprised at the rate of the rise of Islam. According to the Pew Research Center's Forum on Religion & Public Life, the Muslim population in sub-Saharan Africa is projected to grow by nearly 60 per cent in the next twenty years, from 242.5 million in 2010 to 385.9 million in 2030, almost double the projected rate of increase for the Muslim world as a whole.

'It would take more than this to take away my sanity.'

Bibi looked weary, though, as his mobile rang yet again. This time, Will answered and propped the phone next to the speaker of an iPod he had set up. The caller, had they gone on listening, would have been treated to a diverse playlist containing everything from Eminem to Supertramp.

Nuisance-calling sounded a childish tactic, but it had in fact significantly hampered the ability of both AMISOM and the TFG to communicate. Al Shabaab's access to the mobile phone companies' customer databases was so total that Mogadishu's residents had learned not to answer any incoming call unless they recognized the number. I also suspected that the never-ending death threats, however empty they might have been, were far more wearing than Major Bibi was prepared to admit. In the digital age, the most effective response to a technologically superior enemy was often surprisingly low-tech, as al-Qaida first spectacularly proved with their attacks of 9/11.

This memorable evening unfortunately had little effect on my bid to secure a seat in an outgoing Casspir, and the waiting about at the Bancroft Hotel continued. A pair of lion cubs in a cage at the back of the camp provided an unlikely distraction when there was no one around to talk to. The animals, thought to be orphans from the south of Somalia, had been captured by smugglers hoping to sell them on as pets to rich Arabs. Port officials had found them in the hold of a UAE-bound ship docked at Mogadishu and, not knowing what to do with them, passed them on to Bancroft. They were kittens then, perhaps just three months old, but they quickly grew into cubs that paced purposefully around their enclosure, and devoured a dead goat every three days. Like the outcome of the AMISOM mission itself, the eventual fate of the beasts was uncertain. The original plan was to have the Somali president present them as a gift to his Ugandan counterpart, but that scheme had fallen through. Returning them to their natural habitat had been suggested, but this was rejected on the grounds that they were already too domesticated to survive. The truth was that no one quite knew what to do with them – a bit like the international community's attitude towards Somalia itself.

When I last saw the cubs in 2011, they had fallen gravely ill with a respiratory disease that no one could diagnose, and had lost so much weight that they tottered when they walked. The Ugandan orderly who had been put in charge of them shook his head sadly, and explained there were no zoologists or lion experts in Somalia. The lions wouldn't eat goat any more, or even the cooked chicken he tenderly proffered them. The only hope, he said, was outside help, perhaps from the Born Free Foundation based in South Africa. So far, though, no lion vet had agreed to undertake the journey to Mogadishu; and very soon, he thought, it would be too late for these animals anyway. For both the lions and the state, foreign intervention, if it was to have any chance of succeeding, had to arrive in time; and it had to be the right kind of intervention, or it could easily end up making matters worse.

3

The field hospital: What bombs and bullets do to people

AMISOM HQ, March 2011

There was almost no need, in the end, to leave the base to discover what the war had done to ordinary Somalis. AMISOM's field hospital, barely a quarter of a mile along the edge of the runway from the Bancroft Hotel, turned out to be packed with wounded civilians.

The hospital had opened in 2007 as a tented triage station for wounded AMISOM personnel; the decision to treat civilians alongside the soldiers had come later on. At first, senior UN officials in Nairobi noisily disapproved. Allowing civilians in for treatment, they argued, risked compromising the base's security, and breached the terms of neutrality under which, as 'peacekeepers', AMISOM technically operated. But the commanders in the field had taken the view that since their mission was to help the people of Somalia, it would be absurd to deny them medical assistance on grounds such as these. Enemy combatants were treated at the hospital too, after all. Winning over hearts and minds is a cornerstone of modern counter-insurgency theory – and what better way was there to achieve this when first-class trauma clinics were practically non-existent anywhere else?

Nairobi had grudgingly conceded this point, since when AMISOM had taken the principle further, and dug into their own budgets to open a civilians-only outpatients department near by. The OPD, as it was then known, was an instant success. On three mornings each week, about eight GPs treated as many as six hundred patients who came not just from Mogadishu but in some cases from as far away as the Ethiopian border, a dangerous 500-kilometre journey that could easily take several days to complete. This said much about the availability of medical treatment in this ruined country. The clinic was yet another bombed-out seaside villa. Although it did not open until nine, a long queue had always formed before dawn at the entrance in the camp perimeter, a narrow chicane of razor wire and Hesco barriers that AMISOM's enthusiastic press officers had dubbed 'the Gate of Hope'.

Medicine's power to impress the locals was quickly demonstrated when al-Shabaab announced on the radio that anyone obtaining or even seeking treatment from the infidels would be considered 'unclean'. When this admonition was ignored, an edict was passed warning that anyone found in possession of an AMISOM medical form risked having their tongue cut out. The militants also occasionally tried to mortar the OPD. And yet by ten o'clock on the morning I visited, the open-sided shed lined with crude wooden benches that served as a reception area was already full to bursting. Al-Shabaab's threats, or the risk of a lucky mortar strike, were no deterrent at all.

The patients had segregated themselves, men to the right, women to the left where the shade was fullest. A hundred pairs of eyes swivelled in unison as this sweating *mzungu* advanced towards them, their teeth ethereally white against the darkened ovals of their shrouded faces. The atmosphere was very subdued, both here and in the clinic itself, where they queued for medicine with an almost bovine patience, dull-eyed and dazed. The patients exuded dejection, not hope, however the PR men tried to spin it.

At the head of the queue I found Sister Mary, a warm-hearted, big-bosomed Ugandan in combat fatigues, dispensing medicines from a table in the ruins of the villa's kitchen. She offered me her wrist to shake – a frequent gesture in this infection-prone part of the world – and told me that the complaint she dealt with most often was diarrhoea; before adding that there was an even more common disorder, just as potentially serious, that the OPD was unable to treat.

'The people here are very stressed,' she explained. 'They are traumatized. They do not know where to turn.'

This was literally true in the case of one elderly patient I watched being steered into the room by the shoulders, his eyes glazed and his jaw working from side to side: the effect, Sister Mary told me once he had stumbled out again, of too much qat.

'You talk a lot in the West about PTSD – Post-Traumatic Stress Disorder,' she said, shaking her head, 'but for these people there is no "Post". The trauma never ends. Psychologically, that is so much worse.'

Mogadishu was a city where violence was so endemic that it had become the norm. The sleep of its citizens was no longer disturbed by the sound of shooting at night; small boys thought nothing of playing football in their street while a firefight raged up and down their neighbourhood. In 2011, according to the World Health Organization, nearly half of Somali victims of weapons-related injuries were children under the age of five. An entire generation of Somalis had grown up knowing that they could be violently killed, at random, at any time. Fatalism of the deepest, darkest kind was inevitable in such a place – and who knew what long-term effect that might have on a person's mental well-being?

The suffering up at the hospital was at least easier to discern. Most of the patients there had been injured by bombs or bullets. The wards were no more than large canvas tents, arranged either side of a dust and gravel roadway wide enough for the lumbering armoured ambulances to turn. The whole place bore a striking resemblance to the set of *M*A*S*H*. A new casualty, a TFG soldier, was being stretchered down from the back of an ambulance as I arrived. The bandages around his stomach were soaked in blood and his face was twisted with pain. A white-coated reception committee clustered around him, conferring rapidly, before reaching a decision and bearing him away. Among them I recognized Ed Parsons, a bearlike Canadian medic whom I had befriended back at the Bancroft camp, who held aloft a saline drip with a rubber-gloved hand, comically taller than any of them.

Demonic laughter came from above as the wounded man passed. I looked up and saw a monkey – very obviously a male monkey – reclining deckchair-style in the concavity of the hospital tent roof. He suddenly jumped up and, still cackling, swarmed down a guy-rope to join the cavalcade of medics, strutting along behind them on his hind legs with his chest puffed out. The medics paid no attention to this freakish apparition. I later learned that the monkey was the hospital mascot, a clever animal that had learned to lick the sugar coating from painkiller pills. The risk that it might bite and seriously injure someone had been removed by the surgeons, who had drawn its fangs under anaesthetic.

Ed came back a few minutes later, explaining that the soldier had been shot 'through and through', but that the wound had begun to bleed into his abdominal cavity, necessitating a rush into theatre. A veteran of military hospitals in both Iraq and Afghanistan, Ed knew a great deal about the lethality of gunshot wounds. A through-and-through wound, he said, was typical of a medium calibre round like an AK-47, and was the best kind to get. Smaller rounds such as a .22 could actually cause more damage because they tended to 'tumble' on impact, after which they could bounce around the body like a pinball, tearing through delicate organs and ending up almost anywhere.

'Finding a tumbled bullet can be guesswork. A small one can even travel in the veins. People don't fall dramatically backwards when they're shot. That's a Hollywood thing left over from the days of silent movies, when directors were always looking for drama. Getting shot for real is more like "bang – crump – down". In fact, gunshot victims quite often just slump forwards. The real drama is all internal, invisible to the camera.'

The smell of stale sweat inside the ward tents was nostril-flaringly strong, as was the occasional cheesy whiff of suppurating wounds. The men in the TFG soldiers' ward were thin and tough, and not all of them were welcoming. They were mostly locals from the same Hawiye Abgaal clan, one of the big players during the civil war and traditionally the major power in the Mogadishu region. I suspected it might not go well in here for a patient from a different clan. The new Somali national army that AMISOM were busily training up was supposed to be ethnically balanced, because favouring one clan over another during the recruitment process risked creating one more clan-based militia. But if this hospital ward was in any way representative of the new army's make-up, AMISOM's training programme risked ending up doing more harm than good.

I spoke to Mohammed, a 28-year-old shot laterally through the hips, a complicated wound that had also destroyed his bladder. He had been in various hospitals for over a year, but was now two days away from being discharged back to his family.

'I bet you're looking forward to that,' I said. 'Do you have children?'

'Two,' he replied, 'but they are both dead.'

'I'm sorry.'

'No problem.'

'So what will you do?'

'I've always been a soldier. I want to go back in the army,' he said.

I glanced down at the long metal rods that still protruded awkwardly from his sides, pinning his body together at the waist like one of those nail-through-finger tricks you get in joke shops. It was hard to imagine him ever returning to active service.

'So many of my friends are dead,' he went on. 'All I want is peace.'

'But if you want peace, why do you want to go back to fighting?'

'It is my duty to fight the foreigners.'

By now, two or three other TFG men had gathered around Mohammed's bed, nodding their agreement.

'Al-Shabaab is led by people from Eritrea, from Afghanistan, from Pakistan, from India,' Mohammed went on. 'People with problems in their own countries who want to hide in ours.'

'You don't think al-Shabaab are fighting for Islam?'

The TFG men all shook their heads.

'No,' said Mohammed. 'They are fighting for their own ends – for al-Qaida's agenda against America. They only say they are fighting for religion. But Islam is based on peace and forgiveness. Al-Shabaab do not want peace.'

The tent reserved for injured civilians was just as hot and full as the TFG soldiers' one, the wounds on display just as severe. I was met with more blank stares. A mood of sullen anger prevailed. A man with wild, crusty hair and a heavily bandaged arm lay on his back on a cot in one corner, quietly mouthing nonsense at the canvas ceiling, his ravings ignored by those around him. A portly Ugandan nurse explained that he was a mental case, a homeless beggar whose arm had been sliced open by a stray bullet. It was very common, he said, for non-combatants to be wounded or killed in this way. A lot of the gunfire in the

city was speculative rather than deliberately aimed at anyone. Sometimes, in the case of weddings or birthdays, it was
celebratory. Either way, the shooters apparently gave little
thought to what their bullets might do when they came
down.

On the way out I stopped by the bed of an elderly man,
Abdulkarim, who had been brought in a week previously
with a bullet-smashed thigh. His young grandson sat beside
him, waving flies off his still blood-soaked bandages with a
square-shaped, wickerwork fan. The bullet that hit the old
man had dropped at random from the sky one morning as
he sat on the porch of his home. He stared into the distance
as he told me his story, his speech halting and barely
audible. Perhaps understandably, he seemed terribly
depressed. He was a retired agronomist who had learned a
little English over the years, working alongside UNFAO,
the United Nations Food and Agriculture Organization.
He shook his head when he had finished and looked
at me for the first time, his watering eyes filled with an
immeasurable sadness.

'I just don't know what we're going to do about our
young men,' he said.

'Young men' was a literal translation of the imported
Arabic word, *shabaab*. But coming from the mouth of this
blameless senior citizen, it somehow took on a deeper
meaning. Abdulkarim was expressing the despair of a
patriarchal society that had lost all control of its successor
generation. With the traditional bonds broken, the young
men were rudderless, and now, exploited by foreigners and
misled by extremists, their mad and endless violence was
slowly destroying Somalia, a country he loved and whose

people he had served all his life. His words struck me, in that moment, as one of the most succinct analyses of the Somali tragedy that I had heard.

The violence between Somalia's young men was hardly a new phenomenon. As a nation of nomadic camel-herders in one of the world's hottest and driest regions, where access to water and grazing is often literally a matter of life or death, the competition between the clans has long been noted for its viciousness.

'"Conscience",' wrote the famous explorer Richard Burton in *First Footsteps in East Africa*, published in 1856, 'does not exist in Eastern Africa, and "Repentance" expresses regret for missed opportunities of mortal crime ... Murder – the more atrocious the midnight crime the better – makes the hero. Honor consists in taking human life: hyena-like, the Bedouins cannot be trusted where blood may be shed: Glory is the having done all manner of harm.'

Somali society, though, had learned over the centuries to control the violence through the application of *xeer*, an ancient and highly developed system of customary law traditionally administered by the elders of the rival clans, who would sit down and negotiate a compromise in the event of major disputes. Somalia's real troubles began in the late 1970s when Siad Barre began to exploit and exacerbate the old clan rivalries in order to maintain his grip on power – a classic instance of divide and rule – while simultaneously running down the xeer system in favour of scientific socialism. The old social contract was then further destroyed by years of terrible civil war.

Somalia's tragedy is that the differences between the four

major clan groups – the Hawiye, the Darod, the Dir and the Rahanweyn – are not as entrenched as the bloodshed between them since the early 1990s suggests. For instance, no Somali can tell a Hawiye from a Darod or a Dir merely by looking at them. They tend instead to identify their compatriots by listening for subtle regional differences of accent, to which they are acutely sensitive. Genetically speaking, the main tribes are all close cousins. For example, the Darod and the Isaaq (the dominant tribe of Somaliland, so closely connected to the Dir that they are sometimes described as 'northern Dir') both say their progenitors came over from Arabia in the tenth or eleventh century, and that both these men – Sheikh Abdirahman bin Isma'il al-Jabarti for the Darod, Sheikh Ishaq ibn Ahmad al-'Alawi for the Isaaq – were members of the Banu Hashim, the tribe of the Prophet Mohammed. The conflict between them was not like the dispute between, say, the racially distinct Hutus and Tutsis which led to the Rwanda genocide of 1994. Somalia's long clan war, of which the battle against al-Shabaab was arguably just another manifestation, was more like a petty family feud that had run horribly out of control.

I had been warned that a visit to the AMISOM field hospital would require a strong stomach, and nowhere was this truer than in the women's ward. Set slightly apart from the others, the nurses called it the 'Fistula Clinic', so often did they find themselves treating that serious obstetric disorder. A fistula is associated with the tearing of the perineum during childbirth, which frequently happens when the mother is a girl who has yet to reach physical maturity. Almost unheard of in the West, the condition is common in Somalia, where in some rural communities girls are still married off at the age of nine. In this war-ravaged country, furthermore, young girls are everywhere and forever being raped. Even al-Shabaab, the self-acclaimed defenders of Islamic probity, allowed its foot soldiers to force families to hand over their daughters for so-called 'battlefield marriages', a type of contract that tended not to last for more than a few weeks, and that really amounted to a form of sexual slavery. It was no coincidence that the patients in the fistula clinic were above averagely pretty as well as young.

The first patient I saw here was a beautiful young woman lying back on a cot and cradling a tiny newborn baby. She was smiling broadly, and I grinned my congratulations back, before noticing there was something not quite natural about her expression, a certain glassiness in her eye that hinted at heavy sedation. The sister in charge confirmed it. She had been brought in that afternoon, seven months pregnant and with a shell fragment lodged in her spine. She had just undergone an emergency Caesarean, and was still so full of drugs that she hardly knew where she was, nor why. This was perhaps just as well. The shell fragment, the sister explained in a kind, low voice, had gone too deep for the surgeons to remove safely. The patient was paralysed from the waist down, and it was unlikely that she would ever recover the use of her legs.

'But what will happen to her?' I said, aghast.

'Who knows?' shrugged the sister. 'At least the baby is healthy.'

The baby's mother gazed vacantly ahead, understanding none of this, her pearly smile as broad and beautiful as ever, a vilely tainted vision of the black Madonna and child. I could not bear to look any more, and hurried on down the ward. I mentioned what I had seen later to Richard, who remarked that it was nothing very unusual.

'The worst thing I ever saw in there was a woman giving birth just after both her legs had been blown off,' he said.

For the hospital staff, the catalogue of suffering never seemed to end. I was intrigued by the chief medical officer, Colonel James Kiyungo, a slight man with an intelligent, sensitive face, and a reputation for efficiency and calm, very popular with the internationals at the Bancroft Hotel. I was in moralistic mood after the fistula clinic, yet he refused to condemn the militiamen responsible for the carnage he dealt with every day.

'You have to understand what motivates the violence,' he said, collapsing into his office chair. As the hospital's senior surgeon he was fresh back from theatre, where he had succeeded in stemming the abdominal bleeding of the TFG soldier I had seen earlier. 'These people survive on the absence of government. The only hope they have is chaos.'

A few months previously, I had been told, the hospital had detailed a detachment of Ugandans to install a stand-pipe in a city district suffering from an outbreak of cholera. The standpipe went unused, however, because al-Shabaab had – allegedly – threatened to kill anyone caught using it. Was the story true?

'I ordered the installation of that standpipe myself,' Kiyungo said, swivelling in his seat and tapping a spot on the map of the city on the wall behind him. 'Al-Shabaab want to prevent *anything* that might make people support AMISOM.'

'But – don't you think that action was wholly evil?'

'I suppose you could characterize it that way,' he replied

after some thought, 'but then: what is evil? Some people say eating meat is evil. For others, it is fornication. Or building a nuclear power station in the path of a tsunami – is that evil?'

He had seen more than his share of horror in the course of his military career, including during the campaign against the Lord's Resistance Army in northern Uganda in the 1990s, yet his faith in humanity remained deep-seated, his compassion apparently unshakeable. It was hard not to be impressed. Even the previous summer's devastating suicide bomb attack in his home city of Kampala, he said, was 'part of the price you pay to redeem these people'. The root problem, he thought, was lack of education. 'The fighters here learn to read the Koran, but they have no skills. There are no carpenters, no cooks, no plumbers – only the gun. I think it was Roosevelt who said that the security of a nation depends on ammunition in the short term, but that it is the economy that counts in the long run.'

I recounted something I had heard in a bar in Nairobi, how during Ramadan for the last two years, al-Shabaab had run a Koran-recital competition aimed at children, and broadcast the results on one of the radio stations they controlled. In 2009, the first prize was an RPG; runners-up received an AK-47 or a pair of hand grenades. Some of the competitors were as young as ten. (Al-Shabaab ran the competition again during Ramadan in 2011, when they handed out more weapons along with religious texts. 'Youths should use one hand for education and the other for a gun to defend Islam,' the adjudicator reportedly told the prize-giving ceremony in Elesha Biyaha, 20 kilometres from Mogadishu.[1]) The audience in Nairobi had reacted to this story with a breathless whistle, but Kiyungo simply laughed. To him, the competition was a sign not of evil but of misguided idiocy.

'If people are hungry they will cling to almost any organization,' he said.

Kiyungo's generosity of spirit was exemplary, but I still found the idea of arming ten-year-olds hard to forgive. There is no ignoring or escaping the damage that Somalis have inflicted on one another over the last twenty years. No one knows for certain how many people have been killed since 1991, whether by bombs or bullets or by the effects of the famine that the fighting exacerbated, although the figure usually given is 500,000. The AMISOM field hospital proved an old observation – almost an East African adage – that the introduction of modern weaponry by *gaalo*, foreigners, in the nineteenth century was a particular disaster for Somalia.

Somalis resisted the new-fangled weaponry to begin with. In the 1850s, firearms were still considered 'cowardly weapons with which the poltroon can slay the bravest'.[2] In the 1900s, however, firearms began to leak into Somalia from Abyssinia – modern Ethiopia – where the tribesmen had been armed by the French during negotiations to build the Addis Ababa–Djibouti railway in the 1890s. In 1903 a British political officer, Major Harald Swayne, wrote: 'The result of their contact with civilisation, to one who has watched the Somalis for nearly twenty years . . . has known them at their camp fires, and had their interest at heart, gives rise to melancholy reflections.'[3]

Swayne's foreboding was soon justified. Somali society could accommodate killing in the name of honour in an era

when men were armed with arrows and spears, but technology soon turned the old rituals on their heads. Somalia's
addiction to the gun first flourished during World War
One when the 'Mad Mullah', Sayyid Mohammed Hassan,
led a rebellion against the British in their northern Somali
protectorate, Somaliland. Armed with rifles provided by
the Ottoman Turks – the 'main cause' of the uprising,
according to Swayne – the Sayyid's campaign took inter-
clan killing to a new level. Then, at the beginning of World
War Two, Italy and Britain fought back and forth across
the region, bringing mechanized warfare to Somalia for the
first time. In 1941 when Mussolini withdrew from
Mogadishu, the capital of *Somalia italiana*, his troops
abandoned their ammunition dumps and turned their
locally levied recruits loose with their guns, creating a
whole new class of bandit *shifta* and ushering in another era
of lawlessness.

Somalia's independence in 1960, which came after ten
years of administration by the UN and the unification of
the former British protectorate and Italian colony, was at
least a relatively bloodless affair. But a military coup in 1969
brought General Siad Barre to power, along with a flood of
Russian weaponry from his Communist sponsors. Henry
Kissinger accused Somalia of hiding missiles in its
minarets.[4]

In 1977, Barre invaded Ethiopia, hoping to annex its
Somali-inhabited eastern region, the Ogaden. Moscow,
however, sided with Ethiopia's Communist Derg regime –
as did Fidel Castro, who agreed to send 5,000 of his troops
to stiffen the resistance. When Siad Barre's troops were
repulsed, he switched his allegiance from Moscow to

Washington, turning his country into one of the hottest fronts of the Cold War. Between 1979 and 1980, the US spent $35m upgrading the former Soviet naval facility and airstrip at the Somaliland port of Berbera. With Washington's help, Siad Barre set about expanding and modernizing his army until it was the largest in Africa, a force he didn't hesitate to unleash on Somaliland when the former protectorate rebelled against his regime a decade later. Two-thirds of the Somaliland capital, Hargeisa, were flattened in an aerial bombardment that killed tens of thousands of its inhabitants.

Siad Barre was ousted in 1991 by clan-based opposition groups backed, once again, by foreigners: Ethiopia and even, this time, Libya's Muammar Gaddafi. By then Somalia was super-saturated with weaponry. When the clans fell out with each other (as the clans always did), the stage was already set for one of the longest and cruellest civil wars of modern times – and it was all made possible by the machinations of foreigners over the preceding century.

The gaalo, furthermore, are still supplying the country with weapons. Al-Shabaab and their allies obtained at least some of their guns from jihadist sympathizers in Yemen and the Gulf states, or from rogue states like Eritrea which was intent on destabilizing their arch-enemy, Ethiopia. AMISOM's weapons are also paid for by foreigners. In 2011, the US granted Uganda and Burundi $45m in military aid. In December of that year even Beijing joined in, when the Chinese defence minister, General Liang Guanglie, pledged $2.3m to the Ugandan military. It is small wonder that so many Somalis blame outsiders for their country's ills. If Afghanistan is the 'Cockpit of Asia', as the Viceroy of India Lord Curzon once said, then Somalia is Africa's unfortunate equivalent, a nation strategically located at the crossroads of competing powers and ideologies, whose fate it is to be endlessly fought over by foreigners.

4

Aden's story

AMISOM HQ, March 2011

I was fortunate, up at the OPD one morning, to meet a young man called Aden Ibrahim who had come in complaining that he felt 'dizzy'. The cause was never diagnosed, although I suspected that straightforward hunger had much to do with it. Aden's cheekbones were protuberant even for a Somali; his black trousers and spotless white shirt hung off him in folds. He spoke a little English, but at first seemed so shy of using it that I gave up, and moved off to find someone else to interview. But he came after me and tugged on my sleeve, murmuring with a backward glance that he did want to speak to me, but in private, not here by the reception area where there was no telling who might be watching from the crowd. And so, with some misgivings, I led him back towards the Gate of Hope, and sat him down beneath the gaze of the AMISOM sentries among some sandbags in a half-built machinegun nest.

The story of what had happened to him and his family turned out to be so engrossing that we didn't stand up again for two hours. He was only twenty, yet almost every terrible thing that can happen in a person's life seemed already to have done so. He was a walking epitome of the Somali catastrophe.

Aden was born in Tieglow near Baidoa in the south-central region, the son of a poor sorghum farmer. His parents, two sisters and a brother lived together in a three-roomed mud hut built by his grandfather. They belonged to an obscure sub-clan of the southern Rahanweyn people, a background that came to determine the family's fate.*

The Rahanweyn, who account for perhaps 20 per cent of all Somalis, have long been marginalized by the other clans. They are marked out by the 'Mai Terreh' Somali they speak, a dialect quite different to the 'Maxaa Tiri' used everywhere else. Like many Rahanweyn, moreover, Aden's clan were settled farmers, who have always been looked down upon by the nomads, the country's 'aristocracy', even though all the farmers had done, over the centuries, was to

---

* I later asked Aden to write down his full clan lineage, although I quickly wished that I hadn't. He wrote:

A – *Rahanweyn*
B – *Jilible*
C – *Ilkole*
D – *Abow enow hasan*
E – *Gasaro gud*
F – *Bagadi*
G – *Abasad*
H – *Diile (Dhiigle in Somali)*
I – *Yamen orgin is Yamen*

adapt to their environment. As inhabitants of the south, a fertile region irrigated by Somalia's only two significant rivers, the Shabelle and the Juba, why would they be nomads? But in the nomads' eyes, the settled life was an easier life that had softened the Rahanweyn farmer clans, and that made them degenerate.

As the civil mayhem of the 1990s took hold, the farmers were at first persecuted and then pillaged by the mainstream clans. This is one of the reasons that a disproportionate number of Rahanweyn, the great losers of Somali society, later came to support al-Shabaab, a movement whose back-to-basics Salafism theoretically transcends the clan system. The south, in fact, was al-Shabaab's heartland from the start. In 2011, an estimated 30 per cent of the movement's foot soldiery, over 4,000 fighting men, were Rahanweyn, with another 1,000 classified as 'students and farmers' from southern minority clans.[1]

Despite the dangers of belonging to a Rahanweyn farming family as the civil war ignited, Aden remembered his childhood in Tieglow with fondness. Although his district was tribally mixed, it managed to escape the worst depredations of the clan militias. Many of his family's relations lived close by, providing a sense of security and community. Aden's father had brought his children up in the gentle old Sufi tradition, where food and work were shared equally, and neighbourly relations were governed by a culture of mutual respect: 'The complete opposite,' Aden remarked bitterly, 'of the clan system in Mogadishu.'

In a good harvest year his father's farm produced twenty sacks of sorghum; almost double what the family needed. But the rains were uncertain throughout the 1990s, and when the sorghum failed, life became much harder. In one year, Aden remembered, the family went without a proper meal for three months. But the drought of 2000–1 proved too much even for these hardy survivors, and the family were forced to shut up the house and trek east to Mogadishu to find an alternative living. The move was supposed to be temporary, but when the time came to return to Tieglow, the family refused to go. Mogadishu offered a far better chance of survival than the drought-stricken region they had left behind.

The city was kind to them at first. His parents opened a small shop on the edge of the Bakara Market, selling combs, mirrors, pens and other bric-a-brac. They made enough money to send the children to school, which Aden loved. His mates called him Ateera ('Body Slam'), a typical Somali joke nickname, since his skinny build was the exact opposite of a wrestler's. He recalled playing football as a young teenager inside the roofless wreck of the old parliament building, where he said a journalist from the *New York Times* had once interviewed him, a memory that I guessed had prompted him to ask to talk to me.

These were years of genuine hope for many Somalis. A Transitional National Government was formed in 2000, ostensibly offering the country its best chance of peace in a decade. But ultimately neither the TNG, nor the Transitional Federal Government which succeeded it in 2004, was able to secure a lasting political settlement. Both were fatally weakened by corruption and the vested clan interests that had dragged the country into civil war in the first place.

From their outset, the fledgling government institutions

were challenged by the Islamic judiciary who thought, perhaps understandably, that they could do a better job of running the country. The collapse of Barre's dictatorship had left a vacuum that had to be filled by something, and since 1991, starting in the south of the country, a system of government by judges had evolved – a historically rare example of a 'krytocracy' – under which local courts offered not only Sharia justice but, eventually, police services, education and even healthcare. In April 1999 they took control of the Bakara Market, the commercial heart of Mogadishu. Five years later, in 2004, the courts had formally amalgamated into the Islamic Courts Union, or ICU.

By Somali standards, the ICU's administration was not a bad one. Civil society functioned without the corruption that plagued daily life in the areas supposedly controlled by the TFG. The streets were policed by officials wearing distinctly Arab-looking *thobes* and *keffiyehs*. Serious crimes such as rape and murder were sometimes punishable by stoning. The strict Salafist doctrine that the ICU judges imposed was in fact imported from Arabia, and was almost the antithesis, within Islam, of the liberal, hymn-singing Sufism traditionally practised in Somalia. The movement was not popular with everyone, therefore. Richard Burton wrote that 'though superstitious, the Somal are not bigoted like the Arabs, with the exception of those who, wishing to become learned, visit Yemen or El Hejaz, and catch the complaint. Nominal Mohammedans, El Islam hangs so lightly upon them, that apparently they care little for making it binding upon others.'

On the other hand, the ICU did bring security to the areas under their control – and to a people weary of war, that could easily overcome any ideological misgivings. In this respect, the ICU's support was comparable to that enjoyed by the Taliban when they took over Kabul in 1997. Those Afghans' brand of Islam (and the harshness with which they sometimes enforced it) was not always popular either. But they did restore order to a city that had suffered years of brutal civil war, and that, to Kabulis, was worth almost any sacrifice. For a while, Mogadishu's Bakara Market became one of the safest places in the whole country, as well as the obvious choice of destination for a family of refugees like Aden's.

In 2005, however, a group of clan warlords, jealous of the ICU's grip on the Bakara Market and its revenue-raising possibilities, stopped fighting each other and agreed to turn their guns on the Islamists. Crucially, the 'Alliance for the Restoration of Peace and Counter-Terrorism' – some of whose members were also ministers in the TFG government – was supported by the US, who were concerned that the ICU was a front for, or at least sheltering members of, al-Qaida. This was precisely the same concern they had had about the Taliban, who sheltered Osama bin Laden in Afghanistan in the years before 2001. The CIA, who reportedly funnelled $150,000 a month to the anti-ICU Alliance, was particularly interested in Comoros-born Fazul Abdullah Mohammed, an al-Qaida leader implicated in the cataclysmic US embassy bombings in Dar es Salaam and Nairobi in 1998, which killed 223 and injured more than 4,000.[2]

The ICU may have harboured extremists, but it was not an extremist organization per se. It actually encompassed quite a wide range of Islamist doctrine, from Sufi moderates to Salafist hardliners, which meant, among other things, that its ideological direction was never very fixed. Even in 2006, the UN secretary-general Kofi Annan was unable to say if the ICU was a good or bad thing for Somalia.

'I don't know much about the Islamic Court group,' he told a reporter. 'What I can say is that the people of Somalia are totally fed up with the warlords, that I suspect that most Somalis, except those with vested interests, will say good riddance.'[3]

After the outrage of 9/11, however, the Bush administration was in no mood to pay attention to such nuances. Any friend of their enemy was their enemy.

'We certainly want to work with people in Somalia who are interested in combatting terrorism,' said Sean McCormack, a spokesman for the State Department. 'We do have concerns about the presence of al-Qaida.'[4]

Kofi Annan, using remarkably frank language for a secretary-general of the UN, said it was unequivocally 'wrong' of the US to support warlords, but even that criticism was ignored. The US decision to take sides against the ICU was to have profound unforeseen consequences – for Aden's family, for Somalia, and for the world.

The showdown came in May 2006, when street fighting for control of the Bakara Market blew up into a full-scale battle in which more than three hundred people died. Cowering behind the shutters of their little market shop as the fighting raged outside, Aden's parents and older sister were all killed instantly when a TFG mortar shell plunged through the roof. Aden, his brother and his other sister only survived because they happened to have gone to visit some neighbours that day, and had taken shelter there as the fire-fight intensified.

'We all have to submit to Allah's will,' said Aden tonelessly.

Allah hadn't finished with the family yet. In June 2006, the TFG was driven into exile in the western town of Baidoa by the Islamists, who took control first of Mogadishu and then the entire south of the country. This greatly alarmed Christian Ethiopia, Somalia's historical rival in the region. Backed by the US, President Zeles Menawi ordered an invasion in support of the TFG. The ICU people's militias were no match for Ethiopia's well-equipped military, who advanced until they occupied Mogadishu, an occupation that was to last until 2008.

The ICU was now in crisis. Some of the moderates among them, led by Sheikh Sharif Sheikh Ahmed, a former secondary school teacher and the movement's one-time commander-in-chief, favoured negotiating with the newly reinstated government. Sheikh Sharif eventually signed a peace deal with the TFG, in Djibouti in 2008; he was rewarded with the presidency of Somalia the following year. The hardliners, however, refused to have anything to do with the TFG. They were led by Sheikh Sharif's great friend and mentor, Sheikh Hassan Aweys, a former army colonel who had been decorated for bravery during Siad Barre's Ogaden War.

Presenting himself as a rallying point for outraged Somali nationalism, Aweys and his allies launched a ferocious guerrilla campaign against the TFG and their Ethiopian supporters, whom they portrayed not just as infidels but as proxies of Uncle Sam, the Great Satan himself. Soon they were being reinforced by foreign jihadis from around the world, bent on a fight against the latest army of *kuffar* to taint holy Muslim soil. The hardliners were badly divided at first, and even fought each other, notably in a ferocious battle for control of the important southern port of Kismayo in 2008. But the factions overcame their differences and eventually united under the banner of al-Shabaab in 2010, with Sheikh Aweys emerging as their spiritual head. As a former colonel, Aweys insisted that his new troops were properly drilled and trained. The force that emerged was highly disciplined by Somali standards. Later propaganda videos made much of their ability to parade in formation and to march in time. Many units even wore matching camouflage uniforms beneath their keffiyeh-swathed heads, adding to the impression that they were, as they claimed to be, a legitimate army of national liberation. The world's newest and potentially most dangerous Islamist insurgency had come of age.

None of this was good news for the surviving members of Aden's family. The fighting in Ethiopian-occupied Mogadishu was intermittent, but could flare up at any time, deadly and unpredictable. After the destruction of Aden's parents' shop – later made irreparable when al-Shabaab dug a communications trench through the middle of it – he and his siblings went to live in a neighbouring district with an aunt and uncle who had moved, like them, from Tieglow to Mogadishu some years before. Soon afterwards, the youngest of the children, Aden's nine-year-old sister Xawl,* was shot through the kidney by a stray bullet. Then

---

* 'Aden and Xawl', Aden explained, is the Somali equivalent of 'Adam and Eve'.

their uncle, a bus driver, was killed by Ethiopian army gunfire as he plied his usual route near the port.

At sixteen, Aden was now his dwindling family's main breadwinner. Remarkably, considering the dangers of travelling about the city, he continued to attend school, where he was employed as an assistant teacher when he was not in class himself. He was paid between $15 and $20 a month. In 2008, though, even this meagre income dried up as the school was finally forced to close by the fighting.

'I never managed to graduate,' he said sadly. 'I never won any certificates to help get me a good job.'

He was lucky to find work as a porter at the Keysaney Hospital, a converted prison in the north of the city, which always seemed to be overflowing with maimed civilians and was itself frequently shot at or shelled. Aden's 14-year-old brother, Mohammed, briefly managed to open a stall in the Bakara Market, a smaller version of the bric-a-brac shop his parents had run. Aden helped him when he wasn't at the hospital, but the venture came to an end when the shop next door was hit by a shell which started a fire that destroyed all his stock. Meanwhile his sister Xawl, now eleven years old and only recently recovered from the bullet that had cost her a kidney, was hit again, this time in the head by a fragment of shrapnel.

The fighting in the city the following year, 2009, was the fiercest Aden had ever experienced. Al-Shabaab had driven the last Ethiopian soldiers from Somalia by then, leaving the TFG defended by an uncertain alliance of clan militias, supported by an African Union peace-keeping force judged by most to be still too small and under-equipped to hold the line. As the militants closed in on the AMISOM base, all flights in and out of the airport were suspended, heightening the sense of isolation and abandonment among the city's beleaguered inhabitants.

'The shelling from both sides was indiscriminate. Our house was shaking from the rocket fire. It went on 24 hours a day, for weeks. I remember the hunger when we ran out of food. It was impossible to leave the house to search for more . . . Our neighbour was killed during one fight for our street. He lay outside, and no one could bury him. If you stuck a finger outside, it would be shot off. There were a dozen bullet holes in our door . . . I hid under a bed, and prayed to Allah. I was sure I was going to die.'

It was his brother, Mohammed, who cracked first under the strain.

'He couldn't stay in Mogadishu any more,' said Aden. 'He told me: "I prefer to die than to go on living like this." The pressure was too much for him. He had to go somewhere safe.'

Such places were not easy to find in Somalia, though. Mohammed decided instead to make the perilous journey to Yemen, adding another epic subplot to the family saga. Not long after his fifteenth birthday he took the last few dollars from the family savings tin, crossed through al-Shabaab lines and bought a place on a truck heading north to the port of Bossasso. Here he paid $80 to a gang of people-smugglers to take him across the Gulf of Aden. The boat was overloaded, however, and half way across when the weather turned rough, the smugglers forced some of their passengers to walk the plank. Anyone who resisted or

even objected was either shot or beaten to death.*
Mohammed, thankfully, survived to tell Aden the tale in a
phone call a few weeks later, by which time he was somewhere near Sana'a, the Yemeni capital, hoping to find work
as a labourer.

'My brother is very brave,' Aden said.

For the last eight months, though, there had been no
word from Yemen. Aden was naturally desperately
worried. He had heard that it might be possible to trace his
brother through the International Committee for the Red
Cross, but only if Mohammed had thought to register himself with them when he arrived in Yemen, and he had no
idea if his brother had done this.

'I just hope he isn't dead,' he shrugged.

Aden was also anxious to escape Mogadishu in 2009. The
city was becoming impossibly dangerous, with suicide
bombings ever more common, although even Somalis were
shocked by an attack in December at the Shamo Hotel that
killed twenty-five people, including three government
ministers, and injured sixty more. Aden had no time for the
moral equivocation displayed by Colonel Kiyungo. The
attack, he said, was 'very evil'. Most of the dead were
medical students who had gathered for a university enrol-
ment ceremony, a rare cause for celebration in Mogadishu
that had drawn a crowd of hundreds. Carnival turned to

* Such horror stories remain distressingly common on the well-
established smugglers' run over to Yemen. In 2009, according to
the United Nations High Commission for Refugees, some 78,000
Somalis and Ethiopians made this voyage, of whom 376 people
were categorized as 'dead or missing'.

carnage when the bomber, who was dressed as a woman, approached the speakers' panel and said 'Salaam' – Peace – before detonating the explosive belt hidden beneath his jilbab. Sheikh Sharif called the atrocity 'a national disaster' and blamed al-Shabaab, although they denied responsibility; according to one report, the bomber was a 23-year-old loner from Denmark.[5]

Whoever was responsible, al-Shabaab, now unconstrained by any rival ICU faction and in full battle cry, had become a truly terrifying organization. As a young man of fighting age, Aden was in particular danger.

'The streets were filled with al-Shabaab press gangs,' he recalled. 'All men were targeted, but especially young men like me. And so I ran, alone, back to Tieglow.'

His home town, however, was not the place he remembered. Half the population had disappeared, either killed or driven out by the fighting or the famine. Many had fled to refugee camps in Ethiopia, or Kenya, or further abroad; and al-Shabaab, he discovered, were as firmly in charge here as in Mogadishu. Empty houses were looted or squatted in. Houses still in use were requisitioned at gunpoint. Aden had planned to hide in the countryside with any family friend or distant relative he could find, but he was picked up almost immediately by an al-Shabaab patrol, and imprisoned.

'There were twenty-two of us, all young men like me,' he recalled. 'They were trying to make us join them. We were shackled together and put in a cell four metres square. For three days and nights they preached at us – especially at night. We were not permitted to sleep, or eat, or to go outside except at prayer time. They kept asking, "Are you ready to martyr yourselves, are you ready to die?"'

The pressure was intense, and eventually around twelve of the captives succumbed. Aden knew one of them slightly, a lad his age called Gumo Shahi* from Beledwayne, 100 kilometres away. Gumo's home had been destroyed in recent fighting, and his family, always very poor, were now destitute. He agreed to join al-Shabaab when he heard that a small salary was on offer.

'I stayed in touch with Gumo for a while,' said Aden. 'He used to call me from Bur, near Baidoa, and then from central Somalia. He changed his mind about al-Shabaab. He said they never paid him anything. They only gave him food to eat. But it was too dangerous to desert, and then he was killed in fighting near Guri'el.'

Gumo's new career had lasted all of two months.

Aden was not fooled by al-Shabaab's promises. He had seen enough of them in Mogadishu to know what they were about, and had no intention of fighting for their cause, let alone dying for it. He spoke as little as possible and kept his eyes on the ground and eventually his captors grew bored of taunting him and let him go. Aden's contempt for them was total. There was no manufacturing the hard, bright look in his eye as he listed a long catalogue of abuses.

'They stop people from playing football – even kids. They beat people for being late for prayers; teachers are beaten for teaching girls. If you have a mobile phone, they check to see if you have any films or music on it. They even check the ringtone. And if they do not like it they will destroy the phone and take your money and make you

---

* An odd nickname meaning 'Pigeon Tea'. Aden's explanation – that he 'used to drink tea like a pigeon' – was unconvincing.

swallow the SIM card . . . Their culture has nothing to do with us. Somalis are naturally moderate, not extremists. We can't make sense of any of this.'

In one notorious example of over-zealousness, in Jowhar in April 2010, al-Shabaab banned the use of bells in schools, on the grounds that bells were 'a sign of the Christian churches'; henceforth, the teachers were to signal the end of class by clapping their hands.

'What they are doing has nothing to do with Islam,' Aden repeated. 'They just want to control people.'

(Their zealotry, however absurd, was no laughing matter for the Somalis forced to live with it. In 2009 in the Bakara Market in Mogadishu, a young man called Ismael Khalif Abdulle was arrested on what he later claimed were trumped-up charges of theft, and subjected to a Sharia punishment rarely practised in the Islamic world: cross-amputation. Along with three other youths, in front of a crowd forced by the militants to watch the spectacle, Abdulle's right hand and left foot were hacked off, without anaesthetic, with a knife usually used for the slaughtering of camels. His suffering did not end there. A fortnight later the al-Shabaab commander Fuad Shangole, a Swedish passport-holder who for twelve years had run a mosque in Stockholm, arrived at the house where the four youths were recovering to announce that the judges had made a mistake. 'He told us that our legs had been cut too low down, and would have to be shortened,' Ismael Khalif explained later to a British reporter. 'He took the end of my leg, and put three fingers above the stump and said: "That's where it should be."' This time the operation was carried out with a plumber's saw. Once again, there was no anaesthetic.⁶)

To Aden, the hypocrisy implicit in the way they extorted money from people in the name of Islam was almost worse than Shangole's barbarity. In the coastal town of Marka in 2009, al-Shabaab decreed that gold fillings were a sign of vanity and therefore unIslamic. The decree was enforced by patrolling militiamen who mounted spot checks on the passing citizenry, and yanked out any offending teeth they found with pliers.[7] Aden described how another gang took to stopping buses and ordering all young boys to drop their trousers to prove they were circumcised. If they were not, they were subjected to instant surgery with a kitchen knife, right there at the side of the road – a 'service' for which customers were charged $3.

'These are bad, bad people,' he concluded, shaking his head and clicking and sucking through his teeth in the Somali way. 'They are not acting like human beings.'

Aden thought that al-Shabaab's extreme youth was partly to blame.

'Even the commanders are only nineteen or twenty,' Aden explained. 'They are very ignorant, and that ignorance is easily manipulated. They have no understanding of the world: no BBC, no Voice of America, no access to foreign media at all since 2009. They collect hordes of youngsters to do the cooking and the shoe-cleaning as well as the fighting . . . some of their recruits are as young as nine. If you tell them, "We are going into attack, we are going to destroy America", they won't question it; they will just reply, "OK: let's go."'

At the level of the street, normality had been replaced by a kind of mad children's crusade where chaos and sadism ruled. It was like *Lord of the Flies* with automatic weapons.

In the old days, said Aden, the young men of al-Shabaab would have been brought into line by their elders and betters. The problem was that the war had destroyed that system. 'It is not possible to convene a council of elders because there are no elders,' he said.

The collapse of the old order had been exploited most of all, in his view, by brainwashing foreigners. It was well known that al-Shabaab's leadership was mostly foreign. Did al-Shabaab's fighters not have to wear 'Pakistani' clothes, the baggy trousers and long-tailed *shalwar kamiz* favoured across central Asia? In Mogadishu, furthermore, he had once seen with his own eyes Omar Hammami, the famous white American al-Shabaab leader known as Abu Mansoor Al-Amriki, whose mother was a southern American Baptist and who was raised in Daphne, Alabama.

Al-Shabaab's leaders, Aden believed, were engaged in a systematic assault on Somali values and culture. The destruction of an important Sufi shrine at Biyoley, 20 kilometres from Tieglow, was a case in point. Biyoley was the burial place of Sheikh Aweys Al-Barawi, a national hero in the late nineteenth century, as well as one of East Africa's greatest proselytes for Qadiri Sufism.* His grave attracted huge numbers of visitors each year, some of them from as far away as the Congo or the Comoros Islands.

---

* The Qadiriya is one of three Sufi brotherhoods with strong representation among Somalis; the others are the Ahmediya and the Salihiya. Aweys Al-Barawi was murdered in 1909 by the Mad Mullah, Sayyid Mohammed Hassan, who was jealous of his influence.[8]

'Busloads of pilgrims used to come, especially on the Sheikh's birthday,' Aden recalled.

Al-Shabaab soon put a stop to that. As Wahhabi Salafists they disapproved of shrine worship, which smacked to them of idolatry. In 2008, therefore, they smashed up the grave and scattered the saint's bones in the desert.* The pilgrim buses were turned back at gunpoint, the hawkers and traders driven off with sticks.

'We all hated al-Shabaab for what they did,' said Aden. 'In Tieglow we reject them in our hearts, 100 per cent.'

This was not just because of the affront to the local saint. In a region devastated by war and the weather, the shrine's reliability as an income generator made it a mainstay of the local economy. Al-Shabaab could not have done more to alienate the people of Tieglow if they had tried.

Amazingly, this tactical error was repeated in many other places in Somalia. Al-Shabaab was a dogmatic organization that seldom acknowledged its mistakes. The country is peppered with Sufi shrines, and from 2008 the militants took every opportunity to desecrate them, a policy that enraged Sufis everywhere. The Red Mosque in Mogadishu, which I had peeked out at from the Ugandan lines in Hawl Wadaag, was one of the shrines that suffered in this way. Although a professedly non-violent religious order – 'Sufi Islam is gentle Islam,' Aden insisted – in 2008 the Sufis formed a multi-clan militia, the Ahlu Sunna

---

* Wahhabis abhor shrine worship so fiercely that in 1913 they razed all the domed graves around the holy city of Medina, including those of the uncle, father and wives of the Prophet Mohammed himself.

Waljama'a or ASWJ, which soon scored several victories over al-Shabaab, notably in central Somalia. Aden's childhood acquaintance Gumo was in fact killed in one of these battles. By March 2010 the ASWJ had become the TFG government's most important local ally, and so powerful that they were granted control of five government ministries.

It was six months before Aden could scrape up the money to get out of Tieglow again, by when he had been picked up three times by marauding al-Shabaab gangs. On one occasion a fellow detainee revealed to their bullyboy tormentors that Aden spoke English. This was easily enough to warrant a death sentence among some al-Shabaab. 'Sometimes it can be dangerous just to talk,' as Aden pointed out. He was already in trouble with this particular group of fighters because his hair was unshaven at the sides, the style supposedly advocated by the Prophet. Once again, he was lucky: the group's leader told him he was in a good mood that day, and booted him back on to the street with orders to get his hair cut.

He knew his luck would not last for ever, however.

'I had three choices,' he said. 'To fight for al-Shabaab, to be killed by them, or to run away again.'

Aden fled back to TFG-controlled Mogadishu in the summer of 2010, and had been here ever since. He arrived just in time to witness al-Shabaab's latest offensive, which was timed, as in 2009, to coincide with Ramadan. This one was called *Dhameytirka Dabadhilif*, 'the War of the Elimination of the Stooges'. An al-Shabaab spokesman, Sheikh Ali Mohamud Rage, issued a statement calling on 'all al-Shabaab troops, beginning at this hour, to invade and destroy all entrenchments of the apostates and Christians'. The offensive opened with a suicide attack on another hotel, the Muna, a favourite meeting place for TFG politicians. Six MPs were killed. It was just the beginning: in the course of 2010, the city ambulance service recorded over 2,300 violent civilian deaths, and 6,000 more who were injured.[9]

Aden got into trouble with al-Shabaab yet again when he tried to bring a friend of his, a paraplegic gunshot victim, across the lines to the doctors on the AMISOM base.

'He'd been at the Benadir Hospital but all they could offer him was a wheelchair,' he said.

The patrol that stopped him said they would kill him if they ever found him in an al-Shabaab-controlled area again. For that reason, he had not been into their territory for eight months.

'Never mind having your tongue cut out,' he snorted. 'There was a time when they'd cut your head off with a sword if they caught you with Ugandan medical papers.'

Life was as hard as it had ever been for Aden's few remaining family members. The house he had shared with his aunt and sister had been destroyed. Home was now a shell-scrape in the Medina district, with walls formed of sacking strung between trees and a tarpaulin for a roof. They were not alone, for the district was crowded with refugees living rough – there were, he said, three hundred people living in his 'village' among the ruins – although there was little sense of community because the refugees tended to keep themselves to themselves. This was for fear of the *Amniyat*, al-Shabaab's 'security' wing, whose frequently murderous agents were everywhere.

'It is not possible to tell who is Amniyat and who is not, because they are ordinary people, from soldiers to shoe-cleaners. You cannot trust anyone; you have to watch what you say all the time.'

His was a feral existence, a Hobbesian struggle for daily survival. Food prices were going up, and the only income came from the handful of Shillings his aunt earned by taking in washing. Aden never ate more often than twice a day, therefore.

'We eat bread. Or maize is cheap. We get beans, some-times. We used to buy powdered milk, but that has become too expensive. We can't afford oil or sugar, either.'

It was little wonder that he felt dizzy. On this meagre diet, Aden went out into the city each day, walking the sizzling streets for hours – because he couldn't afford the buses – in an endless search for work. His current plan was to get a job as a guard at the Villa Somalia presidential complex. The chief of security there belonged to the Jilible sub-clan, the same as him. The problem, he explained, was getting into the chief's office.

'Do you think,' he coughed, 'that you could help me with an introduction?'

I thought at first that he must be joking. Did he really think I could have such influence? It was the mark of a desperate man, if so; and showed that the power of clan patronage had its limits in Mogadishu, at least if you were a Jilible.

It was still no simple matter to travel about the city. That very morning, he said, his route here had been blocked by a fierce gun-battle, obliging him to make a lengthy detour that caused him to miss a place near the front of the queue for the OPD. On reaching the gate, he discovered a new regulation was in force: all patients had to surrender their wallets and phones to a gang of guards who were charging a dollar to get them back again on the way out. He sucked through his teeth, and sadly shook his head. Such petty official corruption, he meant to say, was the norm here.

The OPD was closing by this time, and the AMISOM sentries, relaxed until now about our occupation of their unfinished machinegun nest, were anxious for us to be gone. Aden, I suddenly guiltily realized, had not seen a doctor, the whole purpose of his coming here. But he said it didn't matter because, as a matter of fact, he no longer felt dizzy; and added, as we walked together back up to the gate, that he felt much better for having spoken of his troubles to me.

I wasn't sure how to interpret this. At the time, I cynically took it as a coded, and not inelegant, request for money. I was happy to give him some: $50, enough to keep his family group in wheat or maize for a hundred days. He looked surprised, then very pleased. He quickly folded and refolded it and then, with a glance left and right to make sure no one was looking, slipped it into his shoe. Later, though, I concluded that I was wrong to be so cynical, and that Aden had meant what he said, at least in part. Talking to an outsider really had made him feel better. I was an emissary of a different world, who had affirmed to him merely by showing interest in his stories that Mogadishu was not normal, and that life did not have to be governed by poverty and savagery.

I gave him my contact details and he still emails me occasionally, short letters in shaky English, that always begin 'dear freind'. He even phones sometimes, always from a different borrowed mobile, his voice pursuing me all the way back to Britain. His letters contain interesting snippets of news from Mogadishu. Once, he wanted me to investigate an organ-smuggling ring he believed was operating out of one of the city hospitals; a friend of his had apparently had a kidney stolen while under anaesthetic for an operation for a gunshot wound. (A story I never pursued, beyond asking the Canadian medic Ed Parsons about it. 'Anything is possible in Mogadishu,' he said.)

> hi jmaes dear freind
> this is a picture's of the person that I had told you who his kindey was stolen I summitted all of his evidence like computer result anad ather letter U will see into your box byee adden

Most of the time, though, he just wanted help finding work, ideally with one of the foreign NGOs in Somalia, Care or Save the Children or Médecins Sans Frontières – a favour I have never been able to swing for him, although I did try.

> My personality I am still jobless
> The country's job opportunities are under hand of special individual not easy to get a job in Somalia with out help special in Mogadishu. Without outside help or inside. Things which encourages that some persons to hold all jobs under their hands are tribalism and corruption which is part of the manner.
> I need your support most if you have any contact with

NGOS and agencies in the home link me to them if you
can.
It is good for me having your contacts

We stay in touch. As a Somali fisherman might say: If
Aden insists on seeing me as a lifeline to a better future,
who am I to cut him adrift? All I can do for now is to tow
him through dangerous waters. It would be good, one day,
if I could find a way to reel him in.

5

The failure of Somali politics

Villa Somalia presidential complex, March 2011

Mohamed Omaar, Somalia's Minister of Foreign Affairs, leaned back in his office chair. He was just explaining to me why he had returned from the safety of exile to take on this most challenging of jobs, his sense of national duty and the need he felt to form a bridge to the rest of the world, when he was interrupted by an ear-crushing *BADOOOOOM* from outside. The office's single window was protected by sandbags piled up on its sill, but the blast was so near and so powerful that the glass briefly rippled, like the surface of the water in a bath when you bang the side of the tub. One of my eyelids slowly dipped of its own accord. It was a comedy twitch, worthy of Herbert Lom, the Inspector Dreyfus actor in the *Pink Panther* films.

'Shelling?' said the minister with a thin smile. 'It is like water off a duck's back to us . . . But don't worry, I expect that one was outgoing.'

Before I could answer, a machinegun opened up, loud and near, and then, just as the noise stopped again, all the lights went out. From a chink in the sandbags the gloom was pierced by a hot needle of sunshine that fell across the desk between us, the beam filled with motes of crazily tumbling dust.

'Don't worry,' he said again, his glasses glinting. 'This is normal. All normal.'

When the lights came on again – the presidential complex was equipped with back-up generators, so we didn't have to wait for long – he checked to see I was still listening before carrying on exactly where he had left off; although I was, frankly, having trouble concentrating. It was less than twenty minutes since a Casspir had dropped me off on the parade ground outside, and my shirt was still sticking to my back from the flak-jacketed, sweat-bathed drive through the centre of town. It had taken many days of difficult phone calls to secure an interview with any TFG minister, and more effort still to persuade AMISOM to give me a ride, despite the shortness of the journey here, a mere ten minutes from the airport. In any normal city, I would certainly have walked it. But now that I was here, the Villa Somalia complex, the seat of every president since in-dependence in 1960 and the country's most conspicuous symbol of political power, felt a lot more dangerous than I had expected. Set on high ground in the centre of the city, it commanded an excellent view of the port area and the ocean beyond. The walls facing inland, though, were dis-concertingly peppered with bullet holes. It seemed an extraordinary place from which to try to govern a country. Omaar's sangfroid was not put on: this really was his ordinary working environment.

His point, in the end, was a simple one: the keys to

Somalia's future lay in the hands of the country's immense diaspora.

'The speaker and the prime minister have put aside the vested interests of the warlords,' he said, 'and for the first time, they have reached out to the diaspora – to our skilled people, our trained people, our *educated* people – with the message that *they* are the ones we need to rebuild our country. There is no shortage of talent out there. The only question is: do we have enough carrots to lure them back?'

The civil war, he explained, had driven perhaps two million of his countrymen abroad, and they had gone to every corner of the globe. An entire generation had since grown up there, absorbing not just foreign educations but different languages, values, ideas. It was not just that the diaspora could, potentially, provide Somalia with all the petro-engineers or investment bankers it needed (although Omaar's assertion that the London equities desk of Goldman Sachs was filled with Somalis, or that one in six managing directors at Morgan Stanley was Somali, was surely an exaggeration). What he meant was that, through their discovery of a viable alternative to the stultifying clan system that had perpetuated the violence here for so long, those exiles could have a civilizing, almost revolutionary influence on the home country. They represented the best chance of modernizing Somali society since Siad Barre's experiments with socialism in the 1970s, if only they could be persuaded to come back and impart what they had learned.

Omaar and his ministerial colleagues were not hypocrites in this regard. Almost all of them were returnees from abroad, half of them from America, who had given up good jobs and safe, suburban homes in order to come here.

The prime minister, Mohamed Abdullahi Mohamed but universally known as Farmaajo,* was entirely typical of the cabinet he appointed: he was from Buffalo, New York, where he had worked for years as a commissioner for equal employment in the state's Department of Transport.

Unusually in this cabinet, Omaar was from Britain: the brother of Rageh, the well-known television presenter who made his name covering the Iraq invasion for the BBC in 2003. There was only a faint resemblance to the 'Scud Stud', as the *Washington Post* once dubbed Rageh. Mohamed's build was broader and he was considerably older, with a neatly trimmed moustache and hair that had receded to a corona of grey. Their father, a Somaliland businessman and property magnate, moved his children to London in the 1960s in order to educate them. Mohamed duly attended a smart boarding school in Dorset, and went on to graduate from Trinity College, Oxford. I found him an eloquent, civilized, thoughtful man, the complete opposite of the Western warlord stereotype. He spoke fluent English but with a slightly patrician accent that somehow added to his gravitas and plausibility. You could see at once why Farmaajo had chosen him as foreign minister.

'Somalia's problems can easily be solved, but only if the West has the political will,' he said. 'Sierra Leone is the proof of what direct intervention can achieve. If it worked there, why not in Somalia?'

I thought perhaps he had a point. For almost a decade now, the international community's strategy had been

* The nickname means 'Cheese', a word lifted directly from the Italian colonists who popularized the commodity.

focused on 'containing' Somalia's problems rather than on helping to solve them. The TFG, formed in 2004 with the backing of the UN, was the country's fifteenth attempt in twenty years to form a functioning central government. It was by definition a temporary institution, intended to be replaced as soon as possible by an elected government rather than an appointed one.* Yet the transition to a proper federal democracy had been dragging on for seven years now. There had been two presidents since 2004, and Farmaajo was the fourth prime minister. No doubt the international community did need to apply more pressure, although that was never going to solve the country's problems by itself. Somalis also had to want to help themselves. Sadly, though, not all of them did.

The most pressing political problem was that the TFG's mandate was due to expire in four months' time, by when the parliament was supposed to have ratified the new federal constitution necessary for a general election. It was looking highly unlikely, however, that the deadline would be met, because parliament had been paralysed for months by a bitter power struggle between 'the two Sharifs', the president, Sheikh Sharif Ahmed, and the powerful speaker of parliament, Sharif Hassan Sheikh Aden.

Their animosity was exacerbated by the politics of the clumsy 4.5 power-sharing formula, according to which the position of president had always been reserved for a

---

* Government positions were divvied up among the clans according to the notorious '4.5 formula', which is to say, equally among the four main clans, with the remaining ethnic minorities swept up into that '0.5'.

member of the Hawiye clan, and that of speaker for the Rahanweyn. Later that year, at the fortified entrance to the Villa Somalia, four men were killed when a gun battle broke out between the president's guards and the speaker's Rahanweyn entourage, who objected to surrendering their weapons as they came in. Political reformers were appalled, although to ordinary Somalis, the shoot-out was no more than a reversion to the national norm – for was not violence the traditional way of resolving a dispute between clans? The TFG's problems were certainly huge, and in Mohamed Omaar's view, unless the UN started knocking heads together, then the TFG's mandate would run out and the country would soon arrive at yet another morale-sapping, war-prolonging political impasse.

The parliament was singled out by many as the greatest block to progress. I saw the debating chamber for myself, later that summer: a small, hot, low-ceilinged basement, safe from al-Shabaab mortar fire beneath the post-apocalyptic remains of the old Italian-built Parliament House in Wardhiigley. It was empty when I visited, save for a sleepy janitor and several tall piles of blue plastic chairs, and seemed to exude bureaucratic lassitude. An extraordinary 550 MPs were supposed to work here: more, even, than to be found in democracies the size of Nigeria or India.* Furthermore, on the rare occasions that it met, this bloated body frequently struggled to reach the quorum necessary to legislate.

* When the TFG was established in 2004, there were 275 MPs. That number doubled when the TFG reconciled with ARS, Sheikh Sharif's Alliance for the Reliberation of Somalia, following the Djibouti Accord of 2008.

Efforts to reform the institution had so far been resisted by the speaker, who effectively controlled it through his large faction of MPs. He treated parliament as his private fiefdom. A former international qat trader, as well as a former finance minister, he was reputed to be a very wealthy man, with a stake in every large government contract going. His nickname was Sheikh Sakiin – Sheikh Razorblade – because you never noticed the pain of the cut he inflicted until afterwards. Nothing got in the way of his business interests. He was even rumoured to have links to fellow Rahanweyn clansmen within the high leadership of al-Shabaab.

Sheikh Razorblade was naturally suspicious of the reform-minded new prime minister, and tried to block his appointment from the start. Parliamentary business was halted for a fortnight while he and Sheikh Sharif squabbled over whether a parliamentary vote to confirm Farmaajo's nomination should be done by a show of hands or, as the speaker wanted, by secret ballot. The speaker's position was absurd: MPs had voted with their hands on this matter for over fifty years. Yet it took the intervention of the Supreme Court to resolve the impasse, along with delegations from the UN, the AU and IGAD, the region's Intergovernmental Authority on Development. Afterwards, the head of the UN, Ban Ki-Moon himself, was moved to write the Somali leadership a letter of congratulation. It was outrageous, but it seemed that Somalia's speaker of parliament could hold the world to ransom if he chose.

Considering the obstacles, Farmaajo's cabinet of technocrats weren't doing at all badly. They had only been in power for four months but had already instigated some significant reforms. The regulations governing loans from the notoriously leaky central bank had been tightened. A report had been published on the profit and expenditure details of the government's numerous foreign contracts, an exercise in transparency previously unheard of in Mogadishu. Farmaajo had halved the number of ministerial portfolios, and put a stop to the private jet travel that the previous government enjoyed. In short he was behaving like a public servant rather than a kleptocrat, and that was unusual in Somalia, a country widely considered the most corrupt in the world.*

Farmaajo's stand had made him popular in many circles, but it had also created some dangerous enemies in certain others. Omaar was too much of a diplomat to say whether or not he thought the speaker was corrupt. We talked instead about the role of Islam in Somalia's future. Surprisingly, considering his Westernized background, Omaar envisaged a very substantial one. He had no wish to reverse the process of Islamification that had swept his country since the early 1990s. On the contrary, he regarded Sharia law, properly applied, as an important part of the solution to Somalia's problems.

'Sharia only becomes a danger when it is not properly

---

* Somalia has come bottom of Transparency International's annual Corruption Perceptions Index every year since 2007. In June 2012, the World Bank reported a $130m (£85m) discrepancy in the TFG's accounts over two years. In July 2012, the UN Monitoring Group alleged that $7 in every $10 of international aid received by the TFG from 2009 to 2010 never made it into the state's coffers. President Sheikh Sharif dismissed both charges as 'baseless and unfounded propaganda'.

codified through the central intellectual and judicial institutions,' he said. 'The Council of Ulema [religious scholars] in this country is a reasonably broad church. Unfortunately, the extremists got a head start when the ICU collapsed. But there was a period of about six months when the ICU successfully imposed law and order – which is what Somalis want and need more than anything.'

He went on to describe how, in his native Hargeisa, female money changers were able to operate in perfect safety on the street, even after midnight.

'And when they go home, they simply lock their money in a metal mesh box, which they leave right there on the street. No one ever steals it!'

Islam, he was convinced, was more than merely popular among Somalis. Over the years, it had become the very basis of civil society.

'When I am in Hargeisa I like to go for walks in the very early morning. There are mosques everywhere – three of them within five minutes of my house – and each morning, for the *fajr* prayer at 5 a.m., they are always completely full.'

It was far too late, he said, to turn back the clock. Islamification had happened by a process of what he called 'force majeure'. The Italian civil code applied by the judiciary in the 1960s had been 'unpicked' by the years of socialism in the 1970s and 1980s, before being smashed altogether in the chaos of the 1990s; and only the imams had proved able to fill the void. The West had therefore better learn to work with the grain of Islamic tradition instead of always struggling against it, a message which he had put at the heart of his mission as Minister of Foreign Affairs.

'The president is regarded with suspicion when he

speaks up for Islam, but I am perceived a little differently ... I spoke on this subject at the UN Security Council in 2009. I think I have sold the idea to the US. We *have* to be practical.'

His notion of practicality did not extend to negotiating with al-Shabaab.

'The leadership is hard core, and I think there is no cure for them. The educated ulema in America and elsewhere have declared their jihad illegitimate. When they declare every member of the government, from the president down to the humblest cleaning lady, to be an apostate or a *kafir* – how can anyone take that seriously?'

His question was answered by another burst of machine-gun fire from outside. As before, Omaar simply ignored it.

'The threat here is not al-Qaida,' he went on. 'Somalis by character are too independent-minded to follow any foreign ideology for long. That is part of the reason for the chaos. Everyone is a prima donna. You can't get them to agree on bloody anything.'

There was nothing new about this characteristic. Their innate belligerence was not so much described as celebrated in this well-worn Somali proverb:

> I against my brother.
> I and my brother against the family.
> I and my family against the clan.
> I and my clan against Somalia.
> I and Somalia against the world.

The parliament, although characterized most of the time by inertia, was also the occasional scene of spectacular drama, as arguments between MPs got out of hand. In January 2012, a dispute led to a fist-fight so intense that it had to be broken up by AMISOM troops, and four MPs were taken to hospital with serious head injuries.

Omaar thought that the greatest danger was not Islamism but the country's 'statelessness', which made it susceptible to hijack by warlords and, particularly, pirates.

'Al-Qaida is a poor, miserable thing, but the piracy is El Dorado. There are 20,000 vessels passing through Somali waters every year, and millions – billions – to be made. The young here are already at great risk. They have never even *seen* a functioning state. And when you add in the temptation of that waterway to a fierce fighting tradition . . . if the West doesn't get serious about this place, we could end up with a variation of the Colombian narco-state.'

Yarisow, Farmaajo's head of communications, entered the room then, calling Omaar 'Excellency' and whispering in his ear. Omaar politely excused himself – he was deputizing for Farmaajo, who was abroad, and he had to attend to some state business – but asked Yarisow to show me downstairs to wait in the cabinet room. This nerve centre of Somali government turned out to be a large, gloomy, T-shaped space that smelled of damp and dust, and which appeared not to have been decorated since the 1970s. A low-voltage flicker emanated from a backlit red glass waterfall. Fat, brown leather sofas and armchairs were arranged around the edges of the room, interspersed with shiny reproduction side tables and swirly-patterned rugs. In the centre, beneath a pair of faux-art-deco chandeliers the colour of crème-de-menthe, was an over-varnished, English-style dining table set with eighteen chairs, all empty except at one end where two men sat nattering with their feet up. From the way they scurried out when they saw Yarisow, I suspected they were cleaners on a break.

If the cabinet room felt under-used, that was partly because the government did much of its real business elsewhere, in Nairobi or Kampala or Addis Ababa. Indeed, it was quite rare to find all eighteen members of the cabinet together in Mogadishu at the same time. The city's dangers simply made it impractical for regular meetings. UN officials complained that it was difficult to engage with the political process when the country's top politicians were away all the time. Somalis, however, retorted that UNPOS, the UN's Political Office for Somalia, had been based in Nairobi for more than sixteen years. The UN's Special Representative for Somalia, the Tanzanian diplomat Augustine Mahiga, routinely flew into Mogadishu for important meetings – purely to shake hands in front of the cameras, according to his detractors – before returning to the safety of Nairobi the same day.* Mogadishu, it seemed, was not a place that anyone lingered in longer than they had to.

It was probably significant that the cabinet room hadn't been decorated since the 1970s, for that was the decade when the dream of pan-Somali nationalism really died – killed off, perhaps, by Siad Barre's overweening regional ambitions that culminated in his disastrous invasion of Ethiopia in 1977. In the centre of the conference table was a papier-mâché flowerpot painted in the colours of the

* Mahiga at last took the symbolically vital step of relocating his office to Mogadishu in January 2012.

national flag – blue, with a white star in the centre – and even this bespoke the sad narrative of Somalia's failure as a state.

The flag was designed in the 1950s in preparation for independence, an era of hope and optimism and nationalistic fervour – the last time, perhaps, that Somalis could genuinely look forward to the future. The star was a 'star of unity', the points of which symbolized the five Somali-inhabited regions that nationalists dreamed would one day come together to form *Somaliweyn*, a Greater Somalia: French, British and Italian Somaliland, plus the Ogaden in Ethiopia and the North Eastern Province of Kenya. The blue background, meanwhile, copied and honoured the flag of the United Nations, under whose ten-year 'trusteeship' the colonies were then governed.

But the UN failed in its role of midwife; the infant country it delivered was an unhappy, misshapen thing. British Somaliland – which simply dropped the word 'British' to become 'Somaliland' – immediately regretted unifying with the former Italian colony to the south, and has been trying to separate from them again almost ever since. French Somaliland went its own way and became Djibouti in 1977. The claim on the Ogaden led to a disastrous war with Ethiopia, which destroyed any appetite there might have been to test Kenya's commitment to its North Eastern Province.

The UN, guiltily determined to help its malformed progeny, returned for three years as peacekeepers in 1992. 'UNOSOM' became the largest UN operation in the world, with 30,000 staff and a cost of $1.5bn a year, but it was still powerless to prevent Somalia from spinning even further apart. Now, in the twenty-first century, the UN had returned once more, this time as sponsors – some would say puppet-masters – of the African Union and the TFG. The flag, though, is unchanged: an unhappy amalgam of nationalist white and international blue, and the only one in the world to depict a nation state that has never existed and that almost certainly never will.

The gunfire outside had stopped for a while but now began to pick up again. Yarisow left the room, his fingers jabbing at a mobile phone, then reappeared with the reassuring news that it was all suppressive, outgoing fire. But he also mentioned that the ear-splitting explosion we had heard earlier was caused not by an outgoing shell, as Minister Omaar had suggested, but by a large, incoming one. An 82mm mortar round had exploded in the parade ground right in front of the building's entrace, a spot that I had crossed less than an hour previously. I wondered if Omaar had known all along. Yarisow didn't answer when I asked if anyone had been hurt, but remarked mildly it might be best for me to wait until the exchange of fire had calmed down before leaving.

I wasn't the only one forced to shelter from the metal storm. First came the Minister of Information, Abdulkareem Jama, a clean-cut, bespectacled man with a strong American accent. He turned out to be from Falls Church, Virginia, and used to work as an IT manager for a small commercial publishing firm in Washington. Next to arrive was Mohamed Nur, the speckle-bearded mayor of Mogadishu, a returnee from north London.

I had read about 'Tarzan', as he was nicknamed, because his extraordinary career path had attracted the attention of several British journalists recently. From 1993 until his appointment in 2010, he had lived a quiet life in London with his wife and six children. A local business advisor, he had once run an internet café called Easyreach on the Seven Sisters Road. One of the high points of his previous professional life came when he contested the Camden Council seat of Fortune Green on behalf of the Labour Party in 2006, even though he lost.

He had greater success in Mogadishu, where he was admired by many for his efforts to restore some sense of normality to municipal government.

'My first objectives here were very basic: to improve security, to clean up the markets, to put some lighting on the main streets. But I didn't inherit a single tool from my predecessor. Not even a wheelbarrow.'

His budget came entirely from levies on goods arriving at the seaport, money that for years had been paid in cash straight into the pockets of the city's administrators. Nur made his first, dangerous enemies when he ordered that in future this money should be paid into a traceable bank account. Among the first officials to object was his own deputy. Nur quickly suspended him, but was unable to permanently fire him because he had been appointed, for clan-political reasons, by the president.

'I told my family when I took this job that death was a real possibility,' he said. 'But if I die with my principles intact, that's OK by me.'

There was no mistaking his sincerity. Nur defined his mission in Mogadishu in almost messianic terms.

'Ninety per cent of the people here are traumatized without even knowing it,' he said. 'They have tremendous mental problems. They have been living for years in a dark cage, with no windows, no toilets, with nothing but the awful sound of fighting in their ears, so afraid that they soil themselves . . . and they think this is a normal life. Our job is to break the window, to let in the light and show them, *that* is normality.'

Soon after his appointment, and with this light-disseminating mission in mind, Nur decided to hold a cultural festival.

'I wanted it to be like the market at Camden Lock,' he told me. 'My dream was to have the streets filled with people walking around, enjoying themselves.'

Fairs and festivals were once common in Mogadishu, for Somalia's musical and literary heritage is a particularly rich one, although as Nur pointed out, 'No one has congregated for pleasure in Mogadishu for over twenty years – only for politics.' Armed with $15,000 provided by the UN, he set about hiring troupes of folk dancers, musicians, caterers. Poets were specially commissioned to write, and recite, new works for the occasion. Singers from Waaberi, a famous Somali supergroup, were invited to take part: the first time anyone had heard of them since the late 1990s. Word quickly spread among the public. It was the best and most exciting thing to happen in the city for years.

The crowds were dense from the moment the festival opened, at 8.30 a.m. one February morning. Exactly one hour and ten minutes later, the party came to a sudden end when men loyal to one of Nur's predecessors as mayor, a notorious warlord called Mohamed Dheere, arrived in two armed trucks and opened fire. Four people were killed and sixteen wounded.

'Dheere is just a thug – a cold man,' Nur said bitterly. 'He wants chaos – and he might even get away with it yet.'

Dheere, he explained, had been arrested and imprisoned, and was supposed to be tried by a military court for the attack, but the trial had been deferred following pressure through his Hawiye Abgaal clan.

'My impression is that when someone invokes clan loyalty, they are very often working not in that clan's interests but in their own . . . Dheere has been given special treatment in his cell. He even hired the chief prosecutor's office to defend him! How is that possible? Don't talk to me about an independent judiciary. There is none here.'

Warlordism was evidently still a force to be reckoned with in Mogadishu. The warlords used the clan system against the government, and so did the business community, for whom the restoration of civic order meant the reimposition of taxes they had evaded for years.

'This government is trying to restore a culture of honesty, but it is like trying to swim against the waves of the Indian Ocean.'

Any lack of progress, he added, was not the fault of the government, but of the president: a remark that caused Yarisow, who was listening in to our conversation, to look up sharply. Nur, appointed mayor directly by Sheikh Sharif, was now overtly biting the hand that had fed him. I recalled that the president was a member of the same Hawiye Abgaal clan as Nur's nemesis, Mohamed Dheere.

'The leadership is the problem,' he persisted. 'Sheikh Sharif has not fulfilled our expectations, or those of the Somali people. He is too indecisive. It takes an age to move a bottle from here to here.'

This diatribe was interrupted by the arrival of a stern-looking man in an unusually tall white kufi cap and a heavily embroidered robe. Yarisow coughed and introduced the Minister for Presidential Affairs, Abdulkadir Moallin Noor.

'He is also from London,' Yarisow added, conversationally. 'He is the head of Ahlu Sunna. He is a very important man.'

This was naked flattery, dressed up as an explanation to a clueless gaalo. There were political undercurrents at work here, internal rivalries to do with clan and religion that I, as an outsider, was in no way equipped to detect. As the presidential gatekeeper and the leader of the ASWJ, the government's most important local military ally, the new arrival obviously was an important man. At the same time, he was patently not a member of Farmaajo's club of technocrats. He didn't just dress differently, but spoke differently too. The atmosphere in the room had perceptibly cooled.

'You are British,' he observed, through narrowed eyes.

'Yes. Where did you live in London?'

'Battersea,' he said, in a tone that did not invite further inquiry.

He took me by an elbow then and, leading me to one side, launched into a low, fast monologue, a kind of justificatory introduction to himself that he must have delivered often before.

'I am the Khalifa,' he began. 'It means "the Successor". My father was a big spiritual leader of Ahlu Sunna and I took over from him when he died two years ago. Ahlu

Sunna is a peace-loving organization: a 100 per cent Sufi organization, with followers all over the world. When I fly to London, two hundred people turn out to meet me at Heathrow. With *flags*. My father started over a thousand madrassahs, and built forty-six mosques in Mogadishu alone. We used to be a simple aid organization: we ran food camps that fed five hundred or six hundred people at a time. But when al-Shabaab began to desecrate our graves, we were forced to fight. See?'

I saw; although, privately, I was wondering about the Khalifa's relationship with the enigmatic president. Who was really in charge here?

Earlier that day at AMISOM headquarters, I had heard a rumour that Sheikh Sharif had recently *sold* a truckload of weapons to one of the clan militias fighting for the TFG army – which was supposed to be the nucleus of an essential institution of the state. This was the sort of behaviour Somalis had come to expect of warlords, not of the God-fearing former leader of the Islamic Courts Union. Was Sheikh Sharif merely monetarily corrupt? Or was he, as I thought more likely, another kind of victim, a leader somehow ensnared by the competing vested interests of clan and creed that seemed to dominate all political discourse in this country? If the stories about him were even half true, Sheikh Sharif had surely lost sight of what was best for Somalia.

The gunfire outside had subsided. Yarisow materialized again, a mobile phone still clamped to his ear, informing me that an AMISOM convoy was waiting outside, and that I needed to move fast if I wanted to get back to the base before nightfall. I humped on my soggy flak jacket again, while extracting business cards and promises of another invitation to the Villa Somalia. And then I was running through the gates to the back of a Casspir, which lurched away in a cloud of diesel smoke before the rear doors were fully closed, the top-gunner in his turret crouched and unusually alert.

I didn't know it then, but Farmaajo's promising new administration was already doomed, with less than four more months in office before them. They were the sacrificial victims of the power struggle between the president and the speaker. In June 2011, in Kampala, the two Sharifs agreed to extend their own mandates and postpone a general election for another year. The parliament had earlier unilaterally extended its mandate by three years; the speaker's price for getting parliament to agree to an earlier election date was the dismissal of Farmaajo.

The public was outraged by the so-called Kampala Accord. Sheikh Sharif was clearly taken aback by the strength of public feeling it generated. Thousands of demonstrators took to the streets not just in towns across Somalia but in nine capitals around the world.

'What they have a problem with,' Mayor Nur told the Toronto *Star*, 'is that two people go and decide the fate of this government without considering the feelings of this population.'

Or, for that matter, the feelings of Farmaajo's cabinet – for it was no small risk these officials had taken when they came back to serve their country. In June 2011, just days before the government fell, the Interior Minister, Abdishakur Sheikh Hassan Farah, was killed in his home by a suicide bomber. He was the sixth TFG minister to be murdered by the militants.

What made Farah's death particularly chilling was that the suicide bomber was his own niece, a bright university student called Haboon Qaaf, whose tuition fees he had been paying. According to a family friend I later interviewed,* Haboon had complained about being frisked each time she came to see her uncle, who ordered his guards to make an exception for her. She took advantage of this soft-heartedness on her very next visit. No one had any idea when or how she had been recruited by al-Shabaab, and those who knew her could only guess at what had prompted an act of such nihilism. Just weeks before the attack, according to the friend, Haboon had spoken cheer-fully about qualifying one day as a doctor; her studies suggested an investment in the future that did not begin to fit with the mindset necessary to commit suicide.

The president appeared as unmoved by this tragedy as he was by the Kampala Accord protests, which he declared 'illegal'. Soon afterwards he appointed the Minister of Planning, the economist Abdiweli Mohamed Ali, as his fifth prime minister, a move that sparked further protests from Somalis fearful that he was little more than a place-man. Farmaajo could have joined the protests. He was popular enough, probably, to take to the desert and start a small revolution. But he was not a man of violence, and instead appealed for calm. And then he quietly returned to New York, where his old job with the Department of

---

* This was Abdihakim Mohamoud Haji Faqi, the Minister of Defence.

Transport in Buffalo had sagely been kept open for him.*

The Sharifs were expected to maintain at least some governmental continuity by agreeing to keep on the key ministers, but they were unable to compromise even on this, and in the end the whole cabinet was fired. The exasperation among the international officials whose job it was to mentor the process was palpable.

'It is reptile politics,' said Richard Rouget, AMISOM's French military adviser, who had wasted months building up a relationship with the Minister of Defence. 'Somalis think: "If I kill my enemy, even if killing him kills me too, then I've still won." It is blinkered and destructive: the politics of the playground.'

As before, many of the new cabinet ministers were incomers from the diaspora who would have to learn their jobs from scratch. The calibre of some of them was questionable too. The worldly Mohamed Omaar, for instance, was replaced by Mohamed Mohamud Hajji Ibrahim, a learning support teacher at the Newman Catholic College in Brent, north London. Although Ibraham held a degree in international relations, his main qualification appeared to be that he belonged to a sub-clan of the Rahanweyn, like the speaker. Ibrahim's former employer, Newman College's headmaster Richard Kolka, was as surprised as anyone by the news. 'I was amazed and

---

* Farmaajo's return to the US was not quite the end of his political career in Somalia. To everyone's surprise, in July 2012 he announced he was quitting his job in Buffalo in order to run against Sheikh Sharif in the presidential election. 'I'm giving Somali politics another shot because I believe in serving the common cause for the motherland,' he said.[1]

awestruck,' he told journalists. 'He was always such a humble guy. I'd no idea he was involved in the political life of his country, let alone at such an important level.'[2]

The disadvantages of the crude 4.5 formula were made plain once more. The urgent business of producing a constitution and reforming parliament, Richard Rouget reckoned, was set back by at least another three months and perhaps by as many as six. The self-defeating cycle of Somali politics had begun all over again.

6

What makes al-Shabaab tick?

Hodan district, June 2011

Somalia's political process may have been foundering, but by mid-2011 it was increasingly obvious that AMISOM, against all expectations abroad, were not just making good progress but actually winning their war against al-Shabaab. In three short months, the atmosphere in Mogadishu had significantly changed. Senior UN officials now argued that the rebels could not hold Mogadishu indefinitely. Some even whispered that the insurgency might capitulate, and that a total victory was possible.

The insurgents, it was true, had been losing ground to every AMISOM offensive. Morale among al-Shabaab's foot soldiers was said to be low, and not helped by the fact that their leaders seemed to be in just as much disarray as their opponents in the TFG. So much had happened since the movement emerged in 2006. The successful expulsion of the Ethiopians had removed al-Shabaab's first raison d'être as a nationalist resistance movement, forcing a process of reinvention that was still incomplete. What did al-Shabaab now stand for – what did its leaders really want?

Two distinct factions had begun to emerge that summer. Al-Shabaab's spiritual head, the 76-year-old Sheikh Aweys, and his protégé Sheikh Mukhtar Robow, 42, were the leading figures in the 'indigenous' faction, which was fighting to establish an Islamic theocracy in place of the democracy which, they believed, was being forced upon Somalia by America. Their aims, like those of the Afghan Taliban for whom Robow fought in the early 2000s, were fundamentally domestic: 'Proper Islamic rule within Somalia's current borders', as Aweys put it.[1]

Robow had not just fought for the Taliban. An Islamic lawyer who studied at the University of Khartoum in the 1990s, he also once worked for the Somali branch of the al-Haramain Islamic Foundation, an international Saudi charitable organization accused by the US in 2004 of having direct links to al-Qaida, and subsequently proscribed by the UN. Despite this background, most Somalis considered him a moderate compared to al-Shabaab's other main leader, Sheikh Moktar Ali Zubeyr, known as Godane, who headed the rival 'international' faction within the movement, so-called because its ranks were swelled by foreign jihadist fighters from around the world.

Godane's agenda was much more ambitious and dangerous than Robow's. He had taken over from Robow as al-Shabaab's 'Amir' in 2009 at the age of just thirty-one, and had since pushed him and the old guard to the margins of the debate on the movement's future. Godane had also fought the jihad in Afghanistan, but the conclusions he had drawn from his experiences there were quite different to

Robow's. Godane publicly pledged allegiance to Osama bin Laden when he became Amir, an act that propelled al-Shabaab to the top of the list of proscribed terrorist organizations in half a dozen countries. He became a natural magnet for Islamists from around the world who regarded Somalia as the newest and most promising battle-front in the global war against the infidel. In February 2012 bin Laden's successor, the Egyptian surgeon-theologian Ayman al Zawahiri, announced that al-Shabaab and al-Qaida had formally merged. Did Godane dream, as bin Laden once dreamed, of overthrowing the West through war and terrorism and establishing a new international caliphate? It was the question that kept the chiefs of Western intelligence organizations awake at night.

The version of Sharia that Godane advocated for Somalia was far more severe than Robow's. His ideology was based on a foreign import – Wahhabist Salafism – and, unlike his rival, he appeared to have no respect at all for Somalia's gentler Sufi traditions. For example, although Robow disapproved of the Sufi custom of ancestor worship, he stopped far short of ordering the destruction of shrines. The disagreements between Godane and Robow over such matters were no secret, but were played out in public via Mogadishu's many radio stations. Indeed, the narrative of dissent within al-Shabaab formed an almost constant back-drop to the national news. And although some of this was undoubtedly TFG propaganda, it was clear from Robow's occasional interviews and from intelligence leaks that a great deal of it was not.

The key to the difference between the pair was their clan heritage and where they were from. Robow, who was born in Berdaale in the south-central province of Bay, belonged to the Leysan sub-clan of the Rahanweyn, the clan group dominant in the south of Somalia that had long been subjugated by the 'nobler' clans of the north, and which formed the backbone of al-Shabaab's rank and file. Godane, by contrast, belonged to the Isaaq clan and was born in Hargeisa in Somaliland, hundreds of miles from al-Shabaab's heartlands. There were some who argued that Godane had no choice but to rely on foreign jihadist fighters. Unlike Robow, he was unable to count on the loyalty of any local clan for support. The flipside of this apparent disadvantage was that he also owed no obligation towards the clans of the south. Being an outsider allowed him to pursue any agenda he pleased, and the cruellest of policies, unconstrained by local sensitivities.

No one knew how many foreign fighters Godane really commanded. In early 2012, estimates ranged between 200 and 2,000. The majority were said to come from Yemen, Saudi Arabia, Sudan and the Muslim Swahili coast, although they came from further afield too. Many had simply travelled on from Iraq or Afghanistan, experienced fighters who had made a career out of international jihadism: Pakistanis, Bangladeshis, Middle East Arabs. It was sometimes possible to identify the old hands from the methods they used. Al-Shabaab's snipers, for instance, had been taught to shoot from far back in a building through a tunnel of 'murder holes' dug through a series of walls: a technique much used by the Taliban in Helmand during the urban platoon house sieges of 2006–7. The best al-Shabaab marksman was said to be a Chechen, a veteran of the Iraq war, who had shot so many people with his trademark Dragunov rifle that the medics at the AMISOM field hospital had learned to recognize his handiwork.

And then there were the diaspora volunteers, young Somalis who held Western passports: American, Canadian, British, Scandinavian. This category of foreign fighter worried the security services in those countries most of all – especially, in an Olympics-hosting year, Britain's. A report published by London's Royal United Services Institute in 2012 put the number of foreign fighters in Somalia at just two hundred, but estimated that as many as fifty of these were UK citizens, and spoke of the difficulty of preventing a 'lone wolf' attack in Britain by one of them.[2] Jonathan Evans, the head of MI5, had already warned in a speech in 2010 that it was 'only a matter of time before we see terrorism on our streets inspired by those who are today fighting alongside al-Shabaab'.[3]

Sure enough, a month before the Games in July 2012, a 24-year-old London Somali was arrested after he was spotted on CCTV crossing east London's new Olympic Park five times, in specific breach of an earlier Home Office control order. Identified by police as 'CF', the man was already suspected of having fought for al-Shabaab, of trying to recruit other Britons to the cause, and of attempting to travel to Afghanistan for terrorist training. A Home Office lawyer warned that CF wanted to 're-engage in terrorism-related activities, either in the UK or Somalia' and is 'determined to continue to adhere to his Islamist extremist agenda'.[4]

On 8 June 2011, Western security services received a fillip when Fazul Abdullah Mohammed, al-Qaida's leader in East Africa, was unexpectedly killed in Mogadishu. A suspect in the bombings of the US embassies in Kenya and Tanzania in 1998 that killed more than two hundred people, the Comoros-born Fazul had been bin Laden's *amin sirr* or 'confidential secretary' for over a decade, with an FBI bounty on his head of $5m. He had been one of the al-Qaida leader's closest confidants – so close, indeed, that he managed bin Laden's wives' travel arrangements, and even used to shave his boss's head.[5]

The Bancroft Hotel was still abuzz with what had happened. Fazul and an accomplice had been driving towards the al-Shabaab-held suburb of Dayniile late one night when they apparently took a wrong turning, and ran into a twenty-strong TFG checkpoint. Fazul tried to brazen it out with the sentries on duty by pretending that he and the driver were elders. One soldier, Abdi Hassan, ordered Fazul to show himself by turning on the car's interior light, which he did, although only for a second. But this was long enough for Abdi, already suspicious, to spot that they were armed. He was fully alert, he helpfully explained to reporters later, because his unit always chewed qat when they were on duty at night.[6]

Fazul's driver's last act was to pull a pistol which, fortunately for Abdi, jammed. Both militants died instantly in a hail of return fire. A dusty black Toyota was later put on display for photographers, who counted more than a dozen bullet holes in its windscreen. Among the contents of the car were medicines, three mobile phones, three Kalashnikovs, a South African passport, $40,000 in cash, paperwork, and a laptop. The soldiers immediately took the cash and distributed it amongst themselves, but everything else was recovered by the security services. The laptop turned out to contain much valuable information on, for instance, al-Qaida funding networks. There was also a list of potential terrorist targets which included the Ritz Hotel in London and even the British prime minister's *alma mater*, Eton College.

Perhaps the most intriguing aspect of Fazul's death was an allegation published in *SomaliaReport*, a news website set up and funded by the Canadian correspondent Robert Young Pelton, that it had been orchestrated by Godane. According to *SomaliaReport*, Fazul and his driver had been given instructions to meet some insurgent commanders at a certain al-Shabaab checkpoint outside Dayniile. Godane secretly ordered this checkpoint to be taken down, causing Fazul's companion to drive straight on towards the enemy lines. If true, it was a piece of skulduggery worthy of the Borgias.

SomaliaReport speculated that Godane hoped to curry favour with the new al-Qaida chief, Ayman al-Zawahiri, who had taken over the organization following bin Laden's assassination in May 2011, and whose relationship with the influential Fazul, a bin Laden loyalist, had always been tense. The relationship between Godane and Fazul had not exactly been easy, either. In 2009, Fazul posted a lengthy autobiography online in which he expressed concern at al-Shabaab's political immaturity, and revealed that he had even criticized the formation of the organization in 2006, on the grounds that it was likely to undermine the Islamic Courts Union, which he described as 'an official body ... whose authority ought to be respected'. Bin Laden, no doubt on Fazul's advice, consistently rejected Godane's courtship of his organization. It was not until after his and

Fazul's death that Zawahiri accepted Godane's overtures, and al-Shabaab and al-Qaida merged.

The irony of all this was that Fazul, one of the main reasons that the US covertly manoeuvred to bring down the ICU in 2007–8, probably represented America's best chance at the time of stopping al-Shabaab in its tracks. If Washington had found a way to work with the ICU's moderates instead of opting to destroy the whole regime, how might history have been different?

I had hoped to find a way to get close enough to al-Shabaab's leadership to interview them, but after months of trying I concluded I was probably wasting my time. Godane was a recluse who was said sometimes to issue his orders, Wizard of Oz-style, from behind a curtain. It was a mystique-enhancing trick worthy of Mullah Omar, the one-eyed leader of the Taliban whom no Western journalist had seen for over a decade, and I was discouraged by the *noli me tangere* message behind it. Even the relative moderates such as Sheikh Aweys or Mukhtar Robow rarely granted interviews to foreigners, and then only by email or, very occasionally, by phone. Face-to-face encounters were almost unheard of.

Mogadishu wasn't like Kabul, where with the right contacts, money and patience, a foreign journalist could always find an insurgent willing to talk. The Taliban put great importance on getting their message across to an international audience, and were prepared to take considerable risks to do so. They understood that the continuation of Nato's war depended on Western public approval ratings, and that the foreign media offered them their best opportunity to undermine these.

Al-Shabaab, by contrast, usually just wanted to shoot the messenger. Their common assumption, almost a default position, was that all journalists – even local ones – were traitors and spies. Al-Shabaab knew, or thought they knew, that AMISOM had access to CIA surveillance technology, and were paranoid about being traced. This meant that there was no phone number a journalist could call to request an interview, no email address to write to, and of course no physical office to visit.

The movement had a spokesman, the entertainingly named Sheikh Rage, who regularly issued press releases, but it was difficult if not impossible to speak to him, because his number, like all al-Shabaab numbers, was constantly changing. Then even if you were lucky enough to have the right number, there was no guarantee that he would answer your call, because like everyone else in Mogadishu he tended not to pick up if he didn't recognize *your* number. He must have been one of the least accessible press spokesmen in the world.

Even local journalists struggled in this environment. When I went for help to a friendly producer at Radio Bar-Kulan, an AU-funded station with a well-established news operation, every one of the many phone numbers he produced for Sheikh Rage turned out to be defunct. He rang colleagues on two other radio stations, but neither of them could produce an extant number either. I put this problem to one side, and went to ask the Burundians what they thought about al-Shabaab.

In late February 2011 the Burundians, the junior partners in AMISOM, had attempted to oust al-Shabaab from their main military base in the city, the former

Ministry of Defence headquarters. The government in Bujumbura, facing tough questions about Burundi's apparently open-ended commitment to the Somali mission, was tight-lipped about their casualties. A fortnight later, however, Burundian military sources revealed that they had suffered 43 dead and 110 wounded: one of the costliest operations of the entire campaign.

'They started coming in with bullet wounds the moment the offensive began,' recalled Ed Parsons, the Canadian medic assisting at the field hospital. 'Then they started coming in with knife wounds: deep panga slashes. Then they started coming with blows from rocks. It was basically your worst Oliver Stone nightmare . . . You can criticize the Burundians for their lack of tactics, but there is no doubting their courage as fighters. Boy, they fight.'

The failure to provide the assault force with enough ammunition did not slow it down one bit. One soldier, unable to extract his bayonet from the al-Shabaab fighter he had just impaled, simply disconnected his rifle and charged on using its shoulder butt as a weapon, leaving the dying al-Shabaab fighter skewered to a wall.

It was hard to square such stories with the Burundian soldiers I had met around the AMISOM camp, who smiled shyly whenever I greeted them before answering in courtly, archaic French. They were far less experienced than the Ugandans. Apart from a small policing contingent in earth-quake-struck Haiti, the Somalia mission was the Burundi army's first ever international venture. I found their lack of worldliness rather charming. They had a gentle, curiously artistic side to them, evident in the homely way they marked out the territory around their bivouacs with neat lines of half-buried orange juice cartons and yoghurt pots. Most of them were deeply Catholic, a hangover from Belgian colonial times. They held mass in their section of the base every Sunday, when African harmonies would soar ethereally above the tangled thornscrub where they were encamped. An AMISOM propaganda film showing a new rotation of Burundians on parade had to be scrapped when it was realized that the soldiers were marching beneath a giant illuminated cross, an obvious gift to the crusader-obsessed propagandists on the other side.

But for all their naivety, the Burundians were no strangers to violence. As Hutus and Tutsis, they had been killing each other at home for half a century. Many of the older soldiers had first picked up a gun as children. One of their colonels had started fighting at the age of seven. It was only in 2005 that Burundi, a nation of less than nine million, emerged from a twelve-year civil war that killed 300,000. An end to that bloodbath was negotiated through the African Union, which was why the grateful Bujumbura government had voted to contribute troops to AMISOM, the only African country apart from Uganda to do so.

The Ministry of Defence complex, a collection of identical concrete blocks built in the communist brutalist style by Siad Barre at the height of his power in the 1970s, sat on a hill dominating the district of Hodan, the north-west corner of the city. Mogadishans nicknamed this imposing place Gashaandhigga ('Drop Your Weapons') – a reminder, if any were needed, of the iron fist with which the old dictator ruled his people for so long. The authority of Afweyne ('Big Mouth'), as he was known, rested primarily on the army and the National Security Service, both of which were dominated by his own Darod Marehan clan. Hundreds of his political opponents disappeared into Gashaandhigga during the 1980s, where they were murdered or tortured to death, or imprisoned indefinitely without trial.

The ministry building at the centre of the complex, a famous symbol of Afweyne's regime, had been shot to pieces long before al-Shabaab's time. Gunfire and the elements had continued to round off the corners of its facade, turning windows and monumental doorways into rough-edged holes. Its sweating interior resembled a series of gloomy interlocking caves rather than former offices, with walls so pockmarked by bullets they looked like formations of grey coral.

My guide was the sector commander, Major Gerard Hamenyimana, an officer with a joke-shop scar down his cheek and chin, who grimaced at the memory of the battle he had fought a few weeks previously. Al-Shabaab counter-attacked almost immediately after his battalion's capture of the complex, and went on counter-attacking for ten consecutive days. Three months later, the defenders were still on high alert. Ramadan was due to begin soon, and planeloads of ammunition had been arriving all week from Kampala in anticipation of a repeat of the previous year's al-Shabaab offensive. Yet despite the ferocity of the recent fight for Gashaandhigga, it was the major's confident opinion that the insurgency was now militarily spent. They were losing ground with every AMISOM attack, while the fighters opposing his men seemed to grow younger and more desperate with every passing day.

From a heavy machinegun-emplacement on the roof of

the ministry building, we peeked out at the northern suburb of Dayniile, al-Shabaab's new field headquarters. In between was a no-man's land of cactus and thornscrub pushing up through roofless ruins, a landscape with which I was by now becoming depressingly familiar. To the east were the tower blocks and radio masts of the Bakara Market, with the top of Mogadishu stadium visible just beyond. In the 1990s the stadium had served as the head-quarters of the UN's Pakistani peace-keeping contingent, to whom exhausted US soldiers pelted for safety at the end of *Black Hawk Down*: the finish line of what American military trainers still call a 'Mogadishu Mile'.

The major led us back downstairs and out to the perimeter, which had been massively reinforced with sand-bags. The troops were thickly spread along the fire step: four hundred of them, the major said, around the ministry building alone. The wall was so high that we were able to stroll along the gunline in its shade, safe from everything but a chance mortar strike. Hamenyimana called this a quiet day, and his troops did seem relaxed. Several radios were tuned to Radio Africa, so that jolly pop songs wafted up from their dugouts as we passed. Yet al-Shabaab's fighters were always probing. Twice in five minutes, an enemy bullet snapped overhead, prompting bursts of return fire from the sentries stationed above us.

At one point, surreally, I thought I heard men singing. Hamenyimana grinned: I was not mistaken. It was coming from a couple of hundred yards away, along and back from the gunline, where the battalion choir was at practice for next day's Sunday mass.

'You know, I would like to have been *un prêtre* – a priest,' the major suddenly confided. 'I would like to have studied theology in London.'

We made our way over to the source of the hymn. The choir, all off-duty soldiers in T-shirts and shorts, were sitting in rows of plastic chairs arranged like the pews of a church, facing an altar built of ammunition cases, in a ruined chicken coop of a building that had once housed officer cadets in Siad Barre's army. The major, clearly an aficionado, cocked his head to listen, before nodding with approval and leading us on.

'It is a tragedy, but Somalia was once the *first* military power in Africa,' Hamenyimana observed. 'Officers came from every country to study at the academy here. Even Burundians. We admired the Somalis in those days. We wanted to be like them.'

We picked our way out of the ministry complex on to the Terebunka Road, once a major artery of the city but now blocked with truck containers filled with sand: al-Shabaab had expected AMISOM to attack their position with tanks, not infantry. It was the start of a long morning's hike along the Burundian front. I took photographs of sleeping Burundian soldiers, a pair of emaciated cows grazing on rubbish, and the bullet-pocked front of a grocery decorated with bright little paintings of the goods it had once sold, standard advertising practice in a country with an illiteracy rate of over 60 per cent.[7] We had to sprint across one sniper-exposed section of the line helpfully signposted *DANGER DE MORT*. Beyond was a pharmacy with its side blown off, the shelves within still stocked with tempting-looking packets and boxes, a sign that the shop was almost certainly booby-trapped.

In another wasteland of shattered concrete and tangled thorn, a district known as the Milk Factory although no milk had been processed there for many years, we were high-fived by a TFG soldier, one of the many interspersed with AMISOM's troops all along the line of control. Hamenyimana looked apprehensively at this one, who was wearing combat trousers and a dirty yellow vest that read *FBI: Female Body Inspector*. His nearby bivouac didn't look any more military than his vest. He and his friends had fenced off a large, tumbledown villa, and had brought their families to live with them there, front line or no. A group of women and children were visible in the villa's trash-strewn courtyard, squatting around a fire from which a thin plume of smoke rose. A 'technical', a rusting pick-up truck with a four-barrelled anti-aircraft gun bolted to its load bay, was parked nearby. This weapon of choice for the warlords of the 1990s was a Somali innovation – perhaps the only thing to be created during those years of terrible destruction – that was subsequently copied by everyone from the Taliban to Libya's anti-Gaddafi rebels in 2011.

The sight of these men, all members of the SNA, the fledgling Somali national army on which the TFG's authority supposedly depended, did not bode well for the future. Western advisors had repeatedly pointed out that, to preserve discipline and foster esprit de corps, the SNA's troops really needed to be housed in proper military barracks. As an ex-military dictatorship, Somalia was hardly short of bases. But the ranks of the SNA were filled with ex-clan militiamen like these, who were used to living on the streets 'with their brothers' – and the SNA's officers could not afford to alienate them by ordering them to do otherwise. It was another sign of the fragility of the TFG's hold on power. Could clan loyalty ever be supplanted by patriotism in circumstances such as these?

We came eventually to a district called African Village, built in 1974 to house the VIP delegates to a summit of the Organization of African Unity – the forerunner, ironically enough, of the African Union, the sponsors of the AMISOM troops now in occupation here. The district had been a showcase of modernity in its day, with large, airy accommodation blocks neatly arranged along leafy avenues that must once have been very pleasant.

In the 1980s it was so favoured by senior civil servants and their families that less fortunate Mogadishans nick-named it Booli Qaran ('Stolen Public Money'). That affluent era was long gone now, commemorated by the burned-out carcass of a yellow, American-style school bus.

Back at the ministry complex the major stopped by the eastern gate. This had been filled in with Hesco barriers on which '8 BN AMISOM' had been picked out in empty strawberry yoghurt pots. It was a memorial to his battalion's fallen, spontaneously constructed at the scene of the fiercest fighting of all. Just inside the gateway was a deep conical crater in which lay a blackened engine block and a twist of axle: all that remained of an al-Shabaab suicide truck. Hamenyimana described how, after a week of trying to force the gate, the insurgents had massed for one final attempt. The truck had tried to ram its way through, but the weight of Burundian gunfire pouring through the windscreen was too much, and the driver was killed before he was able to detonate the explosives in the back. The gate was partially blocked by the riddled vehicle, which finally blew up just as al-Shabaab's main force of infantry was trying to negotiate its way around it.

'We picked up sixty of their dead,' said the major, shaking his head. 'Sixty! Can you imagine?'

Al-Shabaab's supply of fighters prepared to martyr themselves did seem inexhaustible, like an industrial conveyor belt of young suicide. I wondered, not for the first time, how their leaders had managed to create this demonic meat-grinder. As Somalis never tired of telling you, suicide bombing was a foreign import, almost unheard of until a decade ago and unfavoured as a tactic even at the height of the civil war. Yet I suspected that many of the traits required in a successful suicide bomber were deeply rooted in the national character. Nomadic warrior tradition, for instance, placed great importance on the obviously useful quality of fearlessness.

'I never saw a Somali who showed any fear of death, which, impressive though it sounds, carries with it the chill of pitilessness and ferocity as well,' wrote Gerald Hanley. 'The Somalis died as they liked to die, contemptuously, throwing off the cloak-blanket and staring at the firing squad, sneering at the trembling rifles. They had had their fragment of living, their brief satisfaction, and they had prayed. Now die. *Hrun sheg! Wallahi!*'[8]

Fearlessness, however, is not quite the same thing as actively seeking to die as you kill your enemy, as these young suicide bombers appeared to do. It is not natural to want to destroy oneself. The mindset it takes to do so therefore has to be nurtured, if not taught from scratch. Al-Shabaab's suicide bomber mentors were skilled theologians, expert at twisting the tenets of Islam to promote and justify martyrdom. Just as importantly, perhaps, they knew exactly which psychological buttons to press in their young charges.

Martyrs for Islam, famously, are rewarded with the attentions of seventy-two virgins when they reach heaven. In Somalia, al-Shabaab's mentors were said to have shown their pupils Bollywood DVDs, and told their young charges that they were watching footage shot by militants who had already blown themselves up and gone to Paradise.[9] It obviously helped that the trainee bombers were uneducated and highly impressionable boys, for the most part, who were easily misled and lied to. Their gullibility was some-times breathtaking. But so, too, was the religious hypocrisy of their mentors. Bollywood movies are a byword for licentiousness in Muslim Asia. Their troupes of gyrating *houris* are seen as agents of moral corruption, to be resisted at all costs. Indeed, the popularity of the genre in Afghanistan was one of the main reasons that the Taliban banned television when they came to power in 1996.

There was no doubt that al-Shabaab's foot soldiers were sexually frustrated. In this, perhaps, they were no different from teenagers in all those other parts of the Islamic world where pre-marital intercourse of all kinds is *haram*. In one recently overrun al-Shabaab position, AMISOM troops were astonished to find the walls covered with doodles of the most obscene type.

'There was a lot of rape imagery – a lot of bestiality, and half-man, half-beast stuff,' said an AMISOM public relations officer who saw it. 'It was certainly not the sort of thing you would associate with pious Islamists.'

The discovery led one UN official in Nairobi to joke that

to neutralize al-Shabaab as a fighting force, all AMISOM needed to do was to fly in two planeloads of prostitutes from Bangkok and ferry them up to the front.

The connection between pornography and Islamic terrorism had been made before. One of the more intriguing discoveries made by the US Navy SEALs who stormed Osama bin Laden's compound in Pakistan in May 2011 was a 'fairly extensive' collection of porn films.[10] Did the puritanical scourge of the 'decadent' West have a porn habit? It seemed so unlikely at the time that many Westerners dismissed the report as black propaganda put out by the CIA. Yet US officials who had seen evidence gathered during investigations of other Islamic militants said it was 'not unusual' to discover porn in such cases.

I was later amazed to discover a large body of psychiatric literature dedicated to the role of sex in suicide bombing.[11] I could just about grasp that to enable them to kill innocent people, suicide bombers commonly 'dehumanized' their target before pulling the pin – and that this process, according to one analyst, was very similar to the 'desensitizing' effect on the male brain of too much pornography. In both cases, I could see, human beings were reduced to the status of objects. But I did not realize that some Islamist suicide bombers literally wrapped up their genitals before their mission in order to preserve them for the promised seventy-two virgins; nor did I know that the act of suicide is commonly described as their 'wedding'. Some psychiatrists interpret the moment of detonation as a kind of consummation, the ultimate physical release of the frustrations of a virgin's life on earth, a grotesque orgasm of body parts.

The US military psychoanalyst Nancy Kobrin delved

even deeper into the suicide-bomber's psyche. She thought suicide bombing was a symptom of early 'problematic bonding' between sons and their mothers, which she regarded as inevitable in Muslim societies where 'the female, instead of being valued and cherished, is denigrated, abused and pathologically controlled from day one. There is no regard for the mother's stress hormone level or her devotion to her newborn. Ultimately, this not only jeopardizes the infant's health but can lead to severe ego dysfunction as well as cognitive impairments, such as flying planes into buildings rather than just fantasizing about it.'

The West had long assumed that Islamic terrorism was primarily about politics. How much of it was actually driven by dysfunction in the terrorist's maternal relationship? It was certainly suggestive that in the 1990s, the Saudis repeatedly sent bin Laden's mother, Umm Usama, to Sudan and Afghanistan in order to get her son to 'behave'. Kobrin noted that *Ummi* – 'Mummy' in Arabic – comes from the same root as *Ummah*, or 'community', the Koranic term for the global Muslim diaspora that bin Laden hoped to unite. 'The Arab Muslim communal self-perception is [thus] linked to the maternal,' Kobrin wrote.

There was no doubt something in this thesis, although again it did not quite explain what was happening in Somalia. From a Freudian point of view the mother–son relationship was 'problematic' for all Muslims, according to Kobrin. Yet the epidemic of suicide bombing was not universally spread, any more than the extremist ideology that underpinned it was. It seemed to me that neither would have flourished in Somalia without the civil war, which had silenced the voices of moderation that might have countered the extremists. There were no schools or teachers, the clan elders had been scattered, and the fathers, very often, were dead.

'One asks – where is the father?' wrote Kobrin. 'The father's absence seems to reflect the frequently heard complaint in the interview literature of terrorists that their fathers were absent. We might conclude that the reason terrorists remain forever tied into their mothers is precisely because of the absence of a father in Islamic regimes.'

Like the first generation of Taliban in the 1990s, many al-Shabaab recruits were indeed orphans of parents killed by famine or war. The careers of thousands of other al-Shabaab fighters had begun, as Mohamed Omaar observed, with the trauma of sudden abduction from the family home, a separation that all too often became permanent. In either case it meant that youths were left vulnerable, hungry, and ripe for exploitation by ambitious ideologues operating *in loco parentis*.

At the AMISOM base, just beyond the north perimeter, was a camp set aside by the TFG for deserters from al-Shabaab. The existence of this place was little advertised, and I was told early on that there was no chance of gaining permission to visit it. The inmates' first-hand knowledge of how the insurgency worked made them a source of intelligence which neither the TFG nor AMISOM much wanted to share. Eventually, however, I and three other foreign journalists badgered the Ugandan civil-military affairs officer, an avuncular lieutenant colonel called Katwekyeire, to let us accompany an army medical officer there on one of his weekly health visits.

There were 168 ex-al-Shabaab fighters living in the camp, almost double the number three months previously, which was another indicator that the war was going AMISOM's way. The numbers were not huge, yet al-Shabaab fighters were already deserting faster than the TFG could handle them. It was not even their intelligence officers but AMISOM's who screened and interrogated the inmates before releasing them into the camp for rehabilitation. There were also dark rumours that TFG officials close to President Sharif had sold some al-Shabaab deserters back to the enemy, with senior fighters commanding the highest prices.

I had come prepared for anti-Western hostility from a gang of hardened jihadist militants. Instead I found a crowd of school-age teenagers, spirited, unruly, and for the most part instantly likeable. Their average age was fifteen. They lived in large, closely packed dormitories that looked out over a sandy parade ground to a huddle of half-built blockhouses on the other side. Dozens of them clustered around the back of the Casspir from the moment we arrived, clearly bored and apparently glad of the novelty of strangers to talk to. It was disorienting, but in their Lakers T-shirts and Nile Sports tracksuits, they resembled schoolboys anywhere in the world. They behaved like them too, particularly in the way they made faces behind the back of Najib, an officious type who 'coordinated' the camp on behalf of the TFG. No one had warned Najib of our visit, and for a moment it seemed we would be ejected from his kingdom, although he was soon calmed by a phone call back to Katwekyeire.

I asked the crowd for their names.

'Saifullah,' said one, after a moment's hesitation.

'Musa,' said another.

'Hizbullah,' said a third, to titters all around.

'Mohamed al-Shabaab,' said a fourth, to guffaws.

It was a good joke – absurd pseudonyms to please the silly gaalo – and they clapped me on the back when I smiled to show that I got it and didn't mind being teased.

'Our real names are all left at the door here,' one of them added apologetically. 'I'm sure you understand.'

The atmosphere felt part army boot camp, part school sports day. There was no perimeter fence to speak of, and no guards, for the inmates here had all volunteered for 'deprogramming', as Najib called the rehabilitation process. There were plans to run vocational training courses in mechanics and electronics when the sheds across the square were finally completed. In the meantime, the boys under-went three mandatory hours a day of 'correct' Islamic instruction, designed to undo the 'lies' they had been taught by al-Shabaab.

At first they answered our questions with platitudes. Al-Shabaab was bad and the TFG was good, they said, because there was 'no life, no prospects' in the insurgency.

'We are taught how to load and unload – that's it,' said one. 'We don't matter to them. I want to fight for the TFG.'

But as the novelty of our presence wore off and the crowd began to thin and break up into smaller groups, the conversations became more interesting. Among the older ex-al-Shabaab, the young men who were no longer in their teens, I detected a troubling level of discontent, and they were keen to explain why.

'Don't let this place fool you,' said one long-faced young

man, glancing over his shoulder. His name, he said, was Jabril, he was twenty-one, and he had been living in the camp for six months. 'Some of the younger ones here are believers, but in truth we are just TFG showpieces. I was promised a better life when I came here – a job, a visa, a passport – but that doesn't happen. So far they have given us nothing.'

'It's true,' said his friend Abshir, a Kenyan Somali who had come to the camp at the same time. 'The TFG have been very welcoming. At least we are alive and well. Yet most of us are thinking every day: how do I get out of here?'

'You ask about our future,' Jabril went on, 'but we cannot think beyond surviving in the present. And meanwhile, we are losing our families.'

Defection, he explained, came at a high cost to the older, married fighters. Jabril had left behind a wife and baby somewhere in al-Shabaab territory, since when the wife had been 'taken' by another fighter. It seemed that battlefield marriages had been forced on the wives of several of the deserters here, no doubt in order to deter others from running to the gaalo.

'So what is stopping you from leaving?' I asked, nodding towards the camp's unguarded entrance. 'Could you not go back for your wife and baby?'

Jabril and Abshir looked at each other.

'Two guys did leave here two days ago,' said Jabril. 'They wanted to find a better life for themselves. They got as far as Afgoye, but then someone recognized them.'*

---

* The so-called Afgoye Corridor just south-west of Mogadishu, home to over half a million refugees displaced by years of fighting in the capital, is a well-known al-Shabaab stronghold.

The author with Ugandan Colonel John Mugarura, of AMISOM, on the front line in Hawl Wadaag district, Mogadishu (top).

Above: Contingency Commander Paul Lokech during an eve-of-battle briefing.

Fighting through this densely packed city required exceptional planning and leadership (*right*).

A captured communications trench, one of a vast network dug through the city centre. AMISOM and al-Shabaab front lines were just 50 metres apart in some places.

Soldiers used 'mouseholes' such as this to pass between abandoned homes: often safer than the front door.

Somalis refer to the years of civil war simply as *Burburki*, 'the Destruction'.

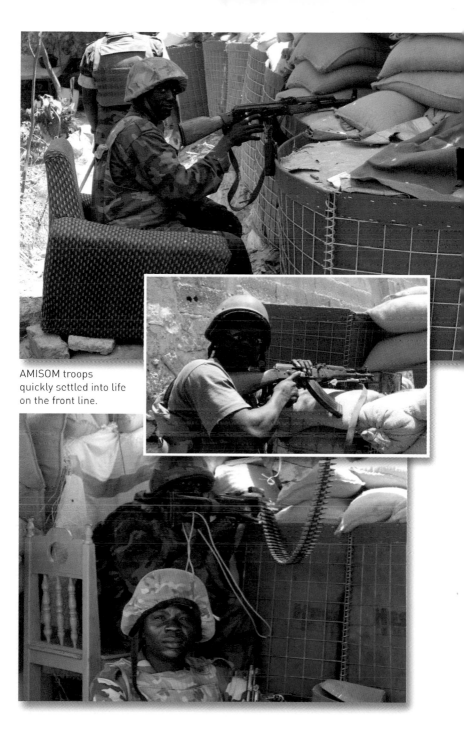

AMISOM troops
quickly settled into life
on the front line.

Above: Somalia has been afflicted by wild street fighting for twenty years. Al-Shabaab (*left*) took power with a promise to restore discipline; footage of well-drilled militiamen in uniform became an important propaganda tool.

Below: Newly captured al-Shabaab fighters, all schoolboys. They said they volunteered in exchange for a daily piece of fruit.

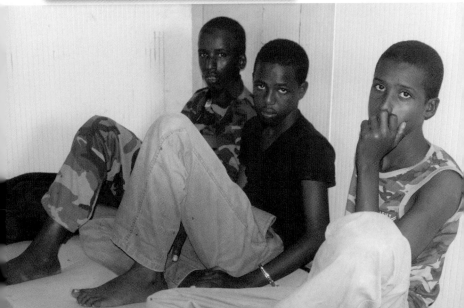

Al-Shabaab's recruitment process often begins even earlier, in a nation said to contain 14 million guns in a population of 8 million. Boys as young as seven have been put to work on the front line.

Top: A food queue at Mogadishu's Badbaado refugee camp where some 35,000 famine victims arrived in the space of three months (*above*). The 2011 drought was the worst for sixty years, affecting over 12 million people. The international aid community were initially slow to respond – unlike the ex-health minister, Osman Ibrahim, here seen dousing a camp latrine with Dettol retrieved from the boot of his car.

Dysentery from contaminated food and water is a major killer in a famine, along with typhoid, cholera, malaria, dengue fever and measles. US officials estimate that 29,000 children under the age of five died between May and July 2011.

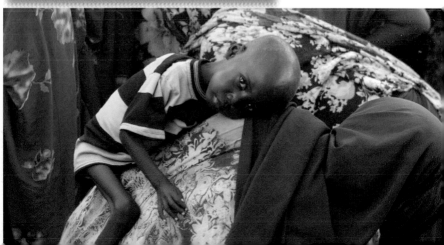

Above: Somali shops advertise their wares with images to overcome an illiteracy rate of over 60 per cent.

Right: Between 60 and 75 per cent of Somalis are thought to be users or sellers of *qat*, a leaf that acts like an amphetamine when chewed.

In Hargeisa (*left*) the streets are so safe that money-changers line the pavements with bundles of bank notes. Further south, however, marketplaces can be deadly, providing easy targets for terrorists (Mogadishu, 2012, *below*).

'And what happened to them?'

There was the tiniest pause.

'They were beheaded by al-Shabaab this morning,' said Abshir.

'But how do you know?'

'We are still in touch with people,' Jabril said. 'We hear things.'

'The hills have ears round here,' Abshir added.

Just then, as if on cue, a third man sauntered up: a fresh-faced 17-year-old who wanted to tell me how he had arrived in the camp just two days before. He had come all the way from Kismayo, he said, travelling at night to avoid the militants who would certainly have killed him had they realized where he was headed. There was a puppyish quality to him that reminded me of 'Young Thing', the naive, wannabe suicide bomber in Nuruddin Farah's novel *Crossbones*. Young Thing was the type of beta-male who would do anything to impress his peers, a willingness to please that also made him highly dangerous. It was clear from their sudden silence that Jabril and Abshir, the camp's old lags, did not trust this newcomer one bit. I could almost see them wondering if he was an al-Shabaab infiltrator. Their camp had no walls but it was a prison to them nevertheless, with all the vicious internal politics associated with such places, and similar behavioural conventions.

'No one in here will tell you if they've killed people, but there's more that have than haven't,' Jabril observed at one point.

I suspected that belonging to the right clique or gang in here could easily be a matter of life or death.

Later that summer, in Puntland, I met a French

criminologist called Daniel LaDouceur, an expert in youth gang culture who knew this deserters' camp well. Gang membership, he explained, was a primitive survival tactic based on strength in numbers. With the collapse of central authority in 1991 and the breakdown of the clan system, Somali society had disintegrated further into a constellation of gangs, the continuing survival of which, he thought, presented the single greatest obstruction to Somalia's civil reconstruction.

'Everything here is about gangs: gangs of kids,' he said. 'Pirates operate in gangs. People smugglers in the Gulf of Aden are gangs. The militias in Mogadishu say they are clan organizations but really they are gangs too ... Al-Shabaab is a super-gang, a collection of small clans ganging up on the big clans. And they are all just kids.'

LaDouceur was piloting a UN-funded scheme called 'Youth at Risk' which aimed to take potential gangsters off the street by paying them to take lessons in citizenship, governance and the rule of law.

'At the moment the international community's strategy is to try to control the violence through the clan elders. But the elders are the wrong interlocutors because, as they themselves acknowledge, they have lost control of their young men.'

In the jargon of sociologists, talking to elders was a 'top-down' approach, when what was needed was a 'bottom-up' one: job-creation schemes, paid community work, and education-based initiatives such as his Youth at Risk programme. Until the UN started viewing Somalia through this prism of gang psychology, he thought, the country would never be demilitarized and nothing would change.

In the deserters' camp I was introduced to a friend of Jabril and Abshir, Abdi-Osman, whose story suggested that the gangs could be literally interchangeable. Abdi-Osman was not just an ex-al-Shabaab fighter: he was also an ex-pirate. He recalled the night when two friends had persuaded him to put to sea in a small fishing skiff, with no plan other than to head out and see what happened. His friends told him they would be gone for a night or two, although the voyage ended up lasting for eighteen. They drifted about, waiting for a ship to pirate, and eventually attempted to board a French-flagged freighter.

'I don't remember its name, but it was pretty big,' he said.

Unfortunately for them, their skiff wasn't fast enough to come alongside their quarry, and the attack was a dismal failure. In fact, the whole adventure was madness. Abdi-Osman and his friends were from Hiraan, an inland state, and had no experience whatsoever of the sea. As he sheepishly acknowledged, they were hopeless amateurs compared to the professional pirates they sought to emulate. He was eventually put ashore at Mogadishu, hungry, sun-burned and destitute. He was picked up in the port by two al-Shabaab recruiters, and immediately agreed to join the insurgency. He shrugged when I asked him what was going through his mind at the time.

'Every man who has nothing will try something to get money,' he replied.

At twenty-three, Abdi-Osman had experienced enough desperate adventure to last most people a lifetime. Al-Shabaab or piracy? Morality simply didn't come into the equation for him.

The two great Somali scourges of the West were simply alternative livelihoods to him. This roguish attitude had a certain charm to it. It was hard not to admire his survivor's instinct and the way he had made his own luck. He reminded me somewhat of the Artful Dodger, the plucky chief pickpocket in *Oliver Twist*. On the margins of another of the groups I spoke to, meanwhile, I thought I spotted innocent Oliver himself, a small child in an embroidered green shirt that was much too long for him. I waved at him, and he was propelled forward until he stood looking up at a circle of his elders, wide-eyed and mute, the reluctant camp mascot. His name was Liban, and he was nine years old.

In a telephone interview in 2011, Sheikh Aweys asserted that 'in Islam, the age of responsibility is defined as fifteen years old', and denied that anyone under that age took any part in the fighting on behalf of al-Shabaab – as well he might, since employing child soldiers under the age of fifteen is defined by the International Criminal Court as a war crime.[12] Liban's story, delivered in barely audible mono-syllables that had to be coaxed from him by the older boys, proved how untrue the Sheikh's claim was. The boy was an orphan – he just looked at me blankly when I asked about his parents – who had been with al-Shabaab since he was seven. To begin with he was used as a runner. Like a Royal Navy powder-monkey in the nineteenth century, he carried supplies and ammunition up to the fighters in the front line; as he grew older he was sent further forward in order to scope out enemy positions because, as an older boy explained, 'children make good spies'.

I asked if he had ever carried a gun, and he replied that

he had; and yes, he had used it once or twice, in order to kill people. I wondered what had prompted him to leave his unit, which after so long must have felt like a surrogate family. An older boy again answered for him: Liban had been starving because his unit, low on food themselves, were no longer able to feed him properly. And so one night he had wandered out to a road and flagged down the first passing car, asking the driver to take him somewhere, anywhere, to find something to eat. It was pure chance that he had ended up in this camp.

'And what will you do next, Liban?'

He looked me in the eye for the first time: here, at last, was a question he understood and recognized.

'I'm ready to fight again!' he trilled. 'I want to fight for the TFG! I'm not scared!'

He said this with such fervour that one or two of the crowd looked away, sucking through their teeth. Liban was no Oliver Twist, I realized, but a deeply damaged little boy, a dangerous, feral creature who knew only how to survive in the dog-eat-dog world of the warzone. His reasoning seemed binary, as simple as a mollusc's: hungry, not hungry, alive, not alive. Did he know that killing people was wrong? I was sure not. His moral compass was terrifyingly absent, and there was no soft-hearted Nancy figure at hand to redeem him.

There was, though, a contender for the role of Bill Sykes. I had been speaking to the boys for over an hour, and was beginning to think I had learned all I could from the deserters, when I fell into conversation with an older man with a skull cap and a long, Islamist's beard – the only beard among the deserters, in fact.

'I can't afford a razor,' he deadpanned when I asked him, jokingly, why he had not shaved it off.

But Abdikadir, 33, was no joke. The other deserters were visibly wary of him. He was not an ex-foot soldier but a former mid-level commander, who had quit the insurgency suffering from what sounded like old-fashioned battle fatigue.

'I still hear the sound of fighting in my head,' he said, with a faraway look in his eye. 'All we ever did in al-Shabaab was fight. The battle against the Ethiopians was the worst. I tell you how long I've been fighting. You see that guy over there? He's twenty-three. I remember when he was turned down by al-Shabaab because he was too young.'

It was another dark joke. Abdikadir had been in the camp for less than two months but was already regretting it. He had expected to be debriefed by the TFG when he deserted, and indeed was willing to share all he knew. Yet no one had so far asked him anything, and now he felt slighted.

'I had a good life in al-Shabaab,' he said bitterly. 'I had a house, and three cars. My family had enough to eat. Look. This was me.'

He produced a mobile phone and prodded at the buttons. Across the tiny, cracked screen flickered some shaky footage of a man in combat gear with his head wrapped in a keffiyeh, posing by a Toyota. In the background was a newly built concrete bungalow.

'I gave all that up for this,' he said, waving dismissively at the dusty parade ground, 'and now, even my wife has been taken from me. Why does the government not want to talk to me? I have a book full of names of people who could help them . . . After Ramadan, if nothing has changed, that might be the time for me to start walking from here.'

He said there had been between three hundred and four hundred fighters in his group, including several foreigners, most of them from Kenya and Sudan but also people from America and Europe.

'The foreigners were mostly being trained as suicide bombers,' he said then. 'They were kept apart from us, in a different camp. Outside, we would walk on one side of the road, they on the other. They had hero status. Even the Somalis from abroad were treated as heroes.'

He recalled a Somali from Britain among this latter group who had been encouraged to take part in a recruitment video, although he couldn't name him. Did he know of any British-Somali suicide bombers; had he heard of Abu Ayyub al-Muhajir, 'the Migrant', the 21-year-old student from Ealing, west London, who blew himself up in Baidoa in 2007?

'You know of one,' he replied. 'I know of many.'

'And what do you think about suicide bombing?'

Abdikadir stroked his beard and looked at me as though the question was strange.

'It was what they had registered in themselves to do,' he shrugged eventually. 'It was part of their path to Heaven.'

The Ugandan medical officer reappeared, his rounds of the dormitories complete. At the sound of our Casspir's engine starting up, a group of 15-year-olds materialized and asked to pose for a team photograph. Abdikadir melted away, and suddenly we were back in the world of schoolboy buffoonery as they crowded in for the shot, laughing, swearing, their white teeth flashing as they jostled for the best positions. They looked like the cream of Somalia youth, in far better condition than the Mogadishu average. The MO confirmed that they were mostly in rude health. The only new medical problem he had found was an infestation of fleas in the dormitory bedding. There seemed to be hope for the future. And yet the horror remained just a step away for all these young men. As we queued to climb back into the vehicle, one of the 20-year-olds pulled me aside again.

'The bearded man – Abdikadir,' he said. 'What did he say to you?'

'Why do you ask?'

'You shouldn't trust what he says. He's a bad one.'

'In what way is he bad?'

'He was one of the executioners. He used to chop off people's heads with a sword.'

7

The famine

Badbaado refugee camp, Dharkenley district,
June–July 2011

In the first week of June 2011, in the al-Shabaab-controlled southern regions of Gedo and Lower Juba, six nomads were attacked and eaten by hungry lions. Local media pounced on this horror story, noting that lions generally only attacked humans *in extremis*. For six people to be eaten within a week was almost unheard of. What could it portend?

A month later, the UN's humanitarian coordinator for Somalia, Mark Bowden,* announced that two al-Shabaab-controlled districts were in the grip of an official famine: an apocalyptic term seldom used by aid officials, and which had not been heard in Somalia since 1992. Yet Bowden made clear that, this time, it was potentially just the beginning. Like some Old Testament prophet of doom, he warned that without immediate foreign intervention the

---

* Not to be confused with Mark Robert Bowden, US journalist and author of *Black Hawk Down*.

153

famine would spread to all eight regions of southern Somalia within two months.

I had seen the effects of famine before, in northern Haiti in the early 1990s, when I witnessed an entire village scrabbling in the dust for the remnants of the contents of an upturned porridge pot. But the scale of this disaster was of a different order. The underlying drought in the region was said to be the worst for sixty years. By late July, 3.7 million Somalis were in need of food aid, almost half of the country's total population. Across the Horn of Africa, over 12 million people were in need of humanitarian assistance. The very young suffered worst of all. Between May and July, according to American officials, the famine claimed the lives of an estimated 29,000 Somali children under the age of five.

I had come to Mogadishu to report on the war against al-Shabaab, but with the city now at the centre of a major international news story I had little choice but to switch horses. Over the course of June and July, an estimated 100,000 refugees arrived in the capital, spontaneously setting up camp among the ruins in over a hundred different locations. AMISOM's rudimentary press facilities were swamped as the A-List media and their camera crews poured in: the stars of CNN and CBS and NBC, along with the chiefs of what seemed like every aid organization in the world.

This famine story wasn't just as big as the one of 1992, when an estimated 300,000 Somalis died. It had the potential to be another 1984, the year of Bob Geldof, Band Aid and Live Aid, when Westerners focused as never before on the suffering of East Africa. An estimated 900,000 Ethiopians died in that famine. On the other hand, the enormous sums of charity raised are said today to have saved the lives of 6 million. This once-in-a-generation moment of solidarity between the First and Third Worlds was sparked, famously, by a single news report by the BBC's Michael Buerk and the Kenyan photojournalist Mo Amin. It was no surprise, therefore, when spare seats in the armoured vehicles became harder than ever to secure, nor that the only places the convoys now seemed to visit were the refugee camps.

The progress of the war was relegated almost to a sideshow, as if it were mere background colour to the new disaster that the world wanted to read and hear about, although in reality they could not be separated in this way. War and famine were two horsemen of the same apocalypse, after all, especially in a country as impoverished as Somalia, where political power has always rested on the control of scant resources.

Al-Shabaab understood this principle absolutely. They also calculated that a famine that only affected parts of Somalia that they controlled was not going to make them look good. Their solution, however, was crazed even by their standards: they simply denied the famine's existence.

'To the latest report by the so-called United Nations about the existence of famine in Somalia, we say it is a 100 per cent lie and propaganda,' Sheikh Rage announced in Mogadishu. 'Yes, there is drought in Somalia, but not to the extent the infidel UN men put it. That is politically motivated and with an ulterior motive.'[1]

The militants had expelled the large humanitarian agencies from their territory in 2009 on the grounds that they were 'anti-Islamic'. Sheikh Rage now made it clear that nothing had changed, and that the ban would remain in place. The international agencies predicted disaster. There was no practical possibility of their ignoring the ban: one of them, the World Food Programme, had had fourteen employees murdered in the south in the last three years. By late July, according to UNOCHA, the United Nations Office for the Coordination of Humanitarian Affairs, aid agencies were able to reach just 20 per cent of the millions of people in urgent need of food aid in southern Somalia.

It seemed that many Somalis agreed with the internationals' assessment, among them my Rahanweyn friend Aden, who came back to see me one day at the AMISOM OPD.

'Al-Shabaab are 100 per cent responsible for this famine,' he said.

He wasn't the only Somali that summer who noted that the al-Shabaab leader Godane was from one of the Isaaq clans of Somaliland, and not therefore predisposed to care what happened to the Rahanweyn peoples of the south.

Aden recalled a visit in 2008 to Wajid in the southern region of Bakool. That small town, he recollected with something like fondness, had in those days played host to all the main relief agencies: Care, World Vision, USAID, WFP. Bakool was now at the very centre of the famine zone, yet not one of the international aid agencies was operating there any more.

'The foreigners were all driven out and their offices were looted. Al-Shabaab said that anyone who worked for them was a spy and would be killed. They were paranoid. Crazy.'

Al-Shabaab was responsible for the disaster in other ways. Although they could not be blamed for the lack of rainfall, they were rightly accused by the TFG of the long-term mismanagement of water resources in the areas they controlled. In other words, the drought underlying the famine was partly man-made. Al-Shabaab failed to regulate the use of wells, or to maintain the decrepit canal systems that once irrigated swathes of the intra-riverine south. Nor did they try to repair the damage done during the civil war, when 95 per cent of bore holes were destroyed by rival clans who filled up each other's wells with rocks.[2]

Meanwhile, deforestation had accelerated dramatically in their territory, leading to a rapid increase in the spread of desertification. This was another ecological disaster that al-Shabaab were disinclined to try to stem, because their insurgency was funded to a significant degree by the trade in charcoal, a minor local industry that had consequently boomed under their tenure. When interviewed, the Gedo villagers being hunted by lions specifically blamed their plight on 'drought and deforestation' in the beasts' usual savannah hunting grounds.

The continuing ban on the foreign agencies that might have helped Gedo was bad enough. As the summer progressed, however, it became clear that the militants intended to go further: they also forbade starving southerners from travelling beyond al-Shabaab territory to seek help. This was the logical extension of al-Shabaab's insistence that there was no famine, and they didn't mean it rhetorically. Reports began to come in that would-be refugees were being stopped on the roads, and ordered to return home with instructions to pray for the rains. Allah would provide if he willed it. Aden regarded this piety as the height of hypocrisy.

'Al-Shabaab are like children: they don't want to be left on their own,' he snorted. 'They need the people to steal from. A fish can't live without water.'

Banning drought victims from travelling was a risky strategy. Moving on when the environment can no longer sustain life is the whole point of nomadism. Roaming is considered an absolute right in Somalia not out of high-minded philosophy, but because it is the only way to survive in an unforgiving land. Nomadism is also a tradition that goes to the heart of the Somali psyche, celebrated for centuries in countless songs and poems. To challenge or remove the right to roam therefore risked alienating millions. I later met an old nomad refugee who had spent all his life in the desert, far from any city. The first time he had even heard of al-Shabaab, he said, was when all his camels died, and a bunch of gunmen in keffiyehs tried to turn back the city-bound truck he had boarded in his quest for help.

'Who are these young men,' he wanted to know, 'that they should treat me so?'

The paradox was that it was not the hated foreigners who were now guilty of 'anti-Islamic' behaviour, but al-Shabaab themselves. Even the term 'Sharia', the system of law that they were so intent on imposing on the country, literally means, in its secondary sense, 'the approach to a water hole'.*

It was not the first time that al-Shabaab had ignored the public mood. This time, though, they had created a

---

* The three-letter root ع ر ش (*Sh Ra I'en*) means to go, to enter or to start; leading to the noun *Shaaira*, a street; which then has the implication of the 'Right Path' and hence *Al Shar*, the Revelation. Sharia law (or more properly, in Arabic, *Shari'ah*) metaphorically offers a path through the dusty wilderness to the cool oasis of salvation: Islam. It is only one of many modern Arabic words that have their roots in the pre-Islamic desert.

backlash that even they were struggling to suppress. In Ruun-Nirgood in Middle Shabelle, villagers were in open rebellion after the militants ordered them to hand over at least one son to join their fight against the TFG, or else to contribute two camels to the cause.

'They asked for the impossible,' said Yahye Alasow, a 57-year-old grandmother. 'If you lock a cat in a room and start to beat her, then in the end she will try to defend herself. We are like that. Al-Shabaab did everything to us, but we will not accept it any more.'³ Was the war about to turn against the militants? It seemed increasingly likely. In Mogadishu, however, the foreign journalists seemed too fixated on the famine to even ask the question.

The surrounding media circus was nothing if not entertaining. That autumn the UNHCR's goodwill ambassador, the actress Angelina Jolie, announced at an award ceremony in Geneva that her experiences among Somali refugees had made her 'a better person, a better mother . . . They've inspired me by showing me the unbreakable strength of the human spirit.'⁴ The same week, the Jolie-Pitt Foundation donated $340,000 to one of the better Somali NGOs working in the camps. Slightly less useful, perhaps, was the contribution of the American rapper Curtis Jackson, better known as 50 Cent, who tweeted: 'So I just got back from Somalia, it was crazy out there. I have never seen anything like it. I'm going to feed a billion people Street King.' The reference was to a brand of energy drink he owned, available in two flavours, orange-mango or grape. 'Fiddy' was offering to pass on a percentage of his sales to the World Food Programme, under the slogan '1 shot = 1 meal for a child'.⁵

Just as controversial, at least in the UK, was a decision by the London *Mail on Sunday* to dispatch their writer Liz Jones to the famine zone. Jones, according to the outraged *Guardian* newspaper, was 'a narcissistic fashion journalist, a lifelong anorexic, a person who just spent £13,500 on a face-lift, and a confessional columnist who charts her obsessions every week in the *Mail on Sunday*'s YOU magazine ... Could there be anything worse than the simple fact of sending such an inappropriate journalist to cover a famine?'[6]

In the end, the *Guardian*'s fury was misplaced. Even Liz Jones's critics acknowledged that the reports she eventually filed were appropriately horror-struck and that she had left her alleged self-obsession at home. The truth was that reporting this story made every Western journalist feel uncomfortable when they stopped to think about it for long enough – particularly if, like me, they happened to be commuting from the famine back to the comforts of the Bancroft Hotel each day. The Bancroft's owners spent $250,000 a year on diesel, mostly just to power its dozens and dozens of ceaselessly whirring air-conditioners. The canteen, anxious to please all those beefy, *braai*-addicted South African contractors, got through as much as three tons of meat each month. Indeed the diet in the cool, clean dining area was so meat-oriented, chops and steaks and sausages and stews for every meal, that the Europeans actually complained about it, although to no avail. A man-sized fridge in the corner was always full of ice-cold bottled water that anyone could help themselves to at any time. As a pleasant hydrating alternative, blissfully chilled orangeade was available on tap, 24 hours a day. One mentally left Somalia behind at the entrance to the Bancroft, a facility barred, for security reasons, to all 'indigenous personnel', as the US Marines called the locals during Operation Restore Hope. With less political correctness, but perhaps more honesty and certainly more accuracy, the Bancroft contractors tended to refer to Somalis as 'Skinnies'.

There were other reasons to feel cynical as the giant international aid machine rumbled into action. For aid workers, famine was a technical term used when more than 30 per cent of a given population were suffering from acute malnutrition, and when the mortality rate had surpassed two people per 10,000 per day. It was merely another notch on the NGO world's sliding scale of suffering, a step up from a food 'emergency' and two steps up from a food 'crisis'. Much of East Africa had been in emergency or crisis for the last two years, teetering on the edge of the present disaster. And yet, during that period, the West had shown no especial sympathy or desire to help the millions in need. UN agencies had received only half of the $1.6bn they said was required for their relief programmes in the region. Oxfam had gone so far as to accuse several European governments of 'wilful neglect'.[7] In a jaded world, it seemed that it took the juju of a full-blown 'famine', with all the biblical overtones of that word, to stimulate anything close to the appropriate response.

I spent a day trailing Jerry Rawlings, the African Union's Special Envoy to Somalia, on his first official visit to Mogadishu. A big, barrel-chested man of sixty-four, and the former president of Ghana, Rawlings cut an unorthodox figure in his baggy embroidered shirt and Polaroid sunglasses. Most visiting dignitaries wore suits; this one presented himself as a man of the people. The son of a

Scottish chemist father and a Ghanaian mother, he had joined the air force in the 1960s, mutinied at the social injustice he saw in his country, taken power in a coup in 1979 and remained in the top job, off and on, for the next twenty years. This classic African career trajectory had drawn him to the attention of Jean Ping, the Gabonese chairman of the African Union, who thought him ideal for the task of 'mobilizing the continent' to assume its responsibilities towards Somalia. This did not prevent Rawlings from considering the African Union a bunch of dilatory bureaucrats.

'Why aren't AU governments doing more?' he growled, during a rare moment of down-time in a Portakabin office on the AMISOM base. 'I'll tell you why. Because they are all too busy holding their fucking arses on to their chairs! When I was president, I was too busy to sit down!'

And he stood up and crabwalked across the office floor, a white plastic chair comically wedged on to his behind.

Rawlings' armoured cavalcade took in the force commander's office, a UN office, the hospital, the parliament. The meetings he was forced to hold in these places were obviously not his forte, and his conversations grew ever more stilted as the day wore on. I wondered if he was out of his depth. At one point I heard him turn to an aide for a reminder of what AMISOM stood for, an admission of ignorance that would have made Jean Ping wince. Rawlings had been the AU's top Somalia representative for over eight months.

The AU was supposed to be his continent's answer to the European Union. It was one of Africa's most conspicuous symbols of a better future: independent, self-reliant, modern, a world away from the old clichés of post-colonial despotism. AMISOM's military success against al-Shabaab was arguably its greatest achievement so far, an impressive advertisement of what could be done when African nations spoke and acted in concert. Rawlings' apparent lack of interest in the institution jarred. On the other hand, he undoubtedly had charisma; and when the armoured cars stopped at Badbaado refugee camp, he at last began to put it to use.

Badbaado, in Dharkenley on the western outskirts of Mogadishu, was the fastest-growing refugee camp in the city, and already the size of a small town. It stood on land that in June had been derelict and empty; by September it would be home to 35,000 people. Dome-shaped tents stretched away from the road as far as the eye could see. In the desert, nomads constructed this traditional shelter, an *aqal soomaali*, by covering a collapsible frame of thorns with woven mats or animal hides. Here they had used anything they could lay their hands on, even bits of old shirt and plastic bags. The luckier ones had been issued with water-proof orange sheeting, but none of their tents looked like they offered adequate protection from the intense heat.

The camp, we had been briefed, was far from being a safe place to visit. Al-Shabaab were assumed to have in-filtrated it thoroughly. The atmosphere here was volatile even without them. A fortnight after our visit, seven people were killed and several wounded following a gunfight that began when a gang of militiamen, possibly members of the TFG army, tried to loot a newly arrived consignment of food aid.[8] Rawlings, showily rejecting the body armour he had been offered, strode purposefully towards a feeding centre in the middle of the camp, leaving a trail of aides, journalists and UN officials in his wake, and even his Ugandan security detail cursing and struggling to keep up.

The feeding centre was a shed in a ring of barbed wire, which a sign announced had been set up and paid for by an NGO called Qatar Charity. Sacks of rice and cans of cooking oil from Pakistan had been laid out in neat lines in preparation for the crowds mobbing the entrance. The refugees, many of them sporting empty food bowls on their heads to ward off the sun, were all women and children. Half a dozen men armed with sjambok-style switches stood on sentry before the gate, but at the foreigners' approach the crowd surged forward, ignoring the flailing guards. Rawlings disappeared in a roiling sea of brightly coloured headscarves, but quickly bobbed to the surface on a pile of rice sacks, his bearded face shining, beatific.

'I hear you,' he shouted in a voice both gravelly and trembling with feeling, 'I have seen your pain! Let me assure you: we, the international community, will never abandon you. Never!'

His eyes glistened as he clenched his fists across his chest in a sign of pan-African solidarity. This was what he had come to Somalia for.

That evening, back at the AMISOM base, I watched in awe as he wept for the refugees on live television. Since there was no studio on the base, the press office had set up a feed camera in the abandoned garden of a once fabulous seaside villa, a building now filled with goat droppings, even upstairs on the second floor. As the sun went down and bats flitted in and out of the glassless windows, each of four, back-to-back evening news programmes received the benefit of his perfect dramatic timing:

Al Jazeera, Channel 4, and two channels of the BBC.

'It was a truly sorrowful sight in the camps today,' he intoned, leaning like a rock star on his microphone stand. 'I'm . . . I'm . . .' (and here his eyes would well up again, his voice blipping with unsuppressed emotion) 'I'm not sure how many of them will even be alive in two or three weeks' time. What we need is a miracle! Not from the Good Lord, but from the governments of countries with money!'

It was a masterclass in manipulation. Even his watching aides, who had seen the show before, were wowed by the performance. It was as if the old man kept an onion in his pocket.

The reality of the Badbaado visit was that we didn't get a chance to see many truly sorrowful sights. The Rawlings party attracted a lot of attention, and the AMISOM organizers were understandably nervous about staying longer than necessary, which to them meant the time it took to take a photograph. An impromptu visit to a refugee camp a few days later in a ruined residential district of Hawl Wadaag provided an entirely different experience.

I and two other journalists were hiking back from another visit to the front line with a platoon of Ugandans when we chanced upon a man digging a tiny grave at the edge of the sandy path.

'My grandson,' he said expressionlessly, barely looking up from his spadework. 'He died of diarrhoea this morning.'

Around the corner we came across a large *zareba* of newly cut acacia thorns protecting hundreds of tents fashioned from white plastic sheeting marked with the logo of the Danish Refugee Council. This detail aside, I could have been standing at the gates of any desert encampment in Somalia. It was a remarkable sight here in urban Hawl Wadaag, less than half a mile from the national parliament, in a part of the city that until very recently had been a no-man's-land raked by mortars and machinegun fire.

We were greeted by the district commissioner, Jaffar, who was passing by in a Toyota Landcruiser. He told us that 2,000 refugees had arrived in this part of Hawl Wadaag in the last four days, most of them from Bakool and Lower Shabelle.

'It has been twenty years since this district had so many residents,' Jaffar observed wryly, 'and now we don't have enough to feed our guests. The Turks brought some food this morning, and the Kuwaitis are promising more. But I do not think they will bring enough.'

I began to work my way around the camp and soon saw what he meant. The children didn't run up to beg here but sat about in listless heaps, showing their hunger by stroking an index finger up and down their throats. The signs of malnutrition were all around: the skeletal limbs, the huge staring eyes, the orange hair falling out in clumps. The stifling interiors of the *aqals* smelled of ripe cheese. In each one I put my head into there seemed to be another motion-less child or two, their eyes white against the darkness, fixed on the ceiling, seeing nothing. They had heads like footballs and sticks for arms, too weak to move and beyond caring anyway about the filth and the flies.

I picked my way over to a party of around thirty women and children who were squatting together along a partially destroyed wall, a classic African tableau in their brightly coloured saris and flower-print shawls. They gazed back at me with the punctured look of the utterly exhausted, and explained that they were Rahanweyn herders who had just arrived from a village near Bardere, 300 kilometres to the west in Gedo. The drought, they said, had killed all their cattle, forcing them to move. Travelling sometimes by truck, sometimes on foot, avoiding the main roads wherever possible and always at night, it had taken them four difficult days to reach Mogadishu. Among their number when they left their village was a sick three-month-old girl, who hadn't survived the journey. Someone pointed out the mother, a young woman crouching silently at the back of the group, who had buried her infant at the side of the desert road. I shook my head in commiseration, which she acknowledged with the faintest of nods, although her expression was inscrutable.

The group had made two attempts to flee. At first they had set out for the Kenyan border, 100 kilometres to the west and much nearer than Mogadishu, but they had been turned back by al-Shabaab at a checkpoint on the road.

'They ordered us to go back to wait for the rains, but there is no food where we lived,' said one woman, Fatima Mohamed. 'Everything is finished. We explained that to go back was to die, but they said, "It's better to die than to accept the help of the gaalo." Al-Shabaab just wanted us to die. They are godless. They have no heart. They were worse than the drought.'

As elsewhere in the camp, there were hardly any men among them: just one old-timer with no teeth. Fatima explained that they had left their young men behind, partly to trick al-Shabaab into thinking they weren't leaving while the women and children slipped out the back, but mainly for fear of the press gangs who would surely have abducted them on the long journey to Mogadishu. There was no doubt in their minds that the militants were directly killing them all with their agenda.

'We are the fortunate ones,' Fatima went on. 'There was another group from Bardere behind us but they were stopped by al-Shabaab, even though many of their children were dying. They are not being Muslims. There is not one Muslim among them. They are only there to mislead us, to lie.'

There were worse horrors in another compound, a hundred yards up the lane. In the shadow of a shot-up minaret, a white-coated doctor and two orderlies, all Somalis, stood Canute-like in a tide of despairing humanity. Starvation, diarrhoea and dehydration were the commonest causes of death in a famine but by no means the only ones. The medics, who were all wearing surgical masks, had seen cases of typhoid, cholera, malaria and dengue fever. Measles was also spreading fast. The doctor explained that the appearance of this disease, a respiratory virus of little consequence in the developed world but a frequent killer when the patient's immune system is weakened by malnutrition, was also partly the fault of al-Shabaab, who for almost three years had rebuffed all vaccination programmes in the territory they controlled.

The southerners dealt with the symptoms of measles in the traditional way, by trying to burn them out with a fire-brand. The doctor led me to his tented field clinic where I photographed a tiny boy with two lines of deep, coin-sized wounds scored across his chest, like the number-six face of a dice. The most recent of these wounds was still open and glistening; my camera caught a fly busying itself at its ragged wet edge like some beast drinking from a water hole.

'These are tough desert people,' the doctor said. 'They are used to going for days without water. Imagine how bad it must be for them to have to come here.'

He said that two dozen children had died in the camp in the last three days, nine of them under the age of five.

As we were speaking a small saloon car arrived, bumping to a halt in a cloud of dust, and a stocky man stepped out, wearing a delicately embroidered kufi cap and an expensive-looking diving watch. He turned out to be Osman Ibrahim, the recently fired Deputy Minister of Health. Known as Libah, or Lion, he was a well-known figure in Mogadishu, whose business interests, principally in shipping, were said to have thrived during the civil war. I watched as he retrieved two bottles of Dettol from the boot of his car. Then he marched across to the blue-painted latrine block that stood in the centre of the compound and began to douse the structure, inside and out, with both bottles at once, like an enthusiastic arsonist spreading petrol.

'At least he's doing something,' said the doctor approvingly. 'He is a good man. He probably paid for that Dettol himself.'

Libah was a member of one of the minority Jerer tribes, the negroid Bantu people historically discriminated against by the Arab-descended majority, and whose traditional homeland was in precisely those areas now afflicted by famine. Was he acting out of clan loyalty, or was his altruism blind? As so often in Somalia, it was difficult to tell. Perhaps he was driven by some confused mixture of the two. But whatever Libah's motive, splashing some Dettol around was no substitute for a proper government strategy for dealing with this crisis.

Al-Shabaab's shortcomings represented a unique opportunity for the TFG, a chance to show southern Somalia what a well-organized central government could do for them. A convincing demonstration of administrative efficiency could deal a deathblow to the insurgency. Yet here in Hawl Wadaag, away from the showboating ambassadors and the set-piece press visits, the authorities were very evidently struggling to cope. Libah's gesture seemed even more futile when, five minutes later and 50 yards away, I observed a woman with a chest like a washboard trying to buy a heap of offal from a rickety butcher's stall, where the wares were so covered with flies that you could barely see the colour of the meat. It was food for thought as we returned for our own surreal banquet of a lunch at the Bancroft Hotel.

The AMISOM base was a good place from which to monitor the increasing pace of the international relief effort. The aid flights had been pouring in for weeks, many of them carrying tons of 'Plumpysup', the sweet, French-invented, peanut-butter-based substance the relief agencies used in food emergencies. I'd also seen a couple of tons of rice rations at Badbaado. But was enough of it getting through to where it was needed – and where was all the Plumpysup going?

According to one UN estimate, up to half of all food aid delivered in 2010 was still being diverted to corrupt contractors, or even directly to al-Shabaab.[9] One of the

South African employees of SKA, the Dubai-based logistics firm that ran Mogadishu's ports on behalf of the TFG, told me that 20 per cent of the Plumpysup landed by ship went missing before it was delivered to the city's emergency feeding centres – a distance in some cases of less than two kilometres. The trucks that were supposed to deliver the rations were operated by local contractors, who naturally had all the usual clan connections. The thieves hardly bothered to conceal this racket. The SKA man recalled how he once caught a dockworker on his lunch break eating some Plumpy he had spent the morning unloading. When challenged, the worker explained that he had bought it in a local shop.

'I don't understand why they don't just get SKA to deliver the goods to the distribution centres,' the logistics man said.

Matters were not as bad as in the early 1990s, when up to 80 per cent of international relief aid was stolen. Regaining control of the aid supply chain was one of the main justifications for the US-led military intervention of 1993. There was no suggestion that the US Army were about to return, but it was nonetheless clear that the lawlessness of that era, when arriving aircraft were sometimes looted before the pilots had switched off their engines, had yet to be eradicated. The concern was that responsibility for the delivery of aid ultimately rested with the government. The hoods who ran the trucking contracts could not operate without top-level TFG protection. Was Sheikh Sharif going to let the political opportunity the famine represented slip through his fingers after all? Senior UN officials were privately worried that he might. At a time of deep national crisis, the worst drought for sixty years, almost none of the new cabinet had any experience of government. In retrospect, the timing of Sheikh Sharif's decision to replace Farmaajo and his ministers could hardly have been worse.

I spent a day following another visiting official around the city, the UN's Under-Secretary-General for Political Affairs, a veteran American diplomat called Lynn Pascoe, who went to visit the president at the Villa Somalia. This in itself was a moment of some significance. AMISOM's latest offensive had pushed al-Shabaab out of effective mortar range of the presidential complex. It was the first time in years that it was judged safe enough for someone as senior as Pascoe.

Sheikh Sharif's state office had mirrored doors and marble floors and smelled strongly of patchouli. The press were herded in for the photo opp. Sharif was wearing the same blue suit and embroidered kufi cap he wore in a framed photograph of himself that hung above the presidential desk. He and Pascoe sat stiff-backed in leather armchairs, grinning furiously at each other across a glass coffee table bearing a small flagpole with the Somali national colours waving from it. The tabletop itself appeared to be supported by a large jar of gobstoppers, which seemed an odd choice for an office that depended as much as Sharif's did on the ability to make small talk. The conversation that ensued was, in fact, desperately stilted.

'So . . . how are you?' Pascoe began. 'It's so lovely to see you again . . .'

Sheikh Sharif nodded and clasped his hands and hoped the Under-Secretary-General had had a pleasant flight to Mogadishu.

'Yeesss!' Pascoe nodded back. 'It's good to see the airport looking so busy!'

There was something about the way they bobbed their heads at each other that reminded me of the courtship ritual of iguanas. They were still nodding in this way as the press pack was chivvied from the room.

Pascoe's formal statement for the cameras afterwards was just as bland. Flanked by the president and the prime minister as well as the speaker, three dark Somalis in three dark blue suits, he spoke of international solidarity and a shared clear vision and of helping Somalia to move forward in the family of nations. It was not until later, as he prepared to board his plane back to Nairobi at the end of a long day, and the mask of smiles was starting to slip in the debilitating heat, that I learned what Pascoe really thought of Sheikh Sharif and the TFG.

'It would be good if there was some evidence of them doing their jobs,' he growled, irritably running a finger beneath his shirt collar. Quite remarkably, this had remained buttoned to the top all day long, and his tie was still pulled up tight. What, I asked, would the UN do if the government failed to meet the latest deadline for drawing up a constitution and holding elections?

'I suppose we'll have to see where we are,' he shrugged. 'If there's no change, we'll just have to start again.'

It was no doubt fortunate for the TFG that, however inadequate their response to the famine, al-Shabaab's was incomparably worse. Godane and his faction simply refused to take the crisis seriously. I met one experienced Somali official, an employee of the UN children's agency UNICEF, who had spent many months trying to persuade al-Shabaab's so-called 'humanitarian committee' to allow at least some emergency food aid through. His job was dangerous as well as difficult: he would only speak to me on condition that I withheld his name.

'I used to have a contact in Shabaab-controlled Mogadishu whom I would go to meet in secret,' he recalled. 'He would take written messages from UNICEF to their humanitarian committee. But one day he just wasn't there any more. I eventually found a new phone number for him. It was a number in Kismayo. I had to beg him to let me email my latest message from UNICEF, but he was so paranoid. He created a new email account especially for my message. One hour after I'd sent it, the account was defunct again.'

Godane's faction in the end simply wasn't interested in cooperating with the foreigners, not even by back channels. On one occasion, while trying to negotiate a delivery to Lower Shabelle, a region in the heart of the famine zone with a population of almost a million, the UNICEF official was told by the militants that he should negotiate exclusively with their 'regional humanitarian coordinator'. This important-sounding officer turned out to be a foot soldier of just sixteen years old.

'The leadership were faceless – pathetic,' he said. 'There was a famine, yet no senior people had been put in charge of relief operations. They only had messengers.'

The hardliners may have been a lost cause, but UNICEF had better success when they approached Mukhtar Robow. On 13 July, two planes carrying five tons of emergency food and medicine were permitted to land at Baidoa. It was the first international airlift to the region for two years. Robow, who was born in nearby Berdaale, was not prepared to see his fellow Rahanweyn clansmen starve to death for reasons of half-baked ideology – and half-baked it undoubtedly still was. Just south of Mogadishu in Afgoye, on the cusp of the fasting month of Ramadan, al-Shabaab was reported to have banned the consumption of samosas, on the grounds that their triangular shape was too similar to the symbol for the Christian Holy Trinity.[10]

Catalysed by the famine, the rift within al-Shabaab's leadership was becoming significant. Aden's aunt, who was in Baidoa at the time of the UNICEF airlift, described to her nephew how Robow had dispatched fifty technicals to secure the airport ahead of the arrival of the planes. No one would normally try to challenge such an impressive array of firepower, yet on this occasion a rival al-Shabaab leader, a known Godane loyalist, also sent fifty technicals to the airport. The day ended in a tense Mexican stand-off, and with UNICEF unlikely to want to repeat their bold experiment.

The argument between Robow and Godane over famine policy rumbled on, but the row was soon eclipsed by developments on the Mogadishu front line. Throughout July, the city had been bracing itself for another offensive over Ramadan, which this year began on 1 August. For this reason, in the last week of July, the Ugandans launched their own pre-emptive strike in Bondhere district in the right-centre of the line. It was another resounding success.

'We heard they'd brought seven hundred reinforcements – all new recruits,' one Ugandan infantry captain told me. 'That was good news for us. It was a walk in the park.'

AMISOM's advance had become relentless. The captain described how his men had laughed as they killed a fighter who had popped up next to one of their T55s and opened fire with a Kalashnikov, the bullets bouncing off the tank's hull in all directions. The Ugandans had every reason to be confident. Their opposition were children. One day, waiting at the base convoy point for another ride up to the front, I came across three recently captured al-Shabaab fighters, the oldest of whom was seventeen, the youngest fifteen. They were slumped along the wall of an administrative Portakabin awaiting transport to who knew where, their hands cuffed behind their backs, dirty and dejected, a look of shock in their eyes. They were volunteers, they said, who had put their hands up when an al-Shabaab recruiter came to their school. This had happened just fifteen days ago. They had decided to surrender when they became separated from their unit and ran out of bullets. Why, I asked, had they put their hands up in the first place? The boys all looked at each other.

'We were given a piece of fruit every day,' said one of them.

For al-Shabaab, the famine was the most convincing recruiting sergeant of all.

Reinforcements of this calibre were almost useless, and turned out to be al-Shabaab's final throw of the dice in their bid to hold on to the capital. On 6 August, the city woke up to discover that, overnight, the militants had withdrawn from eleven of the city's districts, including the Bakara Market. For the first time in four years, the TFG and their AMISOM allies were in charge of the capital. Only the northern suburb of Dayniile remained in al-Shabaab hands. The militants were also reported to have pulled back from a number of other key positions, notably in the Galgadud region in central Somalia. Their military spokesman, Sheikh Abdi-aziz Abu Mus'ab, told the al-Shabaab-run radio station Radio Andalus that the retreat was a tactical one, and that it was only a matter of time before the 'mujahideen' returned to Mogadishu to 'drag their [enemies'] bodies along the streets'. Sheikh Rage echoed him, explaining that the leadership had merely chosen to switch strategy to 'hit and run' guerrilla tactics that would 'break the back' of AMISOM.

Was Rage bluffing? Mogadishu's residents were not dancing in the street quite yet.

'I saw three al-Shabaab fighters throw down their guns and change into civilian dress,' a Dayniile resident known as Casho told *SomaliaReport*.

Aden seemed ominously downbeat when I called him. Al-Shabaab might have retreated from their trench line, he said, but the Amniyat's spies were still everywhere in the city. It was still highly dangerous to speak out openly against the militants.

Two months later, as if in confirmation of Sheikh Rage's promise of a 'back-breaking' guerrilla campaign, an al-Shabaab suicide bomber drove an enormous truck bomb into a complex of government buildings near the junction at K4, killing 139 people and injuring ninety-three. Body parts were flung for hundreds of metres. Among those murdered were several students who had been queuing for exam results at the education ministry, hoping to gain a scholarship to study in Turkey.[11] The famine, combined with their disastrous handling of it, had forced a major tactical reverse for the hardliners. But, as Aden gloomily foretold, they were not yet defeated. The poverty and ignorance of the young which fuelled the insurgency were genuine grievances, and had yet to be addressed. The wider war for control of Somalia was far from over yet.

Part II
NOMADS' LAND

8

In the court of King Farole

Garowe, Puntland, August 2011

August the first was a big public holiday in Garowe. Not only was it the anniversary of Puntland's declaration of autonomy in 1998, but in 2011, 1 August was also the first day of Ramadan. Garowe is Puntland's capital, and the state's president, Mohamed Farole, together with his son – also called Mohamed – had been planning the celebrations for weeks. The centrepiece was to be a parade. At 4 a.m., long before dawn, hundreds of townspeople had begun forming up in their marching squads in the main road out beyond the UN compound, my temporary home in the town. I was woken by the noise of the swelling crowd, a low-frequency rumble of excited chatter interspersed with whistles and snatches of song. Drawn on by the unmistakable atmosphere of a carnival, I dressed quickly and hurried out with my camera.

Puntland looms large in the wider Somali story. It comprises 212,000 square kilometres of territory, a third of all Somalia, the size of England and Wales combined; and it is home to some 4 million people out of an estimated national total of 10 million.[1] These statistics alone mean that if Puntland had decided on full independence from Mogadishu in 1998 – as did Somaliland, their neighbour and rival to the north-west, in 1991 – then Somalia as a unitary state would have been finished. Instead, however, Puntland opted for devolution: self-government from Garowe, while maintaining strong political representation in Mogadishu in a clan-based confederation with all the other states and regions. What the Puntland government said and did mattered, therefore, because this political vision alone kept the dream of a single Somali state alive.

Puntland, however, is known abroad – indeed, it is globally notorious – for something rather different: the extraordinary flourishing of piracy along its thinly policed coastline, which, at 1,600 kilometres, is as long as Portugal's. The state incorporates the whole tip of the Horn of Africa, jutting out into the Indian Ocean to form the southern edge of the Gulf of Aden, through which 21,000 ships plod each year on their way towards the Suez Canal, carrying cargo that includes a tenth of all of the world's petroleum. By 2011, the Gulf of Aden had become the world's Pirate Alley, the focus of a criminal enterprise that, according to one often quoted report, cost the global economy $8.3bn in 2010.[2] The Farole family, meanwhile, had been accused by UN officials in Nairobi of personally profiting from piracy even as they claimed to be tackling it. Was this sensational allegation fair? The answer was important, because even Nato's navies agree that the eventual solution to piracy will be found not at sea but on the land.

Puntland is named after the fabled Land of Punt, or

Pwenet, an ancient Egyptian trading partner known even in the twenty-fifth century BC for its production of gold, frankincense and myrrh. In modern political terms, though, it is Darodistan, the principal homeland of the powerful Darod tribe, one of the big four in Somalia. The clan has produced two presidents and three prime ministers since 1960; and under the 4.5 clan formula, the Darod have been allocated the post of prime minister in the TFG in Mogadishu since 2004.

The Darod claim to be descended from an Arab nobleman named Darud Jabarti, who was supposedly shipwrecked on Puntland's coast in the tenth or eleventh century, although some of the clan's rivals tell the story rather differently. According to them, Jabarti was no nobleman but 'a Galla slave', exiled from Arabia for stealing the slippers of the Prophet himself, who 'dismissed [him] with the words, Inna-*tarad*-na-hu ('Verily we have rejected him'): hence his name Tarud or Darud, 'the Rejected'.[3] The folk tale shows there is nothing new about this region's reputation for old-fashioned thievery.

Farole and most of his ministers were not just Darod but Darod Majeerteen, one of the four main branches of the tribe.* Following the failed invasion of Ethiopia in 1977, disaffected Majeerteen officers of the Somali national army mounted a coup against Siad Barre. This also failed, leading to terrible reprisals in the north-east. The Majeerteen became the first clan formally to renounce the regime in 1979, when the army deserter Colonel Abdullahi Yusuf formed the SSDF, the Somali Salvation Democratic Front.

* The others are the Marehan, the Dolbahante and the Ogadeni.

Yusuf went on to become the first president of Puntland, the first raison d'etre of which was to promote and protect the Majeerteen from the depredations of their chief rivals to the south, the Hawiye, as well as rival Darod clans such as Siad Barre's own Marehan. The statelet had experienced internal unrest in the past, and struggled all the time to maintain law and order throughout the vast territory it claimed to govern. Indeed, *yusuf yusuf* – in dark acknowledgement of the violent legacy of Puntland's founder – remained a common term for a gunfight, an onomatopoeic description of whistling bullets.

And yet, compared to the south, Puntland was a haven of peace and prosperity. There was drought here in the north, but no actual famine, despite the great hardship. Garowe, in fact, had proved a magnet for southern refugees, with new tent villages sprouting along the banks of the dried-out river to the east of town almost as fast as in Mogadishu. Al-Shabaab, meanwhile, had so far failed to exploit the divisions within the Darod sub-clans to establish any mean-ingful foothold here. This was partly because Puntlanders saw themselves as the country's only reliable bulwark against Islamic extremism, a view succinctly expressed by Osman, a local driver for the UN, who told me: 'Al-Shabaab? They are very very fucking people. We hate them. Yes. Thank you.'

The Majeerteen were an independent, aristocratic people who saw themselves as the quintessence of nomad culture, far superior to any other clan. 'The pride the Majeerteen tribes take in being of the Majeerteen, the most barren of all the Somali deserts, is as if that territory was the garden of Eden itself,' observed Gerald Hanley. 'Down south, on the

Juba where the trees drip bananas, lemons, pawpaw ...
where the small, fat, black men can eat chicken, eggs, beef
and have never been without a drink of water, I have heard
Majeerteen askaris sneering at all this, and telling the local
"slave people" that until they see the Majeerteen they do not
know what living is. And in the Majeerteen you would
have to kneel down and pray to a single blade of grass to
come up, and cry on it every day to help it live.'[4]

The Majeerteen hero Yusuf's instigating role in Siad
Barre's overthrow tended to confirm their view of them
selves as lynchpins of the nation's destiny, integral in every
way to a better future for Somalia. In the eighteenth and
nineteenth centuries, Puntland was ruled as a sultanate
known as Migiurtinia. Critics of President Farole sometimes accused him of trying to revive the sultanate's
late-nineteenth-century golden age, and of wielding power
like a *boqor*, or king. He was said, often, to have personal
designs on Sheikh Sharif's job in Mogadishu. Even the
state's motto, Star of the North, was heavy with the clan's
sense of its own importance.

The theme of the 1 August parade was, naturally,
Puntland itself: a none-too-subtle showcase of the splendid
social progress that had been made since 1998. As I made
my way towards the head of the cavalcade, half a mile
ahead, I overtook a company of recent law graduates from
the new Puntland State University, another of freshly
recruited customs officers, a third of policewomen with
uniforms that were pressed and gleaming. The local football team, Daljir FC, was marching in black and claret
tracksuits. The mechanics of the Nugal Electric Company
sported green boiler suits and yellow helmets. Every aspect

of civil society seemed covered, right down to a women's jute-weaving collective, whose members wore light brown jilbabs, and who carried before them the untidy beginnings of a large hessian carpet. It seemed that the spirit of 'scientific socialism' that underpinned Siad Barre's revolution was alive and well in Puntland. The Somali word for socialism, *hantiwadaag*, means 'the sharing of live-stock', and although there were no camels on parade, the nomad herdsmen were well represented. I watched a posse of them go by on horseback, fierce, dark men with pale turbans and richly hennaed beards. Their horses were small and wiry, and wore no saddles; the riders leaned un-naturally far back, and beat their mounts across the withers with long thin canes, goading them into a quick, un-comfortable-looking trot for the appreciative crowds.

It was a greater relief than I had expected to escape the fear and claustrophobia of Mogadishu, 800 kilometres and a world away to the south. In Garowe it was possible, at least at times like this, to mix with ordinary Somalis with-out wearing body armour. Many of the people here were, extraordinarily, smiling. Their costumes were so clean and brightly coloured that they seemed to shine against the dun-coloured, sand-blasted setting of their town. As I walked, I was overtaken by a Toyota containing one of the organizers, the Puntland Youth and Sports Minister Abdiweli Hersi, who stopped to give me a lift.

'What do you think? What do you think?' he said, waving proudly at the crowds through the window.

He dropped me off at the town's main square where a podium had been set up for the president and his entourage. I took up position behind one of the militiamen lining the route – he was wearing standard military camouflage except for the hat, a smart tweed cap that might have been sold in Jermyn Street – and waited for Garowe's elite to arrive.

The presidential entrance was heralded by the arrival of more soldiers – a lot more. Two technicals, their machine-guns swivelling menacingly, lurched to a halt in a cloud of dust and disgorged Farole's Special Protection Unit, a platoon of paramilitaries in mirror sunglasses and bright red berets, whose chests gleamed with ammunition hung in unnecessarily long belts. Farole himself was a dark, squat man in a suit, surrounded by three tall bodyguards, also in suits, whose breast pockets bulged as they scanned the crowds for trouble. They looked as Mafioso as their boss's name sounded: Farole was a nickname that meant 'Missing Finger'.* Their appearance made a sort of sense. Farole, who was born in 1945 and educated in Mogadishu during the UN trusteeship, belonged to that generation of Somalis who still spoke fluent Italian.

On the outskirts of this circus, the president's pencil-moustached son beetled about, harsh and serious as he barked his marshal's orders into a walkie-talkie. He was just as thickset as his father, though more casually dressed in a black polo shirt, chinos and Crocs. This was because the Faroles were diaspora Somalis, from Australia. Mohamed junior had largely been brought up in a suburb of Melbourne.

---

* Although the digit referred to was absent not from the president's hand, but his father's. In Somalia, even nicknames are sometimes passed down the generations.

His father was said to spend two-thirds of his state's income on his own security, and from my vantage point next to the podium I could see it might easily be true. Most of the marchers I had seen so far were civilians, but behind them were hundreds of soldiers, wearing a surprising variety of uniforms. There were also squadrons of police cars and convoys of artillery trucks. Farole took the salute as his troops passed by with their hands on their belts and their knees raised high. He was like Castro in Havana, the Kims in Pyongyang, Brezhnev in Red Square.

Puntland could not well afford this emphasis on the military. Civil society had not yet developed to the point where its citizens actually paid taxes. The state's annual revenue, derived almost entirely from duty on goods passing through the northern port of Bossasso, came to just $26m. For all the pomp of the day's celebrations, Garowe was a small place, with a population of no more than 60,000. The Faroles sometimes jokingly referred to their capital as 'Brasilia' – which meant that Bossasso, with a population of perhaps half a million, was Puntland's São Paulo – although I doubted whether Garowe would ever be more than a raggedy desert road-town. Like a faded staging post on a western US interstate, its heart would always be the highway itself. The road the Puntlanders were parading upon was part of the old Italian-built network centred on Mussolini's *Strada Imperiale* that once connected Mogadishu with Addis Ababa. Eighty years after its construction it was still the country's only metalled road of any consequence. The Faroles were touchy about it, but the truth was that their writ didn't run very far beyond the tarmac.

On the other hand, I had spent enough time in Garowe

to appreciate that however obsessive the regime's concern with its own security might have been, it was not paranoid. On my first visit, four months previously, a well-regarded official called Mohamed Yasin Isse, better known as Ilka-ase ('Red Tooth'), had been killed when his Toyota was ambushed by two gunmen, in broad daylight in the middle of the town. His assassination had nothing to do with Islamic militancy. Red Tooth belonged to a Majeerteen sub-clan called the Omar Mahmud; his killers were thought to be from another Majeerteen sub-clan, the Mahmud Issa. It was a straightforward revenge hit for the shooting two months previously of a Mahmud Issa policeman in Burtinle, a dusty settlement a few miles south of Garowe.

I went with a UN security officer to inspect the aftermath of the killing. Red Tooth had died instantly at the wheel of his speeding car, which had careered on into a street café, killing an unlucky young woman sitting at a table there. The bullet-riddled rear of the vehicle was still visible, poking out from the rubble of the shop. Meanwhile, Farole's secret servicemen, members of the feared Puntland Intelligence Service, had sealed off the town and were engaged in a furious house-to-house search for the culprits. According to the UN man, tit-for-tat clan killings of this kind were still common in Puntland. It made one realize how fragile Puntland's peace was, and that Farole perhaps had no choice but to rule with an iron grip. There was only one road in or out of Garowe, yet Red Tooth's killers were never caught.

The parade became increasingly surreal as it unfurled. The middle section was led by a group of ululating women decked out in green, white and blue, the colours of the new national flag, carrying a banner that read *Xoogsatada* ('the Proletariat'). An absurdly tooting brass band marked the time, led by a baton-twirling drum major with red pom-poms for shoulder flashes, groovy rectangular sunglasses, and a bus conductor's cap. The women's jute-weaving collective reappeared, unsmiling now, and marching with a disturbing, East European-style goosestep. Next came a green, white and blue giant, carrying an orange basketball: the tallest man in Puntland. He waved like an excited child as he loped past the podium, a small state flag held delicately between the forefinger and thumb of an outsized hand. In the same outfit next to him, like a distorted reflection in a funfair hall of mirrors, bustled a dwarf.

That evening, as a guest of the UN, I was invited with an assortment of aid officials to the formal 'Puntland Establishment Day party' at the presidential compound in the centre of town. The middle of it had been strewn with hay, and the surrounding buildings were strung about with coloured light bulbs, a bit like the set of a Christmas nativity play. The foreign guests were ushered to the VIP seats to Farole's front and left, where we were each issued with a small Puntland flag to wave. Behind as well as opposite us sat row upon row of Garowe's political and business elite. In this exposed position there was, un-fortunately, no escape from the floorshow that ensued. The songs, poems and sketches had but one theme – the wonderfulness of the Farole administration in all its forms – and the performers kept it up for over three hours. The comic material was particularly dire.

'I have been so happy these last four weeks!' declared an actor in one sketch.

'Why?' inquired another.

'Because parliament finally approved the law for the new electoral commission!'

This punchline was followed by a Vaudeville-style roll of drums and a cymbal crash. It was truly leaden entertainment. The only real distraction came when we were passed a large wooden bowl of raisin-like nuggets of mutton jerky, called *oodkuc*. This was followed by another nomad delicacy, a communal bowl of camel's milk, *caano geel*, a pleasantly salty, smoky drink I thought I could get used to.*

Farole, who had changed into a loose embroidered shirt and a kufi cap beautifully worked with Arabic script, sat through it all with an impassive expression, speaking little. The audience, who were just as much on parade as the marchers of the morning, sat with stiff backs and fixed grins, smiling and clapping demurely. The evening was being filmed by at least three local film crews, who zoomed in on the foreign guests for the ritual sharing of the caano geel. It was clear enough that we were being used in the crudest way to legitimize the regime. White-skinned foreigners were a relative rarity in Puntland. Our presence as guests lent the party, and its hosts, a certain international respectability. The press here were not independent. The main local media organization, Garowe Online, was run by the president's son.

---

* The 'Somali champagne', as it is known, is as important to nomadic culture as the camel itself. According to the ethnographer I.M. Lewis, the country may even derive its name from the words *soo* and *maal*, which together form an instruction to 'go and milk' – the first words a foreign visitor might hear on the lips of his nomad host.[5]

The Farole family's relationship with the outside world had never been easy, least of all when it came to the question of piracy. The allegation that they were profiting from it personally – an allegation repeatedly made by the UN's Monitoring Group on Somalia – infuriated the Faroles, who emphatically denied it and pointed out, accurately, that there was no evidence for it. It was true that the family had built a large outdoor restaurant, the only secure restaurant in Garowe, called Ruqsan Square, but there was no reason to suppose that this was not honestly paid for. Farole senior had spent many years in the Australian banking sector. In any case, Ruqsan Square could hardly be called opulent, or even much of a commercial success. There were few customers on the two occasions I visited, and those there were seemed mostly to be Farole's ministers escaping the heat of their offices downtown, who paid for their milky tea not with money but with a wink at the waiter. The tables and chairs were arranged into a bizarre approximation of a nomad camp, where each section was cordoned off by an open-sided bell tent. The desert wind blasting through this place was strong enough to toss the plastic chairs about. The pinned-down tablecloths snapped and strained at their moorings like pennants on the mast of a yacht.

Critics in Nairobi, including senior officials at the UN, sometimes described Farole's headquarters as a presidential 'palace', with the clear implication that it was corruptly funded. And yet the compound he occupied struck me as modest. It was certainly much less impressive than the nearby UN headquarters, which at four storeys high was easily the tallest building in Garowe. The UN's building was also heavily guarded and painted white, giving rise to any number of sarcastic local jokes about out-of-touch officials living in ivory towers.

Less amusing was Farole's growled observation one day, to a senior foreign official who had just arrived in Garowe, that there were 'too many southerners' among the UN's local staff. As one of the few sources of a decent income, the UN was an important employer in the town. Farole didn't want those jobs taken by anyone but northerners. The UN interpreted his remark as a scarcely veiled threat, and quietly transferred a number of its non-Darod Somali staff to positions elsewhere in the country. They were in no doubt: Farole's Puntland was at bottom a mono-clan police state, where bad things could and sometimes did happen to people with the wrong tribal affiliation. Yet, that was a quite different complaint to the charge of complicity in piracy – and no matter what Farole did in this regard, the rumours refused to go away.

From the moment he assumed office in 2009, Farole had come under huge international pressure to prove his innocence by taking concrete measures against the pirates. The problem, however, was not just that Puntland was broke. In UN parlance, the state lacked the 'capacity' to deal with piracy on its own. For example, there were an estimated 5,000 pirates operating off Somalia, but with just 350 prison places in the whole of Puntland, there was often literally nowhere to put them when or if they were captured. There was also a shortage of judges capable of trying them, and few courtrooms to hold a trial in. The UN Development Programme was funding dozens of judge-training scholarships at the university in Garowe, as well as building new prisons, notably a 254-cell facility at Gardho. But these projects would take time to mature, and until they did there were genuine limits on what the Faroles could do to oblige the West.

I saw Gardho prison for myself, later in the year. It was a forbidding place, even in its half-constructed state, out on the edge of a remote town half way between Garowe and Bossasso. The desert wind rattled the roofs of the empty watchtowers, and the unfinished cells were inhabited by geckos. The prison represented the first serious money that anyone had spent in Gardho since the Italians, eighty years ago. The former colonists were not forgotten in the town. One local family were even called Duce, thanks to a great-grandfather who adopted the name in honour of the regime that once employed him. The Italians had administered the surrounding region from a Beau Geste fort that still stood in the town, crumbling and forlorn.

Next to it, apparently still in use, was the town jail, a tiny, crenellated blockhouse containing a single, dank cell. Above the door was carved a date, 1933, together with the eroded bas-relief of what appeared to be a saluting fire-hydrant, but that on closer inspection revealed itself to be a *fasces*, the symbol from which the fascists took their name.*

The jail, despite being the only one in Gardho until the new one was finished, was empty when I looked inside. The policeman on duty explained with a shrug that its mud-brick walls were so old and rotten that the last

---

* Mussolini's adopted insignia – actually a bundle of birch rods with an axe-head protruding from it –was a symbol of legal authority carried by magistrates' attendants in Roman times.

prisoner – a 'superthief', he said – had managed to dig his way out with a tin plate. The escape hole was still visible, since no one had troubled to fill it in. Law and order, it seemed, was an optional extra in rural Puntland.

The town jail in Garowe, by contrast, was full to overflowing when I visited. With its two heavily armed soldiers patrolling a parapet around a sandy courtyard that contained a lone, spindly acacia tree, it had a distinct Spaghetti Western atmosphere. Mohamed Abdirazak, the wiry, suspicious captain of the guard, was even wearing a cowboy hat. He led me to the main cell, designed to hold perhaps a dozen prisoners but which now contained forty. It was supposed to be a holding jail, a place to put prisoners in transit to the much larger facility at Bossasso, but due process being what it was in Puntland, most of the inmates here had already been locked up for nine months or more.

They were all young men, most of them under twenty. As I approached, their arms came through the bars of the door like the waving tentacles of a sea-monster. Up close, they pressed their faces into the gaps and protested their innocence, shouting over each other, desperate to be heard. The cell beyond them was a windowless cave, fetid with condensation and stinking of sweat and human waste. You could feel the waves of heat generated by this heap of humanity from ten feet away. Not all the prisoners were shouting. I glimpsed more of them squatting in rows in the darkness at the back, each man shackled to the other by the ankle, mute and depressed.

Captain Mohamed explained that his jail was once notorious for its escapes, but no longer, now that he was in charge. The biggest problem caused by the overcrowding, he said, was that the inmates had to sleep in constant physical contact, shoulder-to-shoulder on the floor, which led to lesions of the skin that became infected. I asked if there were any pirates among them, a question that produced a renewed scuffle by the door.

'Yes! Yes! I'm a pirate!' said one young man, forcing himself forward. 'Can you get me out of here?'

His name, he told me, was Abdikadir, although the details of his story changed so much in the telling that it was impossible to trust anything much he said. At one point he asserted that he was not, actually, a pirate, but a cold chain technician at a Galkacyo maternity clinic. He was like the crucifixion victim in Monty Python's *Life of Brian* who, desperate for a last-minute reprieve, cries out, 'I'm Brian and so's my wife!'

He described how he and his cousins had been travelling the previous year in two cars towards the notorious northern pirate port of Bargal – 'For health reasons,' he said – when they were ambushed by police acting on a tip-off. There was a short shoot-out, in the course of which a cousin was wounded, and all of the travellers were arrested.

'They took three Kalashnikovs and destroyed both of our cars,' he added, still bitter at the memory.

'But what were you doing with three Kalashnikovs?'

Abdikadir ignored this question and merely repeated that he was innocent. He saw no contradiction: why would a cold chain technician *not* be armed, and up for a shoot-out with the police? There was no sense or logic to the way he bent the truth. I was reminded of Richard Burton's frustrated observation that 'these people seem to lie in-voluntarily: the habit of untruth with them becomes a second nature. They deceive without object for deceit, and the only way of obtaining from them correct information is to inquire, receive the answer, and determine it to be diametrically opposed to fact.'

The interpreter I had borrowed from the UN office offered a different explanation, which was that Abdikadir was crazy. This did not seem unlikely after nine months locked up in such a terrible place.

'Now do you see how difficult it is for judges to deal with this problem of pirates?' he said.

Establishing the rule of law was crucial to the fight against piracy. That much was understood in every Western capital in the world. And yet in 2009, when President Farole announced plans to arm and train a new 'Puntland Marine Force' strong enough to take on the heavily armed pirate bases, no foreign donor could be found to fund the programme. The truth was that, despite local help from agencies like the UN Development Programme, the international community still didn't fully trust the Faroles.

In 2010, when Farole turned for help to what was then called Saracen International, a shadowy organization said to be backed by, and based in, the United Arab Emirates (and not to be confused with other organizations and/or companies with the same name), he was publicly denounced by the UN and even the US State Department, who accused him of evading a regional arms embargo. The Puntlanders complained that they were damned if they didn't act against the pirates, and damned if they did. Suspicions were even voiced that the Marine Force's true purpose was not to combat piracy but to secure the state's territory in the north-west, much of which is contested by Somaliland.

A Marine Force had nevertheless come into being, and was said by 2011 to number over a thousand men. They were much in evidence at the parade, easily discernible by their light blue uniforms and a regimental flag displaying a gold anchor and rope. Their marching was better and their weapons seemed cleaner than average. They were discreetly accompanied by two drill instructors whom I presumed to be employees of Saracen, South African-looking white men sporting beards and bush hats, who scowled and looked the other way when I tried to speak to them, press-averse according to type.

An evening or two after the party, I was finally granted the private audience with Farole that I had been looking for, and returned to the presidential compound, which looked even less impressive now that the crowds had gone and the hay and the pretty lights had been removed. Several members of Farole's innermost circle were lounging in plastic chairs by the entrance to his private quarters, chatting and joking with each other. This was always a good time during Ramadan, when the fast-breaking meal, *iftar*, was over, and the cool of the night relieved the tension of the super-heated days. I recognized several of the men here: General Khalif, the Security Minister, Ilkajir Jama, the Interior Minister, Isse Dhollowhaa, the Director of Puntland Petroleum. On a fourth chair, inexplicably, sat the dwarf from the parade, with his legs poking horizontally over the edge. He smiled up at me briefly and shook my hand in a serious way before resuming his conversation with the minister to his left.

The inner sanctum smelled of boiled pasta. An ornate

ceiling fan slowly stirred the heavy air. Farole, sitting stolidly in the centre of a huge brown leather sofa, looked more Godfather-like than ever. His eyes, now that he was no longer wearing sunglasses, seemed small and myopic, while his spoken English seemed surprisingly accented for a man with a PhD from a university in Melbourne. From time to time his utterances were spontaneously interpreted by a small, bald, obsequious man on the adjacent sofa who spoke English like an Oxford grammarian.

'What I think the president is trying to say . . .' he would interrupt.

I wondered who this unlikely court attendant could be. When I found a way to ask he said only that he was a 'friend', newly arrived from Leicester in the English Midlands, where he practised as a fully qualified family doctor.

Farole's antipathy to piracy seemed genuine enough. The damage to Puntland's reputation and to the fabric of Somali society meant that there was 'no alternative' but to fight it. Ignoring the pirate problem was not an option, he said, because it would only spread in a way that could overpower the Puntland government in the end, affecting not just Somalia but the entire world.

'The pirates take drugs and drink alcohol,' he said. 'Both these things were very unusual before they came because they were unaffordable . . . Puntland could become a nation of alcoholics.'

'There's the risk of STDs too, such as AIDS,' chipped in the GP from Leicester.

Farole nodded gravely.

'I have always been against piracy,' he went on. 'Taking young girls by force has never been popular, you know?'

I asked why, if this was his view, the international community persisted in suspecting he was involved. The blame, he said, rested with the UN Security Council's Monitoring Group, whose annual reports had repeatedly alleged that his officials were on the take. In particular he questioned the impartiality of Matthew Bryden, the Monitoring Group's Canadian coordinator. He explained that Bryden's wife, Ubax, was a well-connected Isaaq, the dominant clan in Somaliland, and that Bryden supported Somaliland's bid for independance. That often meant Bryden painting their neighbours, and particularly Puntland, in a bad light as that would encourage the international community to think likewise. The Monitoring Group's allegations, according to Farole, were not objective but 'politically motivated'. Bryden, he noted, had not once visited Garowe while he was president.

'But in the end it doesn't matter what foreigners think. It's what Somalis think that counts.'

Whether Bryden was biased or not, the fact was that in the first quarter of that year, some ninety-seven ships were attacked off Somalia, almost triple the number in the previous first quarter. Even as the new Puntland Marine Force was parading through the centre of Garowe, pirates were holding around six hundred sailors for ransom on board twenty-eight ships.[6]

On the other hand Farole had, in fact, begun to make progress against piracy. For all the shortage of prison spaces, over two hundred alleged pirates were presently locked up in Puntland. Bryden's latest report acknowledged that, thanks to the Farole administration's 'firmer stance' on piracy, the centre of pirate operations had started to shift away from Puntland towards Galmudug, the turbulent region to the south. It was particularly significant that the once notorious pirate port of Eyl was now completely clean of pirates, a development of which Farole, who was born there, sounded very proud.

'It was the community themselves who rejected the pirates,' he said. 'I spoke to the elders and the religious leaders. It was a big campaign. I pointed out the enormous social cost of piracy – how the young men of the coast are in prison in twenty different countries, and how a great many others who put to sea are simply getting themselves killed.'

He was right on this last point. In 2012, the death rate among pirates was estimated by Nato to be as high as one in three.[7]

Farole explained how important Eyl had once been to the Italians for the export of livestock, but that trade had dried up after independence. With the decline of their port, the citizens of Eyl had focused instead on fishing, particularly for lobster. To begin with, Siad Barre had helped with this initiative. The Soviet Union provided training and construction materials for a refrigeration plant, and fishing communities were organized into cooperatives. At the height of the boom, the industry employed as many as 60,000 people.*

Yet after the Ogaden War, Farole went on, Siad Barre

---

* In 1974, Siad Barre relocated large numbers of northern nomads stricken by the so-called 'long-tail' drought to the coast. His idea was to feed the starving pastoralists with the bounty of the ocean, but the experiment ended in failure because the camel-oriented nomads stubbornly refused to eat fish, a foodstuff that they still regard as beneath them. See, for example, Nuur Ciise's poem in Faarax Cawl's 1974 novel *Ignorance is the Enemy of Love*: overleaf.

withdrew his support and concentrated government resources on the 'golden triangle' cornered by Mogadishu, Kismayo and Baidoa. All industries outside that triangle – he listed fisheries, minerals, oil, water and frankincense, as well as the husbandry of livestock – were neglected.

'Whatever else happens, we can't go back to the old system,' he said.

The fisheries industry went into a steep decline. Further disaster struck in 1991, when the collapse of central government opened the door to unlicensed foreign fishing fleets, which devastated local stocks of fish and lobsters. The coastal reefs were desecrated, too, by the unlicensed dumping of toxic waste. Farole explained with something like pride how Eyl had been among the first coastal communities to defend their livelihoods by attacking the illegal fleets. They called themselves, without irony, 'coastguards'. It was the rest of the world, not them, who dubbed them pirates.

That, however, was then; he acknowledged that things were different now. There was no illegal fishing off Somalia any more, and with the re-establishment of authority in Mogadishu and Garowe, 'piracy' no longer served any useful purpose, and had become merely another criminal enterprise. Farole had found foreign funding for 'community projects' designed to entice the young men of Eyl away from the sea and back on to the land. One of the

The grunting grumbler pours tea between his lips,
His nose dribbles as he fills his jaws with fish,
He lives in debt while the man of mettle milks Debec, his
she-camel. See footnote on previous page.

main backers, appropriately enough, was Italian. He described what he called an important 'development opportunity' just south of Eyl, where the commercial production of sorghum and potatoes was possible.

Enticement, however, could only do so much. Farole was adamant that the campaign could not have succeeded without local consent. Most effective of all, he said, had been the moral arguments put forward by the local religious leaders. It was they who had persuaded the people to turn against the pirates by convincing them that their behaviour was 'unIslamic'. The key to defeating piracy, he was convinced, was moral rearmament through the mosques.

The campaign in Eyl, he confidently predicted, was just the start. Other notorious ports, such as Garacad, 130 kilometres to the south, had followed Eyl's example and were driving their local pirates out, too. The whole area of pirate operations was being squeezed southwards and out of Puntland altogether. If I wanted to see pirates for myself these days, he said, I would have to go down to Galkacyo or Hobyo or Harardheere.

There was at least no need to go so far to find the victims of piracy. The following morning in the UN canteen, all the talk among the breakfasting internationals was that the crew of a pirated Thai fishing boat, the *Prantalay 12*, had been rescued and brought into Garowe overnight, and were now resting at the Global Hotel, a run-down establishment barely 200 yards away up the street.

I hurried along there with two UN officials and soon discovered that the rumour was true. There were fourteen fishermen in all. Although the boat they had crewed was Thai-registered, the men were all Burmese – some of the million or so mostly undocumented migrant workers who, over the years, had fled the junta in Rangoon and made Thailand their home. This presented both the Garowe government and the UN with a problem, for these crewmen carried no passports. What country should they be repatriated to, and who would bear the cost? Alan Cole, a British ex-navy officer with the UN Office for Drugs and Crime, had already spoken to the Thai embassy in Nairobi, since there was no Burmese one. The Thais had told him they had never heard of the *Prantalay 12*. Cole shook his head grimly: he had seen this kind of diplomatic farrago before. He recalled an occasion when he had been presented with some pirates who had been shot dead. He had been obliged to organize their burial himself, and even paid for it out of his own pocket.

'The Somalis just aren't set up for this type of thing,' he said. 'I just had to get it sorted.'

The crew of the *Prantalay 12*, he reckoned, could be stuck in Garowe for some time to come.

The crew emerged from the hotel door, blinking in the sunlight and looking comically short next to their lanky Somali hosts. They were fine-boned and caramel-coloured, with tousled hair and light blue food-worker shirts bearing the Prantalay company logo – the only shirts they owned, it turned out. They shook hands with each of us in their demure, super-polite Asian way, the left hand on the right forearm, their eyes cast to the ground. For a group of liberated hostages they seemed very subdued. I guessed they were suffering from a form of shock.

Only one of them, Hassan Pan Aung, spoke any English, but eventually the outlines of an extraordinary tale of

suffering and adventure emerged. They had been in
captivity for fifteen months, and had only been freed following pressure applied by some local elders. Ducaysane
Ahmed, a government official in a smart jacket and tie with
a Puntland flag in his lapel, was on hand at the Global
Hotel to take credit for that – although it was clear that the
poverty of these Burmese had played its part. The pirates
had concluded, eventually, that these men were worthless as
hostages. Five Thai crew members, the master and his four
officers, were less fortunate, and had not been released.

'We were so lucky to be Burmese from a shit-poor
country like our Burma,' as Pan Aung later put it to an
interviewer from the *Myanmar Times*.[8]

Pan Aung recounted how, in early 2010, his boat and two
sister ships, the *Prantalays 11* and *14*, had left the Thai port
of Ranong on the Andaman coast bound for the fishing
grounds off Djibouti, 6,000 kilometres away across the
Indian Ocean. Their trip was certainly not illegal, as
apologists for piracy used to claim. Pan Aung was even able
to produce a licence issued by the Djibouti Ministère de
l'Elevage et de la Mer for the trapping of lobster, mud crab
and blue swimming crab. At 106 tons and 27 metres long,
the wooden-hulled *Prantalay 12* was small and slow, with a
low freeboard designed for the easy recovery of traps and
nets. She was the easiest kind of prey for the pirates, of
whom there were twenty-five, in two speedboats. They
were wearing camouflage uniforms and were so heavily
armed that the fishermen thought at first they must be a
legitimate naval patrol.

'It was only when they were on our boat that we knew
they were mother-fucking Somalis,' said Pan Aung in the

same interview in the *Myanmar Times* (a weekly international journal published, in English, by editors evidently untroubled by profanity).

All three boats in the fleet were taken, along with about seventy crewmen, sixty of whom were reportedly Burmese.

And so their adventure began. Pan Aung's captors were based near the port of Garacad on the southern edge of Puntland. They didn't stay there for long, however, but put the Prantalay fleet to use as 'motherships', with the hostage crews kept on board for use as human shields. Until 2009, the pirates tended to restrict their attacks to their home waters and the Gulf of Aden, but international naval patrols had made that old hunting ground less attractive than before. Motherships allowed them to range much deeper into the Indian Ocean – a response that the world's admirals apparently never anticipated. Pan Aung and his shipmates found themselves travelling half way home again. Their captors took the *Prantalay 12* as far as the coast of Sri Lanka. Eight months after the boat was pirated, they were cruising for a target in the Lakshadweep Islands, 200 kilometres south-west of Kerala, when one of the Burmese, 28-year-old Yan Aung Soe, managed to jump overboard and was rescued by the Indian Navy.

Throughout their ordeal, according to Pan Aung, the pirate bosses back in Garacad were in touch with the bosses of the Prantalay Marketing Company, in whose name the boats were registered, demanding a cool $9m for each of them. Prantalay was a fair-sized frozen seafood specialist with profits of $49m in 2011, but the company refused to pay. The pirates steadily lowered their demands as the months went by, yet Prantalay wouldn't even enter into negotiations. The frustrated pirates began to starve their captives, and kept them hydrated with water contaminated by filth and salt. Pan Aung betrayed no emotion as he described how, one by one, his shipmates succumbed to strange swellings in their limbs and developed breathing difficulties. The sickness was so severe that five of them eventually died and were buried at sea.*

Their troubles were not over yet. One night, back at last on their remote Garacad anchorage, an argument broke out between the pirates. The anchorage was small and crowded with captured fishing boats, and there weren't enough mooring spaces to go around. The squabble turned into a firefight that only stopped when one of the shooters was hit. Pan Aung, who was thirty-six, said the pirates were 'young boys, like my sons'. He added that they were 'always' high on qat, although on that night many of them were drunk as well.

In the melee, a drunken pirate at the controls of the *Prantalay 12* selected the wrong gear and crashed into another boat, splitting her bow. No longer seaworthy, she was moved to another village anchorage where she had languished until one night the previous month, when strong winds had caused the anchor cable to give way. Pirates and captives abandoned ship as the *Prantalay 12* drifted on to rocks and sank. The recriminations on the beach quickly turned violent, and lasted all night. Pan Aung described how the hostages had dug themselves into the sand as the gunfire zipped back and forth above their

---

*The probable cause of death was later identified as beriberi, a vitamin deficiency disease.

heads. The following morning they were marched for two days through the desert, where they were held first at one pirate camp, then at another. This was another fraught period when they thought they might be killed at any minute; no one had told them that the pirate chiefs had in fact begun the negotiations that led to their eventual release.*

The other crewmen sat in patient silence as Pan Aung talked, understanding nothing. I handed them half a packet of cigarettes which they fell upon ravenously, passing it back and back until it was empty. Four or five of them missed out on the windfall, yet I saw no disappointment in their faces or even any change of expression. We sent out for a box of two hundred Marlboros, and asked if they had eaten recently. Not since yesterday, they said; and in any case the hotel kitchens were now closed for the day because it was Ramadan. Ducaysane, embarrassed, went to find the manager, and soon the ship's cook from the *Prantalay 12* was hard at work in the outdoor canteen, cheerfully preparing a tureen full of macaroni.

I asked if any of them had had a chance to contact their families yet, and again they shook their heads. They had been free for nearly 24 hours, but none of them had thought to ask to borrow a phone, and none of the Somali officials had offered. We foreigners produced our mobiles, and a minute

---

* The *Prantalay 12*'s sister ship, the *Prantalay 14*, was sunk off the Lakshadweep Islands by the Indian Navy in January 2012 following a battle in which ten pirates were killed. The *Prantalay 11* was captured nearby a week later, after its captors attacked an Indian Coastguard vessel they had mistaken for a merchantman.

or two later Pan Aung was speaking to his wife in Ranong for the first time in fifteen months. It was the sort of golden emotional moment that in a Hollywood movie would be accompanied by the full string section of an orchestra. Pan Aung, however, merely smiled. He did not weep or dance for joy or even raise his voice much, and he kept his conversation short and matter-of-fact. Alan Cole, the UNODC man, shook his head in awe at this display of reserve and self-control.

'It's extraordinary, isn't it?' he murmured. 'Any European would be in bits after what they've all been through.'

It was three months before the crew of the *Prantalay 12* were able to leave Garowe's Global Hotel. After long negotiations Thailand refused to take them, and they were returned to Rangoon, even though they had been employed by a Thai firm when they were captured, and most of them had families residing in Thailand. Hassan Pan Aung had lived in Ranong for over nineteen years. Their treatment by the Prantalay Marketing Company was disturbing by Western standards, although Alan Cole said it was not unusual.

These Burmese were not high-profile victims like the rescued British yachting couple, Paul and Rachel Chandler, or the proselytizing Californians, Scott and Jean Adam, who were murdered aboard their yacht, the *Quest*, in early 2011. They were stateless, impoverished migrant workers of a sort often found below decks in the Far East's under-regulated and poorly paid fisheries industry. The firms who employed them commonly treated them as expendable. With no family money behind them and no one to champion their cause, trawler crews from the Far East could languish for years in pirate captivity. Or, far from the gaze of the media, unnoticed and unloved, they could just as easily die of abuse, as five crewmen of the *Prantalay 12* had done.

9

Galkacyo: Pirateville
Galmudug, August 2011

President Farole said I would need to go south to see pirates, so I took his advice and joined a UN field trip from Garowe to Galkacyo, Puntland's second city. The surface of the old north–south highway had long since eroded, and for the most part was as rough as a farm track, so that it took well over three hours to cover the 200 kilometres in between. Our white-painted Toyota travelled in the routine UN way, in a convoy between two truckloads of heavily armed SPU. The dust thrown up by the vehicle in front made it hard at times to see out. The desert on either side, dimly perceived through ochre-coloured clouds, was a Henry Moore sculpture park of termite mounds. Here and there we passed an acacia tree, often with a ragged tent pitched in its handkerchief of shade: refugees, the driver said, who had paused in their northward flight from the drought. There was little traffic on the road during the hot mornings, apart from the occasional lorry lumbering towards Bossasso with a cargo of offended-looking camels,

211

their protruding necks and heads swaying in time as their vehicle lurched into another disconcertingly deep pothole.

I was curious to see Galkacyo, one of the great crossroads of Somali trade and an important city in its own right. One of its traditional nicknames was 'the place where the White Men ran away',[1] a reference to a battle won against European troops in colonial times, although its modern reputation was hardly less fierce. Galkacyo lay on the front line between the two main clans of central Somalia, the northern Darod and the southern Hawiye, which made it one of the tensest places in the country. The civil war had not really ended here. The city remained physically divided by an uninhabited no-man's-land, a 'green line' connected by a single road with heavily armed checkpoints at either end. Each side was governed by separate administrations. North Galkacyo was part of Puntland. South Galkacyo was the capital of the autonomous region of Galmudug, presided over by a Hawiye ex-colonel, Mohamed Alin. Those were the basics; it took me some time with a large-scale map to understand the details.

'Galmudug' was a neologism, a composite of the two old provinces from which it was carved, Galgaduud and Mudug (either of which could easily be confused with the nearby town of Galdogob). President Alin, who had returned from exile in Northolt in Middlesex, was a member of the Sacad sub-clan of the Hawiye Habr Gidr. To his south-west was an even smaller regional administration, Ximan & Xeeb, run by Mohamed Aden 'Tiiccey', a returnee from Minneapolis, and a member of the Habr Gidr Suleiman, a Hawiye sub-clan that did not always see eye to eye with the Sacad. Beyond *that* was territory controlled – most of the time – by the ASWJ, the multi-clan Sufi militia, who were battling al-Shabaab to their south. I was not about to attempt it, but anyone driving from Garowe to Mogadishu in mid-2011 was obliged to cross territory controlled by at least six different armed clans or factions, and three active front lines. Galkacyo lay at the sucking edge of a political maelstrom, and that was before taking into consideration the fickle pirate gangs, for whom unstable central Somalia was a true haven, with this city at its hub.

I recalled my visit, earlier that year, to the Northwood, north London headquarters of EUNAVFOR, the naval force spearheading the European Union's counter-piracy mission in the Indian Ocean. I was shown a map marked with blue dots for the pirates' suspected desert camps, around thirty of them in all, with codenames borrowed from Charles Schultz's *Peanuts* cartoons like 'Great Pumpkin' and 'Red Baron'. Galmudug had noticeably more blue dots than anywhere else. The EUNAVFOR operations room resembled the set of a James Bond film. The main feature was a giant electronic wall map, on which the movement of shipping was updated by satellite in real time. At an array of desks facing it worked two dozen officers from twenty different navies, many of them speaking purposefully into the microphones of their headsets.

'When there's an attack on, this place gets as sweaty as a Royal Marine at a spelling test,' said a spokesman, Paddy O'Kennedy, a former RAF Tornado navigator.

The EUNAVFOR operation, although an undoubted

triumph of high-tech, international cooperation, seemed a sledgehammer for the nut of Somali piracy. Its size, its expense, the sheer professionalism represented by so many gold-braided hats and shoulder pips, stood in hilarious contrast to the amateurism of their opponents, the drunk young men who crashed and fought over the *Prantalay 12*. The challenge, O'Kennedy explained, was not the pirates per se, but how to locate and then deal with them quickly enough.

'We're trying to police an area the size of Western Europe with twenty-five military vessels. Once the pirates are aboard their target, it's generally too late to intervene without jeopardizing the lives of the crew. Yet the average time between the first distress call from a boat under attack and the pirates going aboard is about ten minutes. We can't get there fast enough. If we had all the ships of all the navies in the world, we still wouldn't have enough.'

The pirates' success rate had declined recently as merchant ships had learned to defend themselves: by sailing in escorted convoys, by turning their bridges into fortified 'citadels' and, increasingly, by employing armed guards who knew how to repel a boarding party by force. And yet the pirates were not deterred. Indeed, the number of attacks was still increasing: 189 attempts in 2011, up from 152 the year before, according to the shipping industry's Oceans Beyond Piracy project. The main reason, everyone agreed, was that the rewards on offer were bigger than ever. Marine insurance companies paid out $146m in ransoms in 2011, an average of $4.8m per ship, compared to just $5m and $600,000 per ship in 2007. April 2011 saw the highest ransom payment ever recorded: $13.5m for the

Greek-flagged tanker *Irene*, which at the time had $200m worth of crude oil on board.*

EUNAVFOR could go on trying to contain piracy by 'altering the risk–reward ratio' – O'Kennedy pointed out that over a thousand pirates had in fact been imprisoned – but there would be no lasting solution to the problem while the insurance industry effectively colluded with the pirates' mission of self-enrichment. Western governments could legislate to outlaw the paying of ransoms, but O'Kennedy suspected they would not do that, or indeed take any other truly decisive action against the pirates, until they were forced to. There were a handful of potential 'game-changers'. An obvious one was the emergence of evidence of a financial link between the pirates and al-Shabaab. The payment of ransoms would have to stop then because it would mean that insurers were indirectly funding a pro-scribed terrorist organization, which was of course illegal. Conclusive evidence of such a link had so far proved elusive, however. A likelier possibility, according to O'Kennedy, was 'a really big hijacking' in the Indian Ocean.

'A gas or oil tanker arrives in the UK every three days. If two of those get taken, Britain's lights go out,' he said.

The capture of a big cruise liner might also force a change in policy. A handful of liners had in fact already

---

* Although these ransoms sound large, they form only a tiny part of piracy's overall cost to the global economy. According to Oceans Beyond Piracy, hiked insurance premiums, increased security precautions and the extra fuel needed to re-route cargo ships cost the world $6.9bn in 2011 alone.

been attacked, but had so far always managed to escape.

'Three months ago, we received intelligence that a mothership had put to sea with three hundred pirates on board. We can only think they are going after a big cruise ship. Why else would they need so many people?'

In January 2011, the Saga Holidays-owned *Spirit of Adventure* was attacked in the Mozambique Channel on its way from Madagascar to Zanzibar. Its 350 mostly elderly passengers, who had paid £2,000 a head for their cruise, were sitting down to a black-tie dinner when a pirate attack skiff was spotted. Dinner interrupted, they were shepherded amidships to a lounge deck that was then locked from the inside. The atmosphere, according to a lady passenger I later interviewed, was remarkably calm. The passengers drank champagne and listened to the ship's pianist play *Rule Britannia*. It was fortunate that their captain, a former Australian Navy gunnery officer who had seen service in Vietnam, was prepared for this event. Unseen by the pirates, his crewmen deployed a wire trap designed to be towed in the ship's wake below the aft tender deck. This was the point on the ship where the freeboard was lowest, and thus where the pirates were likeliest to try to board. Sure enough, the propellers of the pirates' attack skiff became hopelessly entangled as they closed in, allowing the *Spirit of Adventure* to make its escape at full speed. It was a clever ruse that their attackers were unlikely to fall for again in future.

As President Farole had maintained, the original pirate gangs were dominated by disgruntled fishermen seeking to protect their livelihoods from illegal foreign operators. The coastal communities they came from were made up of skilled old seafaring families, whose ancestors had plied the Indian Ocean's trade routes for centuries in their high-sterned wooden sailing dhows, a boat design that had barely changed. As recently as twenty years ago Puntland's sailors were putting to sea without echo-sounders, and calculating the ocean's depth at night by going down into the hold, putting an ear to the hull, and listening for the knocking sound of rockfish picking at insects in the ship's planking, an indication of shallow waters. The 'aristocratic' nomads of the interior traditionally look down on the coastal communities, but that has never prevented the fishermen from taking great pride in their own distinct heritage. Shuke Osman, the director of the Puntland Development Research Centre in Garowe, noted in a study in 2003: 'In the same way that nomads sing songs of desert hardships to their camels, fishermen sing to their canoes and boats of the dangers of the sea.'

> Dark that which dark is
> Stormy sea
> Morning rain
> A woman's veil is dark
> You, my horned canoe
> May your wood never break up
> Fly over the sea
> Skim to the shore
> Speed us to land
> Driven by our oars and paddles[2]

Their marine subculture is so distinct that until very recently, coastal Somalis used a different calendar to the rest of the country, the Nayruus system, which has its roots in ancient Zoroastrianism. This calendar's most notable feature is that it has no leap year, which meant that the people of the coastal communities had fallen badly out of sync with the rest of the world over the centuries. The first day of 2001, for instance, was on 23 July.[3]

Until 2007, hostages taken for ransom were rarely harmed by the pirates, even by accident. This was partly because the pirates were governed by the marine xeer, the customary law of fishing known as the *'Uruf Alba'hr*, a kind of honour-code of the sea which obliged its followers to respect the lives of other mariners — even foreign ones come to steal Somali lobsters. In 2007, however, as word of the pirates' success spread and the size of the ransoms began to creep up, other Somalis began to get in on the act. The newcomers were not ex-fishermen, or even from the coast, necessarily, but chancers from the south-central interior who knew little and cared less about the 'Uruf Alba'hr. By 2011, the profile of the typical pirate had changed utterly.

'They are really just criminal gangs in boats now,' said O'Kennedy. 'The pirates used to be quite tightly organized along Darod clan lines, but we are seeing many more Hawiye now, and gangs that are much more clan-mixed.'

The consequences for the victims of the new pirate breed could be serious. It wasn't only that their seamanship was often spectacularly poor. Men who didn't know what they were doing in boats were more afraid of the sea, and fear, according to O'Kennedy could make them lose their heads and become 'trigger-happy'. Of the estimated 3,500 seafarers taken hostage by Somalis since 2007, sixty-five had been killed, according to the shipping industry lobbying organization SOS (Save Our Seafarers).

Perhaps even more troubling was evidence that, for the first time, an element of sadism had crept into the way that some pirates now operated. A crew member of the *Beluga Nomination*, a German-owned freighter captured in January 2011 off the Seychelles, was killed while being 'punished' in retaliation for a failed rescue attempt mounted by the Seychellois Coastguard. The crew of the *Marida Marguerite*, an Antwerp-bound chemical tanker, were beaten with iron bars, locked in the ship's freezer, and had cables tied around their genitals. One crewman was even keelhauled – pulled beneath the barnacled hull on a rope, a traditional sailor's punishment unheard of in Europe since the nineteenth century. The pirates reportedly did this 'for fun'.

In January 2012 came the even more chilling news that Chao-I Wu, the Vietnamese skipper of the trawler the *Shiuh Fu-1*, had had his right arm sawn off, in the style of al-Shabaab. His frustrated captors, who had been holding him and his crew near Harardheere for over two years, then allowed his shipmates to phone home, in the hope that their descriptions of their captain's suffering would increase the pressure on the ship's owners to pay up.

And so I felt some unease as our convoy finally bumped its way on to the tarmac that marked the city limits of north Galkacyo. Earlier that week, according to a local radio report, a well-known pirate boss had been injured in a shoot-out between rival gangs, and was being treated at the city hospital, where I now hoped to interview him. August, I had been told, was a good month to find pirates on land, because the sea was too rough for them until September when the south-west monsoon abated. But I did not expect to see so many of them, so soon.

'Look. There,' said the driver as our convoy turned off the city's main drag towards the UN compound. 'Those men are pirates.'

I looked out at a row of tin shack cafés, all closed for Ramadan, where a number of macawiis-clad young men were nevertheless congregated, squatting idly along a wall or chatting in one of two standing groups.

'What – all of them?'

'All of them,' the driver insisted.

I wondered how he could possibly know. They looked entirely ordinary, and no different from the unemployed young men one saw in every Somali town, hanging about on street corners. But the driver was adamant. This was Galkacyo, he said, and the moment the seas calmed down, these men would be off to the coast.

Their ordinariness was, I supposed, the point. Pirates didn't wear tricorn hats or parrots on their shoulders except in the imaginations of small Western boys. Real pirates were part of the people, and so were bound to resemble the other members of the society from which they sprang. Piracy was not something to be conjured from a dressing-up box, but the product of deep social dysfunction and the failure of the Somali state.

It wasn't just small boys who misunderstood this. Piracy had an extraordinary grip on the imaginations of Western adults, too. Between 2003 and 2011, Walt Disney's four *Pirates of the Caribbean* movies grossed over $3.7bn at the box office, with merchandising and other spin-offs worth many millions more.[4] The Gulf of Aden was the modern version of the Spanish Main, and Western imaginations were still in full flight. Several Somali piracy-based thrillers were published in 2011, most of them far too lurid for children. Robert Louis Stevenson, who started the West's romance with eyepatches when he published 'Treasure Island' in a magazine called *Young Folks* in 1881, would have been amazed by Elmore Leonard's novel *Djibouti*, which turns on an al-Qaida plot to blow up a supertanker; or Michael Burns's archly titled *The Horn*, which features a mixed sex team of US Navy SEALs hunting pirates from a decoy yacht; or Wilbur Smith's *Those in Peril* which deals with the kidnap and rescue of the beautiful (and oversexed) daughter of an American oil billionaire.

TV dramatists were no less fascinated. In September 2010, the BBC aired a truly fantastic episode of the drama series *Spooks*, in which an al-Qaida-affiliated gang of Somali pirate suicide bombers try to blow up Westminster using high-speed stealth submarines provided by Colombian drug smugglers. Not even Hollywood had managed to synthesize so many of the West's demons into a single plotline, although it probably wasn't far behind. In November 2011 Paul Greengrass, the celebrated director of two *Bourne* action films, began auditioning among the Somali exile community in Minneapolis for actors to play pirates in *Captain Phillips*, a retelling of the 2009 hijacking of the *Maersk Alabama* starring Tom Hanks. Not all Somalis were impressed. 'I can tell you what the movie is going to be already,' said a Minneapolis restaurateur, Abdi Ahmed. 'They will have a bunch of white American people kidnapped, and Tom Hanks will save them, and a bunch of skinny black guys will get killed.'[5]

A bunch of skinny black guys: to me, in Galkacyo, that was exactly what the pirates looked like. We dropped our bags at the UN office – another prison-like compound with barbed wire on the walls and blast barriers at the gates – and at once headed out again, the SPU men in their vehicles ahead and behind us as before. We hadn't gone far when we came across a cluster of people celebrating the inauguration of a new customs house. Calypso-style music blared from a pair of immense loudspeakers mounted on a van dressed in bunting. We stopped to pay our respects to Cowke, the mayor of north Galkacyo, our SPU men joining us as we mingled with the crowd of officials and onlookers. The mayor was in a grumpy mood despite the carnival atmosphere.

'You've come from Garowe? That nest of vipers,' he said.

And he plunged into an exposition of all the ways the Farole administration was neglecting his town.

'Look at the new police station in Garowe. It is very beautiful. Here, the police sleep in the corridors. Please: take pictures.'

The police, Cowke explained, were appointed not by him but by Farole, according to their clan affiliation. But underinvestment from Puntland's centre – which he called 'an Omar Mahmud mafia' – meant there wasn't enough money to pay the police their salaries, let alone build new facilities. They had therefore turned to corrupt practices in order to survive, practices that even included collusion with pirates.

'The police and the pirates are so intermingled now, but what can I do? The people here are fed up with the corruption. If Farole is not very careful, there will be a revolution here.'

We stayed for his inauguration speech out of politeness. Just as he finished, one of the SPU men came worming his way through the audience and tugged urgently on my sleeve.

'We go. Now,' he said with an anxious look over his shoulder, 'quick, quick.'

Back in the safety of the vehicles, the SPU men described how they had been approached at the back of the crowd by two strangers, who asked if the gaalo they were working for were French. When they asked why, the men – who spoke, the guards said, with slurred voices – replied that they were looking for hostages to exchange for some clansmen of theirs who had been captured by a French warship, and were now in jail in Paris. They had even begun a discussion about how much it would cost for the SPU to look the other way while they grabbed us.

I looked out at the dispersing crowd but could still see nothing unusual. Any one of them could be a pirate. It was uncomfortable to consider how utterly dependent we were on the integrity of our SPU men. How 'special', in reality, was the protection they offered? The fact that they were employed by the UN meant nothing. The pirates could easily trump their paltry salaries, and every man has his price. In October 2011, two staff of the Danish Demining Group, Poul Thisted and an American, Jessica Buchanan, were kidnapped by their own guards on the way to Galkacyo airport.* I later

---

* They were freed three months later in Ximan & Xeeb following a night-time rescue by US Navy SEALs.

223

heard about an SPU man, one of the trusted regulars at the Galkacyo UN office, who had vanished from work a few months previously. Not long after his disappearance he was arrested at sea by the Royal Thai Navy; he was currently awaiting trial for piracy in a jail in Bangkok. I supposed it was simply lucky for us that our guards today had more honour.

If the mayor of north Galkacyo could do nothing about piracy, the powerlessness of the administration to the south turned out to be greater still. Nick Beresford, the Garowe UN Development Programme chief, was keen to show his face in Galmudug, especially as President Alin had recently appointed a new cabinet. And so our little convoy made its way south towards the so-called Green Line, although the only sign of greenery as we approached it was the Somali rose, the local nickname for the shreds of plastic that snag on the thorns that grow in all the country's abandoned urban spaces.

There was no better demonstration of the crazy power of clanism than at the border post, where our guards from Garowe flatly refused to go any further. Instead we were handed over to another, Hawiye, SPU team, employees of President Alin, who were waiting for us at the barrier. I had expected tension, but in fact the handover was weirdly amicable. Indeed, there was so much smiling and back-slapping between the SPU men that I felt certain that we were the focus of a business arrangement of some kind, although I did not actually see money change hands. The new guards then escorted us along a straight, raised stretch of road that ran through a buffer zone of derelict housing to another sandbagged checkpoint on the far side. It felt a little like crossing from West to East Berlin in the days of the Cold War.

The process felt absurd as well as corrupt. It was not just because I was a foreigner that it was impossible to distinguish between the Darod and Hawiye men. In truth, there was no meaningful difference between them. The author Nuruddin Farah made the same point in his 2005 novel *Links*, the action of which is dominated by two rival Mogadishu warlords, characters based on real people, although Farah refuses to name them. He also avoids mentioning which clans they represent, because to do so would be to dignify the absurd cause for which they are fighting. Instead he refers to them throughout the novel simply as 'Strongman North' and 'Strongman South'. It is a piece of satire reminiscent of Jonathan Swift's *Gulliver's Travels*, in which the people of Lilliput are divided into 'Big-Endians' and 'Little-Endians' according to how they think a boiled egg should be eaten – a dispute, wrote Swift, that had given rise to 'six rebellions ... wherein one emperor lost his life, and another his crown'.

We found Mohamed Alin, Galkacyo's Strongman South, waiting for us in a darkened municipal debating chamber with half a dozen of his newly appointed ministers, who sat in a line on a bench to the left of their president with their backs hard up against the wall. Alin, small and bald and spritely looking, introduced them one by one – the Commander of Police, the Minister of Fisheries, the Governor of Mudug, a general called Sed – and explained that they represented all the clans in Somalia, because he had appointed them according to the 4.5 clan formula used in Mogadishu. This, he wanted us to know, was progress; it was the reason he had fired his old cabinet, whose members had all been Habr Gidr Sacad, like him. We sat down on the bench against the wall opposite the ministers. A ceiling fan chugged above, throwing complex shadows from the only light source, a window high up in the wall behind the president. The ministers eyed us in silence, as wary as young teenagers at a school dance. A brown floral coffee table was marooned in the wide space between us, cut into the shape of a five-pointed star.

'Piracy is a *particular* problem in Galkacyo,' said Alin, in a thick English accent, when our conversation finally began. 'Pirates have more militia, more vehicles and more money than we do. No one can fight them at sea. We need assistance to fight them on land, but no one in the international community is listening.'

He wanted help with the funding of schools – 'to educate the young men about the perils of piracy' – and with skills training to provide alternative livelihoods, such as carpentry and electrical engineering. The courts needed restructuring. There was no proper prison in Galmudug. The few police available to him were under-trained, they had no transport or communications equipment, and their uniforms were worn out. The shopping list went on and on in a tone that suggested it was not the first time he had itemized it. Nick Beresford, a man with a UN budget and thus the main intended audience, nodded extravagantly and took copious notes.

If Alin was bitter about foreigners ignoring him, he was bitterer still about their support for the TFG in Mogadishu, which he accused of abandoning Galmudug, for they had contributed nothing to his fight against the pirates either. I noticed that he was clutching a copy of *The Law of the Somalis* by Michael van Notten, which was not exactly a TFG-friendly polemic. The author, a Dutch lawyer, argued passionately that xeer, Somalia's ancient customary law, should be allowed to form the basis of Somalia's reconstruction, and that the international community had made a critical error when they opted instead to try to create a centralized democratic legislature.

Alin was a former governor of Hobyo, another notorious pirate port on the Galmudug coast, which he announced he was determined to clean up. He said that as soon as the monsoon abated – or by the end of September at the very latest – he intended to move his entire cabinet there.

'We need to show the people we are still here,' he explained. 'We need to mobilize the business community there. We need to clean house.'

I looked across the floor at the ministers, one or two of whom seemed to shift uncomfortably in their seats. Alin said he wanted Hobyo to recapture its nineteenth-century glory days by becoming a commercial port again, an entrepôt as successful as Bossasso. He intended to take not just his ministers there in the autumn, but a cross-section of religious leaders too, who would drive home the message that piracy was not just unSomali but unIslamic. I said it sounded a bold and interesting experiment and asked if I could accompany him to witness the transformation of his old town.

'You will be welcome,' he said.

We were taken, then, to the main police station to see for ourselves how badly Galmudug needed money. The cells, or at least their contents, were suggestive of a society in total meltdown. The division chief, Mohamed Nur Ali, led us into a cell where four young men were shackled together, including a cowed 15-year-old called Fahid.

'That,' said the chief, with the righteous pride of an implacable disciplinarian, 'is my nephew. He was running errands for the pirates. He was well on his way to becoming one of them. I'm locking him up until he sees sense. He needs to listen to his elders and betters.'

He turned on his heel without a second glance at the boy, and led us off to the next cell. Here we found another saved soul, Jamaal, who had been locked up at the request of his father, a friend of the chief. Jamaal, also fifteen, had been inside for five days, awaiting his father's return from a business trip at the end of the week. The chief said Jamaal had been caught skiving off school and hanging out with 'bad characters' who lounged about with guns, chewing qat. 'But you won't do it again, will you, Jamaal?'

'Nooo!' said Jamaal, with a furious shake of his head.

I wasn't sure whether to feel cheered or appalled. The chief had certainly hit upon an effective means of disciplining the young. Like the parents of the teenagers in his jail, he was convinced that disrespect for authority lay at the root of society's ills, and that the best place to start fixing the problem was within the family. Maybe he was right. It was a sentiment often heard on the lips of politicians back home in Britain, after all, particularly in the wake of the urban riots that broke out across England that August, when the British prime minister himself observed that 'if we want to have any hope of mending our broken society, family and parenting is where we've got to start'.[6] The chief saw himself as a rare paragon of order in a world drowning in chaos and violence. There was no arguing with the grue-somely illustrated posters in his office urging children not to play with guns, of which, he said, there were an estimated 14 million in circulation in the country. His stand against the mayhem was not uncourageous, suggesting that society here was perhaps not quite as broken as it was con-stantly made out to be, and that there was hope after all.

On the other hand, Chief Ali was operating his jail as if it were some kind of private borstal, and this was troubling. Imprisonment was supposed to be an instrument of the state. It made one realize how little due process there must be in Galmudug if the head of the local police could act as judge, jury and executioner – a vigilante, in effect. On the way out I caught sight of another teenager, a beautiful girl this time, who was chained like a dog to a courtyard wall. Her name was Kafiyo, and she was sixteen. She had been brought in by her parents that morning, the chief explained, for starting a family fight in the course of which she had bitten her aunt.

'You know,' said the chief, 'in our culture, it is a very serious thing to bite one of your elders. Particularly an aunt.'

Kafiyo scowled and tossed her mane of long black hair at us as we passed, proud and magnificently unrepentant.

We returned to north Galkacyo for an appointment at the medical centre, where I hoped to find my injured pirate. Abdulcadir Giama, its surgeon-director, was a returnee from Crotone, on the sole of the boot of Italy, where he had practised and prospered as an obstetrics and gynaecology consultant for over thirty years. Vivacious, gossipy and instantly likeable, he had become so thoroughly Italianized in exile that he even spelled his name *Jama* with a 'Gi'. He described with glee how he had once been obliged to operate on Guirino Iona, a notorious *capobastone* in the 'Ndrangheta, who had come into his surgery late one night with a piece of glass stuck in his head.

'That was good training for my work here in Galkacyo,' he laughed, his hands flying as he leaned back in his office chair. 'Iona? Eh! All of Interpol were after him!'

Perhaps the most remarkable thing about the medical centre – the only trauma clinic in Puntland – was that he had personally raised the funds to build it. Over 7,500 patients now passed through his doors each year, many of them internal refugees from far beyond the borders of Puntland. The centre was still expanding, and he was so hungry for funding that he had even sold his house in Italy to help meet the bills.

Giama described piracy as a 'pollutant' in Galkacyo, a city that in the last few months had become a magnet for unemployed militiamen from all over the country. Ninety-nine per cent of the pirates, he thought, were ex-military.

'We are seeing more and more things happening that are alien to our culture: rape, abductions, drive-by shootings,' he said. 'They are always getting into car smashes, or injuring each other in drunken shoot-outs. I get two or three gunshot victims in the hospital every day.'

My hopes rose but were just as quickly dashed when I explained what I was after. The radio report I had heard was wrong: there was no injured pirate boss in the hospital at the moment. But Giama, sensing my disappointment, offered to introduce me instead to a patient of his who was 'a good friend of the pirates'. I had no idea what this might mean but accepted anyway, and followed him out of his office and through the half-finished hospital to a small, hot ward that smelled of sweat and cheese, just like the wards in Mogadishu.

Propped up in a bed at one end of the room was a tall man with an imperious, pockmarked face. He had one arm in a cast in a grubby grey sling, the result of a car accident. There was a subtle menace in his bloodshot eyes, a repressed violence that one instinctively knew it would be unwise to provoke. From the way the ward's other patients all looked to him as we entered, it seemed that they knew it too. He gruffly agreed to speak to me so long as I hid his identity with a pseudonym. I suggested Abdi.

'No,' he said firmly, 'I want to be Guled.'

'OK then. Guled.'

He grunted his satisfaction, but still would not speak until we had gone somewhere private. It was no wonder, because Guled turned out to be more than a playground bully. He was a killer with a past, an Omar Mahmud gun for hire who had once fought Islamic militants for President Yusuf in the Galgala Mountains, before switching sides and fighting for al-Shabaab – although he was now back with the government, working undercover for PIS, the Puntland Intelligence Service that was supposed to be under the control of President Farole, but which was often alleged to be trained and funded by the CIA.

'We are under the Americans,' he confirmed flatly, as if this were of no interest. 'I saw their trainers in Bossasso. The training programme is continuous.'

Guled had been charged with the extraordinarily dangerous task of infiltrating the pirate gangs in order to establish whether or not they were in league with al-Shabaab. He had begun by infiltrating the main pirate network around Garacad in Puntland, and found that there was no such connection. Al-Shabaab's presence in that small, Darod-dominated port was minimal.

Then he had proceeded to Harardheere to ask the same questions, an even riskier enterprise considering that Harardheere was under the control of al-Shabaab, the local pirates were all Hawiye Suleiman, and he was a Darod Omar Mahmud. He found what he was looking for, though. In Harardheere, he said, al-Shabaab routinely took a cut of between $200,000 and $300,000 for each pirated ship brought to anchorage there.

'Are you sure?' I said, startled. 'Does the CIA know this?'

'I suppose so,' he shrugged with the same supreme indifference as before. 'I passed the information up the chain.'

The pirate–al-Shabaab relationship, Guled explained, had nothing to do with shared ideology. It was purely a business arrangement, and not a very happy one at that.

'The Harardheere pirates would normally use a different port rather than pay al-Shabaab, but as Hawiye Suleiman they are forced to use Harardheere. They can't go to Garacad, and Hobyo is difficult for them now.'

Al-Shabaab, in other words, was extorting cash from the pirates. This was not the same thing or as dangerous as a merger between the groups, as postulated in Elmore Leonard's novel *Djibouti*. Nevertheless, it sounded as though Western insurance money was finding its way into the pockets of designated terrorists: one of the piracy 'game-changers' muttered about at Northwood. If

Guled's findings were provable, they were important.

He had little respect for the pirates, although not because their immoral behaviour was tearing at the fabric of society, but because they were so foolish with their money.

'They flash their money around. The price of everything goes up when the ransoms come in. Even the dollar exchange rate goes up, but they still spend everything. They buy cars from Dubai, alcohol from Ethiopia, qat from Kenya, beautiful girls from Djibouti. They will drop $40,000 on a new car, no problem. It's all fun, fun, fun.'

The solution he proposed was predictable: he wanted them all put down by military force.

'The marines would close them down,' he drawled. 'If the marines had enough weapons, they could go wherever they liked.'

Like so many among his damaged generation, Guled had known nothing but violence in his life, in the course of which he seemed to have developed a frightening indifference to pain and suffering. I doubted whether he had lost his moral bearings. He struck me rather as someone who had never had such a compass in the first place. He was an ugly, feral, dangerous man, and thus, I supposed, well suited to the job of infiltrating the pirate boss underworld. I wasn't sorry when, as though suddenly bored, he cut our conversation short and sloped off back to his ward.

Dr Giama, who never passed up a fundraising opportunity if he could help it, wanted Nick and me to watch a new PowerPoint presentation he had prepared, an explanation of the work of his hospital. It sounded dull. But this was Somalia, and the frank, before-and-after surgery photographs he had taken turned out to be some of the most riveting I had ever seen, as well as some of the most horrific.

Only a few of the images were to do with war, such as the eight-year-old boy who had been brought in with both hands reduced to bloody stumps by an IED. Most of the operations Giama performed were on congenital or cancerous deformities that, like so many evils in Somalia, had been allowed to fester for far too long. His slide show was thus the starkest illustration imaginable of the human cost of the state's twenty-year failure to provide basic healthcare or education. The projector whirred through close-ups of every kind of tumour, a Victorian freak show of suffering: an advanced sarcoma, a huge angioma, an inoperable mesenteric carcinoma.

'Just look at that myoma,' said Giama at one point, in amazement still at the obscenely glistening mound of matter that he had chopped out of some poor woman's uterus, 'How big is *that*?!'

The horrors grew worse: a baby with a malignant, foot-ball-sized growth on its backside; two still-born Siamese twins, a starburst of misdirected eyes and hands and limbs, spatch-cocked on a mortuary slab; and a calcified ectopic pregnancy, a creature from the scariest science-fiction film, removed from its mother after six years of mummification.

'In Europe you would just never see such things,' Giama murmured.

I looked away, and saw Nick sitting ramrod straight with a hand over his eyes, peeping out through a slit between his fingers. It seemed that he hadn't been prepared for this, either.

But Giama wasn't finished yet. As a gynaecologist he had a fascinated hatred for Somalia's continuing adherence to the old African practice known to the World Health Organization as FGM, or Female Genital Mutilation. I had read a great deal about this infamous cultural oddity, which Giama called Somalia's 'silent tragedy'. But actually seeing the surgical reality of FGM, especially in such lurid, explicit close-up, was an experience that soon had me peeping through my fingers too.

Giama explained, in his mesmerizingly soft and sing-song voice, how Somalis favoured the most extreme, 'Pharaonic' form of genital modification technically known as infibulation, in which both inner and outer labia as well as the clitoris are removed, usually when their owner is between six and twelve years old. Then the labia majora is sewn back on across the top of the vaginal opening, where it eventually heals to form a wall of scar tissue, leaving nothing but a matchstick-sized hole below. This procedure, he said, was almost always carried out at home, on a kitchen table, without much antiseptic and never with any anaesthetic. The thread used was often the same as the kind used to make sacking. There were, inevitably, many complications, physical, psychological and social.

We heard the story of a 'beautiful, beautiful' young girl brought into the clinic by her father, who couldn't understand why his daughter kept refusing the hand of any of the many suitors he had brought her. Giama soon discovered his patient's secret. Out of embarrassment and shame, she had told no one of the dermoid cyst growing between her legs, an object so massive that she could barely walk.

'It is remarkable what you can find hidden beneath an abaya,' said Giama.

FGM, he said, often led to complications like cysts, as his slideshow amply demonstrated.

There was a moment when one of our SPU men put his head round the door to check on us, and stopped dead in the shaft of light streaming in from outside, his eyes popping at another monstrous, mutilated vagina that had just flashed up on the opposite wall. Giama shooed him out and we all laughed at the guard's comic-book confusion, although I wondered whether he had fully understood what we three men were doing, looking at such explicit pictures together in a darkened room. There was, of course, nothing erotic about the experience. Giama's surgery was more suggestive of a butcher's shop than a brothel; the flesh so rudely exposed in his slideshow spoke of carnage, not carnality. Certainly, one was nothing but repulsed by the close-up of a six-year-old girl who had been sewn up so tightly that there was no opening left in her vagina at all: 'The result of a really well-done Pharaonic infibulation,' Giama drily observed. The girl was in agony when she was brought in, suffering from ischuria, or urine retention, so acute that one of her kidneys had failed.

Giama wanted to campaign against FGM in Somalia, to publicize what he had seen in his clinic, but said he didn't have the time. The only good news was that it was in decline in the cities, and rarest of all among the diaspora, which was a 'positive and important' influence on the homeland. He noted that Mohamed Farole, Puntland's Australianized president, was one of FGM's most vociferous critics. On the other hand, Siad Barre had also tried to eradicate it in the 1970s, and failed. The practice today, Giama reckoned, was as widespread as ever among rural communities.

The reasons were complex. Ignorance played a big part. For instance, many Somalis believe FGM to be obligatory under Islam, when in reality there is no such requirement laid out in the Koran.* The underlying cause, however, was Somali society's continuing reluctance to raise women above the status of a chattel. A woman was a possession to be treasured in the way that a nomad values a good camel, and was to be kept 'pure' at all costs. Giama described a 28-year-old mother he had recently seen who had been sewn up for a second time, without anaesthetic, just ten minutes after giving birth. Yet perhaps the most astonishing aspect of this brutality was that it was often not men but women themselves who perpetuated it. In her autobiography *Infidel*, Ayaan Hirsi Ali, who later became a Dutch MP and a noted campaigner for the rights of Muslim women, memorably described how her traditionally minded grandmother orchestrated her own 'cutting', against the specific wishes of her unfortunately absent parents. At the time, Hirsi Ali was just five years old.

'A special table was prepared in [Grandma's] bedroom, and various aunts, known and unknown, gathered in the house ... Grandma swung her hand from side to side and said, "Once this long *kintir* [clitoris] is removed, you and your sister will be pure." ... She caught hold of me and gripped my upper body ... two other women held my legs apart. The man, who was probably an itinerant traditional

---

* In recent years religious scholars in several Muslim countries have issued fatwas against the practice that, as some have pointed out, pre-dates Islam by centuries – as the 'Pharaonic' description of the procedure suggests.

circumciser from the blacksmith clan, picked up a pair of scissors . . . Then the scissors went down between my legs and the man cut off my inner labia and clitoris. I heard it, like a butcher snipping the fat off a piece of meat.'

Grandma was convinced that if left uncut, Hirsi Ali would never find a husband.

'Imagine your daughters ten years from now,' she tells the child's furious mother on her return. 'Who would marry them with a long *kintir* dangling halfway down their legs?'

This attitude seemed old-fashioned to Hirsi Ali's parents in 1975. And yet, thirty-five years on, the preoccupation with purity remains so culturally ingrained that many Somali women still refuse even to shake hands with male strangers, particularly infidel ones. I discovered this when I was introduced to Maryam Qasim, who at the time was Somalia's Minister for Women's Development and Family Affairs. I offered my hand; she withdrew hers to her breast, smiling and shaking her head like someone declining a canapé at a cocktail party. Her experience of exile in Birmingham, where she had worked for years as an officer for Sure Start, a British government programme for pre-schoolers, had not Westernized her.

Pirates were frequently accused of behaving in a way that was 'alien' to Somali culture, particularly in relation to women. They were said to procure prostitutes from Djibouti, and rape was reportedly on the rise. But Giama's slideshow made me think more than ever that these things were symptomatic of a wider social problem, not its cause. The pirates were certainly sexually frustrated, but in that they were no different from al-Shabaab's foot soldiers or, indeed, young men living in any conservative Muslim society. Jay Bahadur, a Canadian reporter who spent several weeks interviewing pirates in Puntland in 2008, recorded a conversation with one of them, Momman, who said: 'The white people we see in porn movies are always so horny. How is it that you're not?'[7]

In early 2011, the Johansen family from Denmark had been kidnapped while on a yachting holiday, and were still being held in the north of Puntland. In a development that sent a frisson around the Western world, the pirate chief had recently offered to release four of the five Danes in exchange for the hand in marriage of the Johansens' 13-year-old daughter, Naja.[8] The Western tabloids were duly convulsed.* And yet, this behaviour was not so hard to recognize. Like young men everywhere, the pirates were desperate to get laid; and big money, to some, was just another means of achieving that. According to one report, proceeds from piracy had caused the traditional bride-price to rise from $5,000 to $35,000 in just six months in 2011, and young women were said to be 'flocking' to marry the men with the new money.[9]

'It really affected me,' said Anab Jama, a mother of two children. 'I divorced my husband and I married a pirate who works in Garacad. For the first few months we had a good time, but then he began to go out with another woman after he got another ransom. Finally I asked for a divorce and came back to my parents' home in Galkacyo.'

Was the pirates' behaviour any surprise when some

---

* The Johansen family were released, unmolested, in September 2011, following payment of a ransom of between $3m and $4m.

young women colluded in it in this way, while so many others did so little to emancipate themselves? The pirates did not invent the attitude that led them to treat women as sex objects. As Dr Giama's slides showed, Somali society had been mistreating their women – and women had been mistreating each other – for a very long time before any pirates came on the scene.

I kept in touch with President Alin after I left Galkacyo, hoping to hold him to his promise to take me with him to Hobyo to report on his crackdown on the pirates. Less than a month after my visit, however, there was a surge in clan violence and kidnappings that put off any further thought of return. A two-day battle erupted in September that left 68 dead and 153 wounded. The Green Line was a warzone again, and the airport, located on supposedly neutral ground between North and South Galkacyo, was briefly shelled. President Farole insisted that his troops had been battling al-Shabaab, but was contradicted by his own ter-rorism advisor, General Shimbir, who noted that the dead and injured were 'mostly from one clan', a local Darod sub-clan called the Leelkase. As so often in Somalia, the true source of the fighting may have been a traditional dispute over water wells.[10]

In any case, Alin's political position was too precarious to allow him to leave Galkacyo for long. The cabinet's move to Hobyo never happened. Instead, at the end of the year, the president was dragged into a power struggle with his own parliament, who voted to oust him for corruption. Alin countered by declaring the vote unconstitutional, and ordering the MPs to be dismissed for incompetence. At the time of writing, the pirates were able to move about the port as freely as they pleased; the latest foreign vessel to be hijacked, the Taiwanese fishing boat *Naham 3* captured south of the Seychelles, was being held in a harbour near by.

At a major conference on Somalia in London in February 2012 – the twentieth such meeting since 1991 – the international community 'reiterated [our] determination to eradicate piracy, noting that the problem requires a comprehensive approach on land as well as at sea'. The foreigners also 'recognised the need to strengthen capacity in regional states' and 'reiterated the importance of supporting communities to tackle the underlying causes of piracy'.[11]

The words were fine, but seemed entirely empty to Abdiweli Farabadane, the commander of President Alin's counter-piracy militia, who in March 2012 was poised for a military campaign against the pirates of Hobyo, although without much expectation of success.

'There are no international organizations supporting us,' he told a reporter plaintively. 'If we had [such support] there would be no pirates in the region. Lack of support is what causes us to be powerless.'[12]

Western leaders liked to assert that a lasting solution to piracy would only be found if it was 'driven' by Somalis themselves. The problem was that Galmudug had lost confidence in its ability to drive anything on its own. The statelet was too frail; and until a surgeon could be found who was able and willing to excise the cancer of piracy, the patient seemed likely to continue to weaken.

10

Hargeisa Nights

Hargeisa, Somaliland, July 2011

My first visit to Hargeisa, the Somaliland capital, came about by accident when I missed a flight to Nairobi and was forced to wait three days for the next one. The portly Indian pilot at the controls of the tiny UN hopper plane that was supposed to connect with the Kenya flight had touched down so hard on the gravel airstrip at Bossasso that he burst a tyre. There was no spare on board, or at Bossasso airport – which was a Potemkin village kind of place, with a swanky new smoked-glass passenger hall, but no maintenance facilities at all – so we were forced to wait while another plane came out especially from Hargeisa to rescue us.

When the new tyre arrived, there was no jack. The pilots then requested the dozen or so passengers to help them lever one wheel of the first plane up on to a rock. It was 35 degrees in Bossasso, and the passengers were mostly UN office workers in suits. 'Only in Somalia,' they muttered under their breath. But no one really minded, because it was better by far than sitting at a desk. UN staffers often have romantic souls –

'missionaries, mercenaries or the broken-hearted', as they like to say about themselves – and there was a definite sense of camaraderie on board when our plane finally reached Hargeisa at sunset, the last possible safe moment for a landing.

Hargeisa was a revelation: a big, bustling African metropolis, the first remotely normal Somali city I had seen. You could understand immediately why so many of Somaliland's 3.5 million citizens wanted independence so badly, for what had any of the neighbours achieved by comparison since the civil war? In their view they owed their fellow countrymen nothing. Much of their capital had been razed literally to knee-height in 1988 by Siad Barre, whose bombers took off and landed from the airport I had just arrived at, on a plateau above and just next to the city. Tens of thousands were killed. The survivors still spoke of how the surgeons had been forced to operate on the dying while lying down, so continuous was the threat from flying glass and bullets. Hargeisa had been rebuilt since then, and it was impossible not to be impressed by the energy its citizens had put into the task, in which they had received no help at all from central government in Mogadishu. The only visible reminder of the past was a downtown war memorial, a Soviet-era MiG in Somali air force colours that had crashed in the act of strafing the city, now repaired and displayed on a plinth like an oversized model Airfix.

I made friends with one of the other delayed passengers, a lanky, easy-going Kenyan Somali called Hassan, an AIDS worker who had previously been posted to Hargeisa and knew the city well. The following day we caught a rickety bus – a bus! – which sped us from the airport hotel down the hill into town, the boy conductor flirting with death as he hung by one hand from a rail by the open door. In the city centre was an immense covered street market, the East African equivalent of a North African souq, bigger by far than any other I had seen in Somalia. We dawdled like tourists in the winding, stall-packed alleys. Here was a shoe stall, the seller half-buried in an avalanche of sandals richly reeking of polish and new leather; there was a sari shop, hung high with bolts of cloth of every hue, like the harem in a folk tale in the *Arabian Nights*. Not for nothing was this region once called the Emporium of East Africa.

Yet Britain's interest here, unlike that of the Italians to the south, was never precisely colonial. Indeed, British Somaliland was never designated as a colony but as a protectorate, which was only formally established in 1888. The original purpose was to secure a steady supply of meat for the British garrison at Aden in Yemen, a critical but resource-challenged coaling station in the voyage between Europe and India – which was why, until 1899, British Somaliland was administered not from London but from Calcutta, and was nicknamed 'Aden's butcher's shop'.

(In the twenty-first century the export of livestock across the Gulf of Aden continues to boom, although the customers are no longer the British but the Saudis, who are obliged to feed the ever-increasing number of pilgrims who descend on Mecca each year. A record 1.83 million pilgrims completed the Hajj in 2011, a 50 per cent increase over the numbers a decade ago, and they were fed by some of the 4.2 million head of camel, sheep and goats that Hargeisa exports to Arabia each year. With half of its GDP and 70 per cent of its jobs reliant on the livestock business, the economy of modern Somaliland arguably depends like that of no other in the world on the growth of global Islam.[1])

So many Indian political officers were employed in the protectorate that Captain Malcolm McNeill of the Somaliland Field Force wrote in 1902 that 'in this manner, Indian ways and customs (and with them Aden prices) came into vogue in the Somali country, where they have remained until today ... the coinage is in rupees, and Hindustani being spoken by very many Somalis is practically the official language of the country.'[2]

However inauspicious its origins, the relationship forged between Somaliland and Britain was a strong one, with a legacy that survives to this day. Local sailors employed by the East India Company settled at the northern end of the trade route in port cities like Bristol and Liverpool, establishing some of the earliest Muslim communities in Britain, which continue to thrive. The first British mosque was established by Somali and Yemeni sailors in 1860 in the Cathays district of Cardiff. Many of their sons and grandsons went on to serve in the merchant navy in both world wars. Hundreds of them gave their lives for Britain on the Atlantic convoys. The maritime flavour of this special relationship was perhaps epitomized by the imam of Cardiff, Sheikh Saeed Ismail, who was born in South Shields in 1930 to an English mother and a Yemeni sailor who was killed when his ship was torpedoed by a U-boat in the Bristol Channel in 1939.* It was no coincidence that the inaugural meeting in 1981 of the SNM, the exiled Somali National Movement which led Somaliland's rebellion against Siad Barre, took place in

---

* Sheikh Saeed died in March 2011, aged 81.

Whitechapel on the edge of east London's docklands.

Like Somaliland itself, the SNM was dominated by a single clan, the Isaaq, who felt they had been marginalized by Mogadishu almost from the moment in 1960 when the British and Italian Somalilands had unified to form modern Somalia. In 1991, with Siad Barre ousted and the victorious SNM in control in Hargeisa, Somaliland unilaterally declared independence from the south. Thirty years after its foundation in London, the SNM was defunct, but its successor, the left-of-centre Peace, Unity and Development Party known as Kulmiye, was still the main force in Somaliland politics, and still closely connected to Britain. In 2010, when the SNM's former chairman, the Manchester University-educated Ahmed Mahamoud Silanyo, was elected Somaliland's president on behalf of Kulmiye, the British prime minister explicitly congratulated him in the House of Commons – although, like the rest of the international community, he fell far short of recognizing Silanyo's goal of Somaliland independence.*

As Hassan and I wandered the city streets it became clear what inveterate travellers and traders the Somalilanders were. The foreign influence was obvious in the business

---

* 'This is an area of the world of enormous importance for our own security ... [I welcome] the peaceful and credible elections in Somaliland. These are an example of genuine democracy in an area of the world not noted for it, and the UK provided funding for election supervision. We are keen to engage with the new government, and I believe the key ... is to prevent terrorist groups establishing their foothold in Somaliland as they have in Somalia. This is vital, and yes, the government will continue to engage.' David Cameron, House of Commons, 8 July 2010

names on display: the Miami Hotel, the Obama Restaurant and Café, even a fashion boutique called Posh, with a sign that read, in English, 'Your elegance is our pleasure.' Hassan put the number of Somalilanders who knew someone or had family abroad as high as 70 per cent, which was almost double the figure given by the UN for Somalia as a whole. Everyone understood that it was remittances from the diaspora that had paid for Hargeisa's reconstruction. In fact, all Somalis, not just those in Somaliland, depended on money transfers to keep the region's economy afloat. The Mogadishu government estimated that friends and relatives abroad sent back $2bn every year, an astonishing sum for a country with an estimated gross domestic product of just $6bn.[3]

Thanks to fierce competition between its six mobile phone operators, Somaliland was one of the cheapest places in Africa to make and receive a phone call. Every second shop in the main trading street seemed to be a mobile phone business, an internet café or a hawala office. Dahabshiil, one of the world's biggest international money transfer businesses, was much in evidence. Founded in the 1970s by a Somalilander, Mohamed Duale, the company now had 24,000 agents in 144 countries, and generated profits of more than $250m a year. 'Dahabshiil' was the Somali word for a goldsmith, which Hassan thought very apt for such a fabulous moneyspinner of a firm. The commercial tradition was as strong here as it must once have been in medieval Genoa or Venice, and quite unlike anywhere else in Somalia.

The state had its own currency, the Shilling, yet it had no central bank. There were no automated cash machines, and no one used credit cards. Instead there were sections of town where the pavements were clogged with money-changers who kept their cash in crude metal cages, so confident in the honesty of the citizenry that they could leave their wads of mouldering banknotes unattended whenever they needed to, just as Mohamed Omaar had described to me in Mogadishu. At the same time there was a strong possibility that cash would be replaced altogether one day by mobile telephone banking, a development that would put Somaliland far ahead of the West. The main mobile banking service, Zaad, had accrued 300,000 users since its launch in 2009. It was even possible to buy qat using Zaad.[4]

As night fell, Hassan took me to an outdoor restaurant called Summertime, set in a pretty, stepped courtyard where a fountain played beneath soft coloured lights. The tables were buzzing with young families out for their evening meal. The normality of the scene was, once again, startling: a vision, perhaps, of what Mogadishu nightlife must once have been like. The atmosphere here put the Ruqsan Square venture in Garowe to shame. A waiter came over to tell us about the wireless internet available – 'A hundred per cent free and superfast,' he said – before producing a menu that listed a dish called Chocolate Fish. ('Actually, it's got nothing to do with chocolate,' he said. 'We just call it that.')

A muezzin sounded, and Hassan went off to pray. When he returned, grinning, he was accompanied by three old friends he had bumped into, Mohamed, Najib and Sabah, who sat down with us for dinner. All three of them were returnees from America. Sabah had been educated in Minnesota and spoke with a pronounced Midwestern twang. They were Westernized, sophisticated, and fun.

'On no account should you touch the chocolate fish,' said Najib sternly as we looked at our menus.

I asked why not, as it was ages since I had eaten fish, but neither he nor the others would tell me. They shook their heads and sucked their teeth in a unified display of mock horror. We ended up eating bread and shredded camel meat, limes and chilli sauce, all washed down with milky Somali tea. I never did discover what the chocolate fish was about.

The talk ranged happily over local politics (only slightly less corrupt than it used to be, they said), some of the surprising advantages of the clan system (it was a useful substitute for car insurance), the prospects for Somaliland independence (fading), and the increasing popularity of the veil over the last twenty years. This prompted an anecdote from Najib who, as a young man in his twenties a decade before, had been at home chewing qat late one night when he determined to go out in search of female company.

'Qat can make you really horny, you know?' he drawled, 'and I was flying that night. My eyes were wide and my jaw was going like a piston . . . Man, I needed to get laid.'

It was a wet evening and so he set off in his car, kerb-crawling the streets of East Hargeisa, until in his headlights he spotted the wiggling backsides of what he thought were two young girls in abayas and headscarves, picking their way through the puddles at the side of the road. It was raining hard by then, and he pulled over to offer them a lift, smugly certain that they would accept.

'But I guess I couldn't see that well,' Najib went on. 'Qat can do things to your eyes sometimes – double vision and stuff, you know? – and it was raining, and the windshield wipers were for shit. And these girls come up and I get the fright of my life, because they've got, like, beards! And they dive into my car going, "God bless you, my son." They weren't girls at all, they were imams on the way back from the masjid ... And I'm driving them along, and my knuckles are white from clutching the steering wheel so hard because I'm so high, and I'm trying to kick my qat bag under my seat so they won't see it. I swear to God, man, I haven't chewed since.'

It wasn't only qat users who were confused by Somali women's steady retreat behind the veil. Everyone around the table had a different theory about why it had happened. The only point of agreement was that the explanation was not simple. Hassan thought that for some women, the veil offered 'solace' for the trauma of the war. The imams, he noted, had been the first to rebel against Siad Barre, and had been 'slaughtered' in the mosques. The veil was therefore a symbol of resistance against oppression, as well as peace over violence, order over chaos. Najib, who ran a rape trauma clinic nowadays, knew a good deal about that. The conversation suddenly turned dark as the old stories of cruelty and sadism from the 1990s tumbled out.

He described one infamous checkpoint where travellers were summarily shot if they failed to recite from memory certain passages from the Koran. Another checkpoint near Baidoa was equipped with a pair of scales. The drug-fuelled militiamen in charge decided that anyone weighing more than 60kg had to pay a per-kilo fine, like a budget airline luggage allowance – except that any traveller who could not pay risked having their excess flesh removed,

Shylock-style, with a panga. One man who objected was directed to go and negotiate with the checkpoint commander, who the militiamen said was asleep on a camp bed in a nearby hut. When the objector tried to wake this man, he discovered a bloody corpse beneath the sheets.

Innocent people could easily be killed out of boredom in these deranged times, or simply on the off-chance that they had a little money on them, a class of murder so common that it was known as a *ncsibso* or 'try-your-luck' killing. There was also, unsurprisingly, a great deal of casual sexual violence. Najib recalled how one fearful elder invited a group of local militia leaders to dinner, hoping to tame their excesses with traditional hospitality. He ended up being forced to watch the gang rape of his wife and teenage daughters. In another notorious episode, a woman was stripped, raped and murdered by checkpoint militiamen who then threw her body into a nearby ditch with several batteries shoved up her vagina. When asked why, the men explained with a giggle that they had turned the corpse into a radio 'in order to listen to the BBC'. The disregard for human life that Najib described was breathtaking, yet that, somehow, was not the worst aspect of the story. Callous evil was not new in the world, after all. What really shocked was the killers' prankish, snickering humour, and the enjoyment they appeared to take in their depravity.

The others around the table fell silent when Najib had finished. They were all in their thirties, which meant that all of their childhoods had been disrupted by the war – and who among their generation didn't have a tale of suffering to tell? It was as though the stories of evil perpetrated by their countrymen offered glimpses of the dark side of their own Somali souls. The serenity of this balmy evening, the good food and company around the restaurant table, no longer seemed banal but, briefly, priceless. The Somaliland urge to cut itself off permanently from the old source of so much horror was clarified for me. The state had cleansed itself of the taint of civil war, and would do anything to avoid recontamination. Peace was a privilege to be treasured and defended at any cost.

This attitude had made Somaliland one of the darlings of the West. Hargeisa's embrace of democracy was one of the developments that led the US to adopt, in 2010, a new 'twin-track' approach to Somalia, which meant supporting both the autonomy-seeking stable regions like Somaliland and the centralizing mission of the government in Mogadishu. The policy amounted to a kind of Plan B in the event of the TFG's failure, for there were many who argued that Somaliland's constitution could provide a model for the rest of the country. Ignatius Takawira, a Zimbabwean UN official who helped monitor the 2010 presidential elections, called Somaliland's election laws 'unique and rather brilliant'. The constitution limited to three the number of political parties allowed to contest the presidency, and all political campaigning was banned until just three weeks before the election.

'The flags go up, the flags come down, and then they vote,' said Takawira. 'That's clever, because it avoids a prolonged fight – and I saw it working. At election time in Zimbabwe, my people just kill each other.'

Somaliland's political elite was unusually well supported in Britain, where a small group of politicians with Somalilander constituencies, led by Alun Michael, the Labour MP for Cardiff South and Penarth, lobbied vociferously on their behalf. London's official Horn of Africa policy was to back the TFG in Mogadishu, which obviously precluded the recognition of Somaliland sovereignty. But this did not prevent Alun Michael from demanding greater 'respect' for the Hargeisa government and its functions. Modern Somaliland, he argued, was 'a beacon of democracy' that deserved to be acknowledged as a 'distinct entity from the rest of Somalia'.[5] When I went to meet him in Westminster, the MP went further, arguing that the case for Somaliland's independence was 'clear and unanswerable' – although he also insisted that it was for Somalis, not him, to assert that case.

Such advocacy irritated many Somalis outside Somaliland. Puntland, which still regarded the SNM's unilateral declaration of secession in 1991 as 'high treason', was particularly touchy about London's perceived doublespeak. In Garowe, President Farole had grumbled about Whitehall's blatant favouritism towards Hargeisa, especially when it came to the distribution of aid. A handful of 'MPs and Welsh lords', he told me, were 'obsessed' with Somaliland. He perhaps had a point. In 2006, the Welsh National Assembly officially invited the Hargeisa government (but not the Garowe one, and certainly not the TFG in Mogadishu) to attend the royal opening of the Senedd in Cardiff. And it was only in 2011 that the All-Party Parliamentary Group for Somaliland, chaired by Alun Michael, had changed its name to include the words 'and Somalia'. Michael explained that Somalia's government had not been elected, unlike the Hargeisa one, and that the whole point of the APPG system was to promote dialogue between democratic parliaments. He was technically correct, although to the Farole government in Garowe, the omission still felt like a slight to Puntland.*

However robust Alun Michael was in his defence of Hargeisa's cause, the case for Somaliland sovereignty did not seem to me to be quite as unanswerable as he claimed. For one thing, according to Hassan and the others at the Summertime restaurant, Somaliland's younger generation were deeply uninterested in the campaign for independence, which Najib described as 'an old man's dream'. There had been no referendum on independence since 2001. Since then, they thought, the true locus of Somaliland as a nation had shifted far beyond the former protectorate's borders. When remittances accounted for a third of all household income, it was clear to them that their nation existed, if it existed at all, somewhere in the international ether. It was not the separatist ambitions of a cabal of ageing revolutionaries that would ensure Somaliland's future, but the power of the internet harnessed to the economic might of the diaspora.

Silanyo had another problem, which was that his Kulmiye Party was still fundamentally a civil war clan organization – and many of the younger generation were out of patience with that, too. For all the proud rhetoric, Somaliland in some ways was a paranoid, mono-clan police state no different from Puntland, its neighbour and chief regional rival: Isaaqistan versus Darodistan. In Hargeisa, non-Isaaqs were almost automatically suspect. In the street market earlier that day, Hassan confessed that he had

* As this book went to press, the APPG's name had still not been updated on the chairman's own website, www.alunmichael.com.

deliberately avoided speaking to anybody for fear that his accent might be identified. As a Hawiye from the Kenyan border town of Mandera, he said, his 'southern dialect would cause problems'. Silanyo's predecessor as president until 2010, Riyale Kahin, had been a high-ranking officer in Siad Barre's feared National Security Service, and hotel guest lists were still rigorously checked every two days by an efficient and well-funded intelligence apparatus on the lookout for any potential enemy of the state.

Hargeisa was not as secure as it seemed. To Silanyo's great chagrin, some of al-Shabaab's most senior leaders were Isaaq clansmen, including Ibrahim al-Afghani and Moktar Godane, who was born in the Somaliland capital. Confidence that al-Shabaab would never gain a foothold here was badly shaken in October 2008 when suicide bombers simultaneously attacked the presidential palace, the UNDP office and the Ethiopian consulate, killing twenty-five. The state's paranoia was perhaps understandable, but there was still much about Somaliland that did not fit with the modern democratic image of itself that it liked to project to the world. Riyale Kahin routinely circumvented the courts via 'security committees' that had no basis in the constitution, and which regularly sent common criminals to prison on the basis of little or no evidence. When human rights observers visited Mandhera prison near Hargeisa in 2009, they found that over half of the prisoners had been sentenced by the security committees, not the courts.[6]

Silanyo had at least abolished the security committees when he became president, but his continuing heavy-handed treatment of the press was hardly the mark of an instinctive democrat. Dissenting journalists were regularly and arbitrarily arrested and held without charge. Ali Ismail Aare, a reporter for the weekly *Waheen*, was detained in 2012 for photographing a service station and a building belonging to the vice-president. So was Yusuf Abdi Ali of the London-based channel Royal TV, after being accused by a local NGO of making false allegations of corruption.

The most troubling incident came in January 2012 when twenty-five journalists were arrested, and a local TV station, Horn Cable TV, was shut down following a raid by a hundred policemen in seven armoured vehicles. Their crime was to have reported on an unauthorized clan meeting in the province of Sool, which bordered Puntland to the east. Silanyo described their coverage as 'anti-Somaliland propaganda'; he later called Horn Cable a 'nation destructor'.[7]

Sool, along with two neighbouring provinces, Sanaag and Cayn, had been causing Hargeisa a headache for years. Although originally a part of the British protectorate, their inhabitants were not Isaaq but Darod. Garowe had always considered them natural citizens of Puntland, therefore. But in 2007, Somaliland re-staked its claim by sending its troops to occupy the region. A bad-tempered dispute had been rumbling between the two states ever since. To make things even more complicated, a local secessionist movement called the HBM-SSC – *Hoggaanka Badbaadada iyo Mideynta*, the 'United Defence League' of Sool, Sanaag and Cayn – had been gaining ground recently. The territory it claimed for itself accounted for perhaps a third of all Somaliland, and included three sizeable towns. The possibility of significant oil reserves being discovered in the region, as well as reports in early 2012 that al-Shabaab elements were infiltrating northwards, made this region even more inflammable. No wonder Silanyo was nervous. The dispute to his east did indeed have the potential to 'destruct' his nascent clan-nation, even before he had achieved the international recognition for it that he so craved.

11

How to start a border war

Taleh, Sool, June 2011

There was, of course, nothing new about the combustibility of the Somaliland border region, as the British discovered in 1898 when Islamist rebels occupied their protectorate's second city, Burao. The rebels were led by a charismatic religious scholar, Muhammad Abdullah Hassan, still known to Somalis as the Sayyid ('Master'), but better known to the British as 'the Mad Mullah'. The nickname, according to legend, dated from 1895 when he arrived back in Berbera from the Hajj and was stopped by a British customs officer who wanted to charge him import duty on his luggage. The Sayyid angrily refused: by what right did this foreigner prevent him entering his own country? Some travellers nearby told the officer to pay no attention to the man: he was just a mad old mullah.

Sayyid Hassan went on to become the focus of resistance against foreign oppressors throughout Somalia. It took the British twenty years and four separate military campaigns to suppress him. Noted for his poetry as much as for his fighting prowess, he is still Somalia's greatest national hero, in a country that has always revered its poets. Siad Barre knew what he was doing when he erected a statue of him, mounted on his warhorse on an immense tiled plinth outside the parliament in Mogadishu. (The statue was subsequently destroyed in the civil war, although the plinth remains.)

The Sayyid's story had many curious twenty-first-century parallels. As a fomenter of jihad he was the Osama bin Laden of his time. Both men managed to unify rival clans and tribes by appealing to their common faith, and exploited that and their own charismas to stir up a powerful rebellion against the infidel oppressors.

'I warn you of this,' the Sayyid once wrote in a letter to the British. 'I wish to fight with you. I like war, but you do not.'

As the *Newsweek* journalist Jeffrey Bartholet pointed out, the sentiment would be echoed almost a century later in bin Laden's 1996 declaration of war against the US: 'These [Muslim] youths love death as you love life.'[1]

The Sayyid, like bin Laden, adapted his revolt to suit the conditions on the ground and the mores of the times. His army wore white turbans and called themselves the Daraawiish ('Dervishes'), a deliberate evocation of a Sufi ascetic tradition dating from at least the twelfth century (and a term that retains semi-mythic connotations in modern Somalia: Puntland's state militia are still collectively known as Daraawiish). The Sayyid may have modelled his movement on that of the Mahdi Army in Sudan in the 1880s, a Sufi-inspired revolt against colonialism that the British themselves characterized as 'Dervish'.*

* According to Shuke, the Director of the Puntland Development Research Centre in Garowe and an authority on East African history, the Sayyid and the Mahdi may even have been taught by the same Islamic scholar, a Wahhabi Sheikh in Mecca called Mohamed Salih.

The Sayyid took Dervishism further than any historical predecessor when he founded a full-blown Dervish state in north-central Somalia in the 1890s. The state was formally recognized by both Germany and the Ottoman empire – a foreshadowing, perhaps, of the Islamic caliphate that al-Qaida theoretically still hopes to establish. Throughout World War One, the Dervish state was the only in-dependent Muslim state on the African continent. It finally came to an end in 1920 when the recently formed Royal Air Force, acting on the orders of the then Minister for War and Air, Winston Churchill, bombed the Sayyid's capital at Taleh. It was the first time in history that Western airpower was used to dislodge an Islamic militant. In the year that bin Laden was trapped and killed in Pakistan by foreign soldiers swooping from the sky, this was another parallel with the present that was impossible to miss.

For all his piety and poetry, the Sayyid was not a kind or gentle man. Clans who resisted the expansion of his state in the 1900s were cut down without mercy, which made him a highly ambivalent sort of hero for modern Somalis, and a tainted symbol of liberty.

'No one dares portray him negatively, yet he killed so many people,' said Isse Dhollowaa, one of President Farole's inner circle, whose father was born in Taleh.* 'Anyone even vaguely associated with the British was

* 'Dhollowaa' meant 'No incisors', the absence of which, he explained, was a genetic trait in his family. 'I think maybe it's because we're nomads and we drink so much milk, so we don't need teeth,' he said.

skinned alive. Children were slaughtered. Pregnant women were disembowelled. It was exactly like al-Shabaab today.'

His notorious livestock raids had not been forgotten in Garowe. On one occasion he sent 5,000 men against the Sultan of Majeerteen, who advanced 'like locusts', destroying and pillaging everything in their path, and eventually drove off over 25,000 camels.

His most famous poem, a work once rote-learned by every Somali schoolchild, was a characteristically gloating account of the killing of Richard Corfield, the dashing but foolhardy colonel-commandant of the British camel constabulary, at the Battle of Dul Madoba in 1913. In the poem, the Sayyid instructs the 'hell-destined' Corfield to explain how he died to the guardians of heaven:

Say to them: 'From that day to this the Dervishes never
    ceased their assaults upon us.
The British were broken, the noise of battle engulfed us';
Say: 'In fury they fell upon us.'
Report how savagely their swords tore you,
Show these past generations in how many places the daggers
    were plunged.
Say:'"Friend," I called, "have compassion and spare me!"'
Say: 'As I looked fearfully from side to side my heart was
    plucked from its sheath.'
Say: 'My eyes stiffened as I watched with horror;
The mercy I implored was not granted.'
Say: 'Striking with spear-butts at my mouth they silenced
    my soft words;
My ears, straining for deliverance, found nothing;
The risk I took, the mistake I made, cost my life.'

Say: 'When pain racked me everywhere
Men lay sleepless at my shrieks.'[2]

The author went on to describe how Corfield's body was
eaten by hyenas, and his veins and tendons plucked out by
crows. He had, however, deployed poetic licence in his
account of what happened at Dul Madoba – or else it was
wishful thinking. In reality, according to Douglas Jardine,
the British Administration Secretary of the day, Corfield
was killed instantly by a bullet to his pith-helmeted head
while trying to unblock a jammed Maxim gun, and his
body was recovered and buried. The British, furthermore,
were not quite as 'broken' as the Sayyid claimed. His
dervishes, marching line abreast towards the enemy line
shouting their 'weird, monotonous war-song, "Mohamed
Salih"', outnumbered the camel constabulary by twenty to
one, and yet four hundred of them were killed to just
thirty-five of the British. When news of the engagement
reached London, the press denounced it as a HORRIBLE
DISASTER TO OUR TROOPS IN SOMALILAND, yet
the Dervish name for their supposed victory told a different
story: it was known forever after as Ruga, 'the smashing or
grinding of bones'.[3]

The Sayyid, of course, was concerned not with historical
accuracy but with firing up a rebellion, and for that, his
poem was perfect. The 'no mercy to infidels' message of
The Death of Richard Corfield was as useful as ever in the
1990s, when militiamen resisting the US military
distributed pamphlets of the poem in Mogadishu.[4] It was
certainly tempting to make a connection between the
Sayyid's imagined version of what happened to Corfield,

and the actual treatment of the US helicopter crewmen whose lynched and semi-naked bodies were dragged through Mogadishu's streets.

Like Richard Burton who wrote that he could not 'well explain the effect of Arab poetry to one who has not visited the Desert', the Sayyid understood intuitively that nothing touched the fierce nomadic soul like a good poem. His modern jihadist successors had the same insight. Osama bin Laden marked the wedding of his son in Kandahar in January 2001 by declaiming a poem of his own composition that celebrated the recent al-Qaida suicide attack on the USS *Cole* as it refuelled at Aden. The text of his verse later found its way into the pan-Arab newspaper *Al-Hayat*:

> A destroyer: even the brave fear its might.
> It inspires horror in the harbour and in the open sea.
> She goes into the waves flanked by arrogance, haughtiness
>   and fake might.
> To her doom she progresses slowly, clothed in a huge
>   illusion.
> A dinghy awaits her, riding the waves.[5]

Until the 1940s, according to the Polish professor of Somali literature B.W. Andrzejewski, oral poetry in Somalia 'was used in inter-clan and national politics as a weapon of propaganda . . . by custom, opinions expressed in verse could be much sharper in tone than anything said in ordinary language.'[6] The poetry itself was highly formalized, and had to follow complex rules of alliteration if it was to be judged any good. The aspiring poet also had to select the metre best suited to the subject matter. The *gabay*, for instance, was favoured for the handling of serious subjects at a leisurely pace, while the *jiifto* was preferred when more urgency was required. Even more urgent was the *geeraar* which, according to Andrzejewski, 'used to be recited on horseback and was associated with journeyings and war'. Although oral poetry is no longer central to social discourse, poetry recital competitions remain popular in the twenty-first century, above all among the eternally homesick diaspora, where the best poets can fill arenas and are treated like rock stars. According to aficionados, though, there is no greater master of the language than the Sayyid, a poet who could write a poem about a camel, and 'capture the inner-most nature of the camel'.[*7]

I badly wanted to see the ruins of Taleh, which enticingly lay just 50 miles north of Garowe. The Sayyid built fortresses all over Somalia in the course of his long rebellion, but the Dervish capital was different: a giant complex of thirteen interlocking stone fortresses known as the Silsillat ('Chain'), a word that also hinted at the holy lineage of the Sayyid, who was said by his followers to be descended from the Prophet himself. The wall encompassed wells, gardens, granaries. There was room for 5,000 Dervish fighters, their horses and camels, and hundreds of head of cattle. There were mighty tomb towers containing the remains of the Sayyid's parents and other notables, as well as an execution area called Hed Kaldig ('Place of Blood'). The whole was overlooked by three further forts

---

* There are said to be forty-six ways to describe a camel in Somali – almost as many as the fifty-two words for snow employed by the Saami people of Lapland.[8]

over 60 feet high, one of which was reserved for the Sayyid himself, and connected to the Silsillat by a tunnel 200 yards long. It was without doubt the greatest archaeological ruin in Somalia.

Nick Beresford, the Garowe UNDP chief, was keen to see it too, and so in early 2011 we began to lobby the Farole government for permission to mount a small expedition there. It shouldn't have been a problem. There seemed no doubt, and Farole's ministers agreed, that Taleh came under their administration. The district's inhabitants were all Darod clansmen, 95 per cent of them Dolbahante, who belonged to the same Harti confederation of sub-clans as President Farole's Majeerteen. There were, however, certain difficulties involved with a trip to Taleh, chief of which was that it lay not in Puntland proper, but in the contested province of Sool. This made it a kind of no-man's-land for the Garowe administration, who tried to avoid antagonizing Hargeisa unnecessarily. The policy was to let sleeping dogs lie, so the Minister for Information, Culture and Heritage, Ahmed Ali Askar, sucked through his teeth when we first asked.

On the other hand, we could see that our request had put him on the spot, for what kind of a heritage minister could not arrange a tourists' visit to the country's greatest ruin, 50 miles from his capital? Farole's critics had always sneered that his authority did not extend far beyond the tarmac between Galkacyo and Bossasso, and Askar's hesitation now suggested that the jibe might be true. It turned out that very few members of Farole's government had been to Taleh since he came to power in 2009. Askar himself had not been since 1978. However, after many days of lobbying it became obvious that Farole himself had been consulted, and that he had ruled in our favour. In fact, not only did we have permission to travel to Taleh: we were to be accompanied there by an official government delegation from Garowe. The president, it seemed, had decided to take advantage of our visit to put down a territorial marker for Puntland.

There were, naturally, several false starts. Various government ministers announced that they were coming, dropped out, changed their minds again, but eventually two of them committed themselves: Ahmed Ali Askar and the Security Minister, Khalif Isse Mudan. At this point the local UN security chief, an ex-Spanish air force officer called Jorge, got wind of the trip and insisted on coming too, along with a paramedic in case of emergency, and an empty spare car in the event of a breakdown. The local press were tipped off, and the Puntland Intelligence Service. With Khalif's heavily armed security detail in two overloaded technicals and our own SPU added in, there were forty-one people assembled outside the UN office on the morning that we finally set out, dispersed among no less than ten four-wheel-drive vehicles.

The journey itself was a delight. We lurched off the tarmac after less than a mile and plunged exhilaratingly into the desert. There was no urban hinterland. One minute we were on Garowe High Street, the next we were streaming across the immense Nugaal plain, the vehicles fanned out in a V-formation to avoid the towering plumes of choking orange sand thrown up by the car in front. The plain was dotted with scrub and the occasional cluster of acacia, and was not empty but teemed with life. I spotted an ostrich bounding along the shimmering horizon with its own plume of dust rising in its wake, its neck outstretched like Walt Disney's Road Runner. Every so often we passed a nomad *zareba* with their attendant herds of goat and camel, some of which numbered in the hundreds. Even the nomad's sheep here were indigenous, although the breed is known, confusingly, as a Blackhead Persian – a small, fat-tailed beast with a skinny white body and a striking, ebony black head. The shepherds were mostly sun-scorched children armed with sticks, looking small and vulnerable in the blazing vastness, yet unquestionably also a part of the ecosystem.

Hyena and cheetahs were said to live here, and East African oryx, and Soemmerring's gazelle. At one point the convoy was obliged to slow to a crawl in order to ford a watercourse, where the spiky greenery flashed with exotic birdlife, weavers and bee-eaters and who knew what else. Back on the plain, a herd of tiny antelope scattered at our approach, bouncing like clockwork toys among the thickets. Our driver said they were dik-dik, although they might easily have been *Gazella spekei*, Speke's gazelle, a species identified by the discoverer of the source of the Nile himself.

When one of the vehicles suffered a puncture, and the convoy stopped and everyone got out while it was being fixed, I looked around to find that everyone was grinning. The sense of space and freedom of the desert made me, too, want to sing, for there was no better cure for the claustro-phobia of the town. Garowe was not a popular posting among the UN staffers, who were forbidden to leave the office without armed guards, and never after dark. Every evening at sunset there was always someone jogging or speed-walking around the barbed-wired edge of the compound, like an animal pacing its cage in a zoo, studiedly ignoring the guards in their watchtowers.

I thought of Benson, the whimsical Kikuyu cook in the canteen on the high top floor of the UN building, who had twice extended his contract in Somalia because of the pay. Benson wore a full chef's toque and whites, which greatly flattered the broiled chicken and rice he seemed to produce every night. His spare time was spent in front of the television or staring through the window at the desert haze out beyond the town, sighing heavily and seeing neither. 'Ohhhhh Gaaarowe,' he would groan, in a way that made the foreign staffers laugh; although the joke never quite concealed the deadness in his eye.

A place like Garowe could easily drive foreigners 'sand-happy', as Gerald Hanley called it in the 1940s. Hanley memorably described interrogating a tall, grey-haired Italian officer who had been found wandering in the desert equipped with nothing but a kettle. When questioned, he explained that he had been walking back to his wife and children in Italy, and begged, with a trembling hand, to be given a pass and sent on his way. One military doctor told Hanley that 'isolation among the wolves can bring about exactly the same effects as a good long drenching of shell-fire', and I had no doubt that was as true now as it had been for Hanley's generation of Europeans.

But our outing was a boon to the Somalis, too. In Garowe, Askar, Khalif and the guards and drivers who surrounded them seldom went further than the Ruqsan Square, the charms of which had palled for me after the first visit. Both ministers had returned from years in exile in order to serve in Farole's cabinet. They had settled in the same suburban Western haven, Woolwich in south-east London, where they must have spent many homesick evenings lamenting the absence of nomads and camels and wondering if they would ever see these things again. So there could be no more satisfying trip for them than this one, particularly as we were heading to Talch, the centre-piece of the Dervish legend that went to the heart of the Somali national identity.

The landscape through which we drove was the setting of a famous Somali novel, *Ignorance is the Enemy of Love* by Faarax M. J. Cawl, in which the hero Calimaax, a Dervish warrior-poet in the mould of the Sayyid, conquers lions and leopards with his bare hands but misses the chance to win the hand of his true love through his inability to read her letters. Published in 1974, Cawl's novel was very much a product of its time, when the country was in the grip of a government education drive. It was also, extraordinarily, the first novel ever to be published in the Somali language. Many cultures define themselves, at least in part, by their published literary canon, but not Somalia, a country whose stories had always been declaimed from memory, and where books other than the Koran barely existed. It was not until 1972, when Siad Barre formally adopted the Latin alphabet and rejected the Arabic one, that Somalia even had an official orthography. So it was highly significant that Cawl's novel, the foundation stone of modern Somali literature, should glorify the Dervishism of the 1910s via a hero who repeatedly recites the Sayyid's actual poetry as the plot unfolds:

The provisions and the clothes which keep people busy
   in the towns
Bustling and trading, are merely lifeless wealth brought
   in from outside.
If the town is cut off from the interior, the Angel of Death
   soon comes to it on his errands.

Taleh, when we finally reached it, felt extraordinarily cut off. The domed tops of the towers of the Silsillat were visible from miles away, rising above the plain like the warheads of missiles from a silo. It was like catching sight of Xanadu for the first time. A senior elder was waiting for us at the city limits in the shade of an old and lonely acacia tree. The ministers got out of their cars and each gave the elder, whom they clearly knew, a manly cheek-to-cheek hug, a small but essential ceremony that signalled our formal permission to proceed.

A crowd of two or three hundred awaited us in the town centre, which was dominated by an acacia even older and larger than the first one. On a low stone wall surrounding this magnificent tree were gathered all the elders of the community, the faces of some of them as gnarled as the bark of the acacia. Each carried a walking stick, a badge of authority in this herding community. The sticks had been customized according to taste. Some were ornately carved, or had been jazzed up with coloured tape. Others had been buffed to a lustrous finish, or were tipped with glittering brass or silver ferrules. All of the elders' sticks, though, were topped with a curved handle, unlike those of the boys and young men standing in the rank behind them, which were plainer as well as straight.

A group of women ululated energetically as the crowd parted, and we were shown to a row of chairs in the centre of the circle, the honoured guests of the village parliament. This was, you could tell immediately, the way things had always been done here. It felt like communing with the Tree of Souls in the James Cameron movie *Avatar*. A hundred yards to the left, tantalizingly, was the crumbling, cream-coloured corner of one of the forts. The ruins, though, would have to wait. First it was time for a speech from the district commissioner.

His tale of woe was translated, divertingly, by a man with a master's degree from Bangor in north Wales. The district commissioner said there had been no effective administration in Taleh since Siad Barre's time. All social services had collapsed. There was no doctor, no police station, no water management, no telephone line to the outside world. The only things that worked here were the school and a mother and child clinic, both of which had been funded by charitable donations from the diaspora. There had been no help from the government in Garowe, let alone the one in Mogadishu, and no help either from the international community, not even from UNESCO, who he thought should recognize the Sayyid's fort as a World Heritage Site. When he had finished I asked how long it had been since a gaalo had been seen in Taleh. The district commissioner turned to consult two other elders before replying that we were the first since some Norwegian aid workers had passed this way in 1997.

Next up to speak was an ancient man with a henna-dyed moustache known as Ahmed Aden Taleexi – 'Mr Taleh' – who turned out to be the community memory bank, a village bard who specialized in the myths of the glorious Dervish past.

'Now then,' he began, 'which one of you is the British journalist?'

I rose to my feet, grinning apprehensively, and he stared at me with bloodshot, rheumy eyes.

'*We* are the ones you fought,' he said, pointing in an arc at the crowd with his walking stick, which I noticed was particularly elaborately carved. 'You British with all your technology and bombs destroyed this place. You can see the damage your warplanes caused with your own eyes, but did we ever receive compensation? We received nothing!'

There was a murmur of agreement from the rapt crowd, and an outbreak of ululating from the women's section.

'The bombing caused great suffering,' the old man went on. 'The British took our young men away to fight in their army – three thousand of them! And we never saw them again. The wounded were left to die of thirst, and their bodies were eaten by hyenas. We wrote to your ambassador in Mogadishu in 1983 demanding recompense, but did we receive a reply? We did not!'

There was more ululating, and I looked at my interpreter in alarm. It was ninety-two years since the RAF had bombed Taleh, but for this old man it was as though it had happened yesterday. Did the younger townspeople share his sense of affront?

'Don't worry,' chuckled the man from Bangor. 'The people here will ask for anything if they think they can get it.'

It was a relief nevertheless when Mr Taleh stopped his Brit-bashing, and launched into a long, florid (and historically inaccurate) account of the rise and fall of the

Dervish state. The ending of his oration was strangely anti-climactic – a meek repeat of the district commissioner's plea for UNESCO recognition of the ruins, and a request to tell the British press – and there was no further mention of British compensation once he had finished.*

Minister Khalif's speech in reply was, as I expected, a brazen piece of politicking. The Puntland government, he said, would soon be opening 'many' offices here. He promised to rebuild the police station, and to put in a phone line. He said he 'fully' supported the elders in their bid for UNESCO recognition of the ruins, which his government would recommend be 'repaired'. This last offer was patently ridiculous – the Silsillat was damaged far beyond any point of repair, even if such a thing was desirable – but it was greeted anyway with cheers and yet more ululation.

Taleh, it occurred to me, was not doing too badly for a community abandoned by government. The townspeople had responded to the delegation from Garowe with energy and discipline, and they clearly knew what they wanted. Somalia might have been the world's most failed state, yet at this local level it had not failed at all, but appeared in some important ways to be thriving. The drought had greatly inconvenienced them, but they were manifestly not

---

* The British ambassador to whom the citizens of Taleh wrote was either Robert Purcell or William Fullerton, who took over from Purcell in 1983. In 1984, Fullerton advised the newly appointed US ambassador Peter Bridges to read *First Footsteps in East Africa*, noting that Burton said Arabs called Somalia *Bilad wa issi*, the 'Land of Give Me Something'. Bridges wrote later in his memoir: '"The longer you are here," said Bill Fullerton, "the more you will think that name is apt." He was right.'[9]

starving. The town was not in a state of anarchy, despite the lack of a police station. All the old social conventions, including the practical application of xeer, customary law, were intact and functioning. Taleh seemed to have achieved a remarkable level of self-sufficiency, which made me think that the district commissioner ought to be careful what he wished for – because in this community's case at least, greater involvement with Garowe could easily cause more problems than it solved.

At last we were released to explore the ruins. We spread out across the interior of the Silsillat with a long chaotic trail of people strung out behind: ministers, civic officials, elders, soldiers, secret servicemen, all mixed in with dozens of curious onlookers from the town. The exterior walls were massive things, 14 feet thick in places, and had evidently been constructed with great skill. The identity of the master-masons responsible has never been discovered. In fact it is not certain that the Sayyid, who only moved his capital to Taleh in 1913, even built the Silsillat. Archaeologists once speculated that the original fort was the work of the Himyarites, a pre-Islamic Yemeni civilization, or even of the ancient Egyptians, and that the Sayyid and his followers had merely crept into the ruins and exploited them.

I climbed a steep staircase to a corner tower roof, and gazed out over the shimmering, dun-coloured plain. The Garowe official, Dhollowaa, had told me that when he was a boy, his ancient grandmother had described how the Sayyid once lived at Taleh 'like a Zulu king', surrounded by the huts of his warriors for as far as the eye could see. There were tens of thousands of them, a roiling, lawless encampment where feuds were common and fights were settled not with words but by the sudden, late-night thrust of a spear through the heart. But the plain was empty of warriors now; only cloud-shadows chased each other across the desert expanse.

We looked into the tallest tomb-tower, a beehive-shaped mausoleum to the Sayyid's Ogadeni father, Sheikh Abdille. The chamber inside was dark and damp and cool beneath a high plastered ceiling that echoed with the chirruping of diving swallows. The Sheikh, I learned, married several Dolbahante women. The Sayyid, born of the first of these, Timiro, was the eldest of thirty children.

'That is why so many of us here are kin to the Sayyid,' the Bangor graduate explained. 'Many of our grandparents were killed in this fort by the British.'

It seemed, however, that there was little ancestor worship in Taleh these days. The raised stone slab covering the Sheikh's grave had been smashed in long ago, leaving a rectangular heap of broken-edged rubble. Bending down to peer through a small opening in the side, I found myself face to face with the eyeless skull of a goat that some joker had placed amid the dust and debris.

We trailed out of the Silsillat to the outlying fort that had once been the Sayyid's private residence: 'Like the White House,' said the Bangor man. The Sayyid began to live up to his reputation for madness as he grew older, a power-crazed monomaniac who eventually became so fat that, according to one envoy prostrated trembling before him, he was unable to cross his legs, and was obliged to sit with them extended straight out in front of him. His subjects believed he had supernatural powers, and that he was protected by an amulet given to him when a lizard whose life he had spared turned out to be a *djinn* in disguise. He kept a semblance of order at Taleh through old-fashioned terror. His chief executioner boasted that he could not sleep at night unless he had achieved at least twenty mutilations and deaths in the course of the day; a sentry who went AWOL was viciously whipped before being burned alive.[10]

The Sayyid's palace was surrounded by a secondary curtain wall built of rocks noticeably bigger than those used for the Silsillat. The front of this stout edifice had nevertheless been blown off, and the roof had caved in. This was the work not of the RAF, as Mr Taleh claimed, but of a camel-borne party of British sappers who followed up the air raids in February 1920. The 20-pound and 2-pound bombs carried by the RAF's Havilland DH9A biplanes were far too puny to dent these walls. As the British well knew, the value of their aircraft was primarily psychological: the Shock and Awe campaign of its day.

The dozen biplanes of the RAF's 'Z Force' had been unloaded in the utmost secrecy in packing cases at Berbera, with their pilots and crews masquerading as a party of oil prospectors. The ruse worked, for the surprise of the attack when it came was total. Not only had the Dervishes never seen an aircraft before: the Sayyid himself had no conception of aviation. So when the first plane appeared over the horizon he anxiously inquired of his advisors what it might be.

'A few guessed the truth, but hesitated to communicate their guess for fear of the death that was the recognized punishment for the bearer of evil tidings,' recorded Douglas Jardine. 'Some, with the Oriental's native penchant for flattery, suggested that they were the chariots of Allah come to take the Mullah up to heaven.'

The Sayyid, concluding that the occupants of the strange machines must at the very least want to talk to him, 'hastily donned his finest apparel. Leaning on the arm of Amir, his uncle and chief councillor, he sallied forth from his house and took up his position under the white canopy used on state occasions, to await the coming of the strange messengers. Then the first bomb fell. Amir was killed outright and the Mullah's garments were singed. Thus the first shot all but ended the campaign.'

The operation to oust the Sayyid actually lasted three weeks. As he and his forces fell back on the Silsillat, Z Force switched from bombs to incendiary rounds and strafing attacks on the Sayyid's livestock, tactics that damaged Dervish morale just as much as the high explosives. The British expected their opponent to make a stand at Taleh, but he fled as the camel corps approached. The Sayyid's caravan was chased and surrounded. Six of his sons were killed in the fight that followed, and six more were captured, although the Sayyid himself, protected no doubt by his magic amulet, managed to slip the net.

The Z Force raids were the toast of London, where they were credited with solving the '21-year-old Dervish problem in Somaliland', although as Jardine pointed out, the achievement was not the RAF's alone.

'Such a legend is dangerous in the extreme,' he wrote, 'leading, as it has done, to a belief in some quarters that the savage peoples of Africa and Asia can be controlled from the air, and that the troops and police on whom we have relied in the past should be replaced in whole or in part by aircraft.'

Jardine's note of caution still resonates in an age when many military tacticians argue that the terrorist hotspots of the world can be policed by unmanned aerial drones in place of ground troops. It was not aircraft or any other British weaponry that finally carried off the 64-year-old Sayyid, but a dose of Spanish influenza contracted while in hiding in the Ogaden later that year.

Our visit to Taleh was not without consequences, for there are few secrets in Somalia, and it wasn't long before the government in Hargeisa found out about it. A week later, another delegation set out to visit Taleh. This one comprised several local Somaliland officials, and was led by a Hargeisa MP. Before they could get to Taleh, however, their convoy was intercepted in the desert by Puntland Defence Forces. A shoot-out ensued in which a Sool province education official was killed.

Nineteen others were arrested and taken back to Garowe, where Ahmed Ali Askar, the formerly mild-mannered Information and Heritage Minister from Woolwich, issued a combative press release that blamed Somaliland's 'provocation' squarely on his opposite number in Hargeisa, Ahmed Abdi Habsade. This individual, he alleged, was a 'known political opportunist' who was 'intending to create insecurity and instability' in the area. 'Recently, he has been busy creating confrontation and continuous crises,' the press release continued. 'Puntland Government believes that the reason behind this provocation is due to last week's visit to Taleh by Puntland Government officials accompanied by UNDP officers and international journalists.'

Was I indirectly responsible for the Sool official's death?

An investigation by the UN's security division later concluded that the Somaliland delegation's presence near Taleh was a coincidence, and unconnected to our visit, whatever Minister Askar said. But I still did not feel entirely comfortable, and nor did Nick Beresford.

'With hindsight it was not a good move,' he told me in an email. 'But it's an unpredictable place: easy for some to be wise after the event.'

Garowe, amazingly, felt that it had still not made its point. A fortnight after the shoot-out, Puntland's chief magistrate found eight of the captured Somalilanders guilty of an 'illegal' incursion that had 'undermined the sovereignty of Puntland', and sentenced them to prison for five to ten years each. This was heavy-handed even by the standards of their fierce border dispute, and three months later the prisoners were granted an amnesty by President Farole and released.

This was not quite the end of the affair. That December near Taleh, unidentified gunmen assassinated Jama Ali Shire, the brother of Puntland's vice-president. Five days later a Puntland finance official was murdered, also by persons unknown, as he left a Taleh restaurant. The region was entering another cycle of the violence that seemed always to have blighted it. These latest killings weren't necessarily the work of Hargeisa, though – because in January 2012, Dolbahante clan elders from three contiguous border provinces, Sool, Sanaag and Cayn, sat down beneath Taleh's acacia tree, and boldly proclaimed a new autonomous state, to be called Khatumo, with Taleh as its capital. The spirit of independence and self-sufficiency I had seen there was real, not imagined. Both Somaliland and Puntland were out of favour. The descendants of the Sayyid had just rejected rule by anyone but themselves. It was news of this momentous decision that Silanyo was so desperate to suppress when he arrested twenty-five journalists in Hargeisa. Abdisaman Keyse, a correspondent for the London-based channel Universal TV, was detained for his 'hyperbolic reporting' of the Taleh meeting a full four months after it had taken place.[11]

Khatumo, geographically, was a recreation of the Dervish state. Some locals even called it Darwiishland, although its leadership this time was rather less charismatic: an ageing ex-prime minister of Somalia, Ali Khalif Galaydh, in allegiance with an exile from Columbus, Ohio known as Xagla-Toosiye ('Hip Straightener'). The new state's parliament was a wall around a tree. Its capital had no telecommunications, no hospital, no road or water or sewerage management, and a police station with no roof. It did, however, have a new state flag. This was the same as the Somali national flag, but with the addition of a white horse rearing to the left of the five-pointed star, saddled but riderless: a clear reference to the mighty Dervish cavalry, or even to the Master himself.

Khatumo, in the end, was absurd: a tiny clan entity, bankrolled by exiles nostalgic for a long-dead state based on robbery and cruelty and a cult of personality. Even Khatumo's supporters admitted that, economically, it had nothing going for it but the livestock trade, although the possibility of oil beneath the ground, however remote, meant that neither Puntland nor Somaliland were likely to give the region up without a fight. The brave act of secession beneath the acacia tree promised nothing but more violence and instability.

Khatumo's first murder occurred just eight weeks after the new state's declaration, when gunmen in Taleh shot and killed a provincial court judge, Abdirashid Igge. The judge had been one of the delegates in the Somaliland convoy ambushed by Puntland militia the previous year, and had only recently been released from jail in Garowe. This unfortunate man was no partisan. Before Hargeisa appointed him a judge, he had been employed by Garowe as an official in the Ministry of Employment and Sport. Khatumo authorities launched an investigation. It was to no one's surprise that the killers were never caught.

Part III
THE DIASPORA

12

The Somali youth time-bomb

London, July 2011

It was late on 1 July, Somali Independence Day, and the crush to get into the Tudor Rose nightclub in Southall, west London, was so dense that my arms were pinned to my sides. The bouncers were archytypes, over-inflated men with shaved heads and earrings and black and orange bomber jackets, who looked on with heavy-lidded eyes from the other side of a strong mesh door, indifferent to the discomfort of the crowd and the cat-calls of impatience from the back. It was a warm evening, for London. The heady smell of scent and soap rose from the women, some of whom had spent a lot of time preparing for this evening, a big night out in the Somali exile calendar. There were hundreds of young Somalis trying to get in, and they had converged on this spot from every corner of the city. The girl in front of me looked understandably grumpy as the blue and white stars painted on her cheeks started to run. There was a sudden forward surge as the door was opened and five more people ahead of us were allowed to wriggle through the crack.

'Good evening, sir,' said one of the bouncers through the grill, 'are you quite sure you want to come in here?'

It was a reasonable question. I was the only non-Somali he could see apart from the other bouncers, a shining white beacon in an ebony sea. I was underdressed compared even to the Somali men here, and a good twenty years older than the average customer in the queue.

'I'm with her,' I said, indicating my companion and guide for the night, Ayaan, who had been channelled away slightly by the squeeze of people.

Several heads turned to look, and the bouncer actually laughed. Ayaan was beautiful, a mesmerizing mixture of African and Arab with her sculpted cheekbones and delicate, ski-jump nose. Tonight she was shimmering like a supermodel. She stood tall and proud in a traditional, off-the-shoulder silk dress called a *guntiino*. Long sparkly earrings dangled beneath her blow-dried coiffure. She was wearing blue eye-shadow and glossy red lipstick, and her breath smelled of honey and menthol from the Lockets she sucked.

'Mind how you go then,' grinned the bouncer, swinging the door open for us. Ayaan sashayed through, and I trailed smugly after her. At last we were in.

Ayaan's outfit had come as a surprise when I picked her up from her council flat in the Ealing suburb of Greenford. Despite the late hour, I had arrived mentally prepared for a work assignment. I had asked her where I could see young Somalis having a good time, for once, and she had offered to accompany me to the Tudor Rose, arguing that I couldn't possibly go to such a place on my own; she said it would look weird, and might even be risky. And now she was making a night out of it, a feisty, 30-something, single Somali girl with an obviously older white man on her arm, determined to have a good time too. She knew she was pushing the boundaries of convention by appearing here with a gaalo. It looked racy. But it was just as obvious that she took a mischievous, sassy delight in that, and especially in the confusion and affront on the faces of some of the younger men, all of whom mistook us for a couple on a date.

We had been introduced by a British journalist friend who had met Ayaan while researching a story about Abu Ayyub al-Muhajir, whose family Ayaan had come to know in the course of her job as a part-time social worker for Ealing Council. Al-Muhajir, whose real name was Ahmed Hussein Ahmed, was a 21-year-old Somali from Ealing who dropped out of his business studies course at Oxford Brookes University in 2007, flew to Kenya, crossed the Somali border on foot, and blew himself up in Baidoa in a suicide attack that killed twenty Ethiopian soldiers.

He was the classic example of a diaspora al-Shabaab recruit, the sort that most alarms the security services; his case was one of those that the former International Development Minister Andrew Mitchell had in mind when he remarked, in late 2011, that there were 'probably more British passport holders engaged in terrorist training in Somalia than in any other country in the world'.[1] The law of averages alone makes it likely that there are other would-be suicide bombers at large in Britain, or, an even scarier possibility, British passport holders who have received explosives training from al-Shabaab in Somalia and have already returned.

No one knows for sure how many Somalis call Britain home. The Office of National Statistics estimated there were 108,000 Somali-born immigrants in 2010, although most other sources, including within the Metropolitan Police, believe the real figure is closer to 250,000 or even 300,000. Even at 108,000, the UK's Somali community is far and away the largest in Europe. Britain's past colonial involvement in East Africa has drawn Somali émigrés to her shores ever since the mid-nineteenth century, forming a natural magnet for the hordes of civil war refugees who followed on at the end of the twentieth. The UK's immigration rules in the early 2000s were liberal compared to most other Western nations – or lax, depending on your political affiliation – leading to even greater inflows, including a significant amount of secondary migration from other European countries, particularly from Scandinavia. By 1999, for whatever reason, over half of all applications for asylum in Europe by Somalis were made in the UK.

Earlier in 2011, in Nairobi, I had met the future British ambassador to Somalia, Matt Baugh, over a beer on the veranda of the heavily guarded British Residence. As a glossy green ibis pecked its stately way across the immaculate lawn below us, he described how Somalia had become the destination of choice for would-be jihadis from the UK. Until recently, he explained, British policy had been to try to 'contain' the security threat these people undoubtedly posed, both to East Africa and to the British homeland. But the government had now realized that 'containment' was never going to work.

'Somalia represents a kind of threat we haven't seen before. It's got the longest coastline in Africa and a huge porous land border. There are massive numbers of Somalis living in all the neighbouring states as well as around the world. It is not a traditional, geographical country, but a diffuse, global entity – and that is not physically containable.'

This was nowhere more true than in London, where the vast majority of British Somalis had settled: at least 80,000 of them, and perhaps as many as 200,000. The enormous size and variety of the capital's Muslim community, of which the Somalis are just one small part, made it almost impossible to police adequately.

'The international community needs to wake up,' said Baugh. 'Will it take another terror attack in the West to make them do that?'

In early 2010, Baugh continued, David Cameron's new National Security Council had formally abandoned the old containment strategy in favour of one of 'engagement' with the 'main drivers' of the security threat. For the Foreign Office, this meant helping the TFG to end al-Shabaab's insurgency much more proactively than before, while urging them on with the process of political reform. For the security services at home, it meant working with Muslim communities to try to counter the causes of radicalization that led to terrorism, instead of just trying to catch the terrorists by themselves. The new emphasis was on prevention rather than cure. This is why, since 2007, the main domestic 'workstream' in the Home Office's counter-terrorism strategy has in fact been called Prevent – a strategy that was formally 'refocused' following a judicial review in 2011.

Al-Shabaab's diaspora recruits have a well-known profile. They tend to be young, disaffected males, alienated both from their families and from their adoptive society, and it was this dark side of the diaspora that I hoped Ayaan would help me explore. As a London social worker, she had spent years working among troubled Somali families, an experience that had made her an almost perfect bellwether of extremism. She had, it seemed to me, an extraordinarily acute feeling for what was happening at the bottom of the Somali exile heap, in part because that was a place where she had once been herself.

Ayaan's life story, told to me a few weeks previously in a scruffy KFC restaurant in Northolt, was like a Dickensian parable of urban suffering and redemption. She had arrived in London alone in 1993 at the age of fourteen. Her father was absent in those days, working as a chef in Saudi Arabia. Her mother, desperate to get her away from the civil violence raging around the family's home city of Burao in Somaliland, had taken her to Addis Ababa, the capital of neighbouring Ethiopia, and put her on a plane to London in the care of a nicely spoken young Somalilander she had just met in the airport, and who was going the same way. This stranger promised to deliver her daughter to a cousin who lived in east London. On arrival, however, he took Ayaan to his own family in west London, where she was effectively enslaved.

'They took away my travel documents and put me to work, cooking and cleaning. I didn't speak any English. I didn't have a clue where I was, and I was very sick.'

She hadn't told her mother that she was, in fact, pregnant.

'That's life,' she shrugged, without rancour or further explanation.

Ayaan never made contact with the cousin from east

London, and was too proud, or too scared, or too broke to phone home. After eight weeks of being shunted between houses belonging to various relatives of the man from Addis airport, she ran away. She ended up in a care home in Wembley, a council-funded orphanage for runaways, where she eventually had her baby, a girl who was now seventeen. The two of them had lived in council care for the first four years of her daughter's life, and still live together in Greenford.

Ayaan was certainly no Islamist, yet that did not translate into outright condemnation of al-Shabaab.

'They're Somalis, not aliens from outer space,' she said. 'They've got a different ideology and I don't agree with it, but they still have to be part of the solution. We have to talk to them.'

She took a dim view of AMISOM, whom she called 'mercenaries'. The Westerners who employed those mercenaries, meanwhile, were 'hypocrites', especially Britain.

'When I arrived here the IRA were bombing London. And I thought, this place is another warzone, it's not so different from Somalia: how interesting! And Martin McGuinness was a hardliner, but now look where he is.'

She disapproved of al-Shabaab's terror tactics – 'Their bombs kill women and children. All Somalis hate that,' she said – and yet she understood why the Ealing student, Abu Ayyub, had felt the need to blow himself up in Baidoa.

'If the UK wants to stop Somalis joining al-Shabaab, maybe the UK needs to change its foreign policy and stop bombing Muslim countries.'

Ayaan's views on everything were shot through with a

fierce, combative pride that could supplant all logic and reason.

'Well done to them!' she exclaimed when I asked what she thought about piracy. 'The shipping is a legitimate target: a gift from Allah. Foreigners stole our fish and destroyed the reefs with their toxic dumping. I think you deserve it. I hate your navy warships. They behave like bullies in a playground.'

Given her upbringing, it was perhaps no surprise that she saw the world as a dangerous, hostile place. More both-ersome was her deep, visceral belief that the only way to survive it was always to fight, as though the best form of defence was invariably to attack, whatever the odds. This was the strategy of the successful street-fighter. It was also the sometimes baffling philosophy of the nomad – what Gerald Hanley called 'this continual challenge, this nomad *machismo* . . . the sharp, impatient bloody-mindedness of the Somali'.

There was plenty of machismo on display in the Tudor Rose that night. The dance floor was hot and dark and packed.

'We Somalis are very strange,' Ayaan yelled in my ear. 'We run away from each other at home, but no matter how far we run we always end up seeking out other Somalis when we get there.'

The music was too loud for a sustained conversation. The club was a regular stop on the London reggae circuit, and the sound system was correspondingly immense. The hall was hung about with Jamaican and other Caribbean flags, and the bar at the back sold Red Stripe on tap, although there were no takers for lager tonight. Indeed, the area in front of the long counter, much to the bemusement of the staff behind it, was the emptiest in the entire room. Whatever vices these Londonized Somalis might have adopted, a taste for alcohol was not among them. It was as though the customers feared contamination by osmosis through the soles of their shoes, for the floor by the bar was gummy with old spilled beer.

From time to time, an MC in a baseball cap shouted incomprehensibly into a microphone on the tiny stage at the front. Later on he was briefly joined by a man in a white *jalabiya* – 'Very traditional!' bawled Ayaan – and, equally mysteriously, a military officer in full dress uniform, who stood at ease with his hands behind his back as he beamed at the crowd below. He never said anything, and no one else tried to explain his presence. It was impossible to tell whether he was a real soldier or a man in fancy dress – a freelance representation, perhaps, of some forgotten hero of the struggle for independence.

The DJ, operating from a kind of cage to one side, played music in the rap-meets-calypso Somali style. The dancers grinned as they moved to the slower numbers with a sinuous African grace, their hips swaying, their hands outstretched before them. I was pleased that I actually recognized one of the tracks, a number called 'Deeqa' by a young exile from Somaliland, Aar Maanta. Written in the pentatonic scale with traditional alliterative lyrics, it was a melancholic protest song about the racist abuse he once suffered at the hands of immigration officials at Heathrow airport: a modern interpretation, perhaps, of the incident in Berbera in 1895 with which the legend of the Mad Mullah began. Deeqa, a popular girl's name meaning 'gift', was also the name of the defunct Somali national airline, a playful double-entendre typical of Somalia's long bardic tradition. The Sayyid himself would have approved of Aar Maanta.

The crowd sang along happily to this music of exile, as they did to the national anthem, 'Soomaaliyeey Tooso' (Somalia, Wake Up!), the words of which clearly still meant something to the audience here, despite having been written in 1947. When it was played for the first time, I was standing near a group of four demure young women dressed in blue and white headscarves, one of whom smiled and shyly offered me the corner of the national flag she was holding. Then we all waved it gently up and down, like nurses changing a bedsheet.

> Somalis wake up,
> Wake up and support each other
> Support your country
> Support them forever.
> Stop fighting each other
> Come back with strength and joy and be friends again
> It's time to look forward and take command
> Defeat your enemies and unite once again.
> Become strong again and again.

The atmosphere in the club changed as it grew later. I spotted one or two toughs who I was sure had not been there earlier, threading their way purposefully through the crowd, their unsmiling eyes bright with the expectation of trouble.

'There's going to be a fight,' yelled Ayaan sensing it. 'Come on, let's leave.'

But we were too late. Back by the ticket office, our exit to the street was blocked by one of the bouncers.

'I wouldn't go out there if I were you,' he said laconically. 'Bottle fight. I'd wait twenty minutes.'

'There's *always* a fight,' said Ayaan, rolling her eyes as we went back inside. 'Every bloody time ... I nearly wasn't going to bring you here.'

The Tudor Rose, it seemed, was well-known for gang violence. In 2002, two men were shot dead on the dance floor during an anti-gun-crime event headlined by the rapper Dizzee Rascal. One of the chief suspects, Wayne 'Brands' Freckleton, belonged to a gang called the Church Road Soldiers from a housing estate in the borough of Brent, a place notorious among Somalis for the earlier stabbing to death of a 15-year-old schoolboy, Mogadishu-born Kayser Osman.

It was a relief when the bouncer announced that the danger had passed and we were permitted to stumble out into the cool of the night. There were no immediate signs of the earlier violence, although that, I discovered, was only because I didn't know how to read them. As we were negotiating the club's outer gate, I was tapped on the shoulder by a shifty-looking teenager wanting to borrow a pen. I offered him my biro.

'That's blue,' he said, peering at it. 'Have you got a black one?'

I said I didn't. He hesitated before taking the blue one anyway, and walking off to the side of the building where he turned his back, hiding something. I couldn't resist sneaking over to see what he was doing, and found him carefully inking a dark round dot on to the back of his left hand. I couldn't make sense of it. Was he mad? A drug casualty, perhaps? Or maybe he was an illiterate, pretending for some reason to be able to write?

It was not until much later that I learned that he was most likely trying to simulate a 'gang mark' tattoo. Like most street gangs, the Somali ones tended to be highly territorial, and many of the people here were a dangerously long way from their patch. There was a particularly big group from Leyton in east London, who had come to Southall when a party there was cancelled at the last minute. It was two in the morning, and Leyton was 16 miles away, which was so far it was 'like going to the moon', according to Ayaan. She had never been there herself, even after twenty years of living in London. I suddenly felt a little sorry for the teenager who had borrowed my pen, for he had only been trying to bluff his way home.

The street beyond the Tudor Rose was not as empty as it first appeared. Here and there we passed parked cars containing young Somalis, all of them men, who were watching and waiting for something, anything, to happen. It wasn't clear how many of them had even been into the club. Ayaan reckoned that most of them couldn't afford the entry price, but had come over to Southall anyway for no other reason than that this was where the action was tonight. Somalis, she said, were 'night people, like the Arabs'. These ones were here, as she put it, 'to see what they could get' – or else, she grumbled, to hassle girls. They were loitering with intent, as the police used to say, and we felt unpleasantly scrutinized as we passed down the pavement.

'Hey, sister,' called one of them, lowering his car window, 'what are you doing with him? You should be with me. Is there something wrong with your brothers?'

Two Somali faces appeared over his shoulder, their eyes and teeth gleaming in the car's dark interior, leering and egging him on.

'Idiots,' Ayaan retorted over her shoulder, without stopping or slowing down. 'Don't you know incest is illegal in this country?'

The catcaller's mates found this putdown hilarious and shouted for us to *Yo, stop!*, but we kept walking.

'God,' she muttered, 'don't you hate that? Bloody kids.'

It was a relief when we reached the safety of the car around the corner. Ayaan knew what she was doing, but there was still a bit more bluster to her streetcraft than felt comfortable.

I wanted to find out more about the gangs, and in particular to explore what connection they had, if any, with Islamic extremism. I had not forgotten the criminologist Daniel LaDouceur's theory in Garowe that al-Shabaab was in essence a big street gang, indistinguishable from those found in almost every big Western city. The impulse for joining any gang, as he told me, was the same: it was a primitive survival tactic based on strength in numbers. The Home Office's Prevent strategy documents identified various places where young Muslims were vulnerable to 'violent radicalization', such as schools, universities, prisons and mosques. Muslims could also radicalize themselves, courtesy of 'Sheikh Google', alone at home on a computer. But the Prevent strategy made little mention of London's gang culture, an oversight pointed out at a Home Affairs committee hearing in 2012, where it was stated that there

was 'a particular risk of radicalization linked to membership of some criminal gangs', especially if those gang
members ended up in prison.[2]

And a great many young Somali gang members did end
up in prison. I spoke to a number of community leaders in
the course of 2011, and they all said the same thing.
Sharmarke Yusuf, the chairman of AMIC, the Association
of Mosques and Islamic Centres, an umbrella group of
seven London Somali mosques, and whose office was
around the corner from the Tudor Rose, told me that a
'majority' of Somali youth was either currently in or had
recently been through the criminal justice system. At any
one time, he asserted, fully two-thirds of young London
Somalis were 'on the street', by which he meant they were
actively involved in gangs or drugs or other minor crimes.
Mohammed Elmi, the Wembley-based head of the
community group Somali Diaspora UK, spoke even more
gloomily of a Somali youth crime 'time-bomb' in Britain.
He had recently visited the Youth Offenders' Institution at
Feltham, and was appalled to discover that, for the first
time, it contained more inmates from Somalia than from
any other foreign country.

'There were over sixty Somalis in there! More, even,
than the Jamaicans,' he added in shocked tones.[3]

Feltham, as the Home Office were all too aware, had a
dangerous reputation for radicalization. Richard Reid, the
would-be 'shoe-bomber' who tried to blow up an American
Airlines passenger jet in 2001, famously converted to Islam
while locked up there for petty theft. Muktar Said Ibrahim,
the leader of the failed suicide attacks against London
Transport on 21 July 2005, also once did time in Feltham for

a gang-related offence. The 21/7 attacks had a pronounced Horn of Africa flavour: Ibrahim was from Eritrea, while two other conspirators, Ramzi Mohamed and Yassin Omar, were born in Somalia. Another former Feltham inmate, Jermaine Grant from Newham in east London, was arrested in December 2011 in Mombasa, having entered Kenya on a false passport; police were convinced that he was a part of an al-Shabaab bomb plot.

The Feltham connection was highly suggestive, yet Sharmarke Yusuf did not think that this institution per se was to blame for the radicalization of Reid and the others.

'There is no overt evidence of al-Qaida radicalization within Feltham,' he said. 'It happens, rather, on Feltham's doorstep, back out in the community, underground.'

He thought that radicalization, like incarceration, was an effect rather than a cause of a deeper, social problem. He pointed out that unemployment among Somali men of working age had doubled in the last ten years, to 40 per cent, the highest rate of any immigrant community. This was just an average, for the rate was far higher in some parts of London, and higher still among the young. Only half of British Somalis had any educational qualifications at all, and only 3 per cent of them had a higher education qualification.

'Life in the UK can be overwhelming for Somali teenagers,' he said. 'They do badly in school, they can't find work, and we have so many prejudices to deal with. We are Muslims, and we are black. To cap it all, we are Somali, which means that we are even rejected by other Africans.'

It was hardly surprising, he said, that so many young Somalis felt alienated from society, and no less surprising that they should turn to Islam as a means of coping with that feeling. As the chairman of an association of mosques, Sharmarke naturally saw nothing wrong with that. But, as he acknowledged, alienated young people were also vulnerable to 'misleading influences' – and that was when radicalization could occur.

The British government, he thought, was partly to blame for this state of affairs. Perhaps like any community displaced by a brutal civil war, the Somalis had special needs, and so needed extra support to help them assimilate into British society. Instead, they had largely been ignored, at least until the London bombings of 2005, when the government properly woke up to the threat of Somali extremism. The early years of the Prevent programme, however, had been 'a disaster'.

'The government saw the issue in black and white, but there are no quick fixes because the roots of the problem run so deep,' Sharmarke observed.

The government was so anxious to be seen to be tackling the causes of extremism after 2005 that they granted Prevent funding to almost any Muslim organization that asked for it, with the minimum of checks as to its suitability, and little control over how the money was spent once allocated. Dozens of new community bodies were set up, some of which appeared to exist almost solely in order to get their hands on the government cash. The budgets were huge. In 2008–9, according to a report by the Institute of Race Relations entitled 'How Not to Prevent Violent Extremism', the government blew £140m on projects such as the Enfield 'Shoot a Ball not a Gun Basketball' project (which received £26,000) and the Edmonton Eagles Boxing Club (£16,000).

'Some mosques accepted the money, others did not,' recalled Sharmarke. 'It caused many divisions, and a whole community was stereotyped as freeloaders and fraudsters as well as potential terrorists.'

Now that the Prevent programme had been refocused, and with funding cuts and a change of government, the Home Office spending bonanza had dried up, leaving the Somali community almost back where they had started in 2005. Sharmarke was still bitter about a speech by David Cameron in Munich in February 2011 in which he declared that multiculturalism wasn't working.

'He said we Muslims need to take responsibility for our own problems – that "if you don't integrate, then this is no country for you". But what we need is greater engagement from the government, not threats.'

It would take time, he thought, to deal with the root causes of radicalization. The key, he said, was 'early intervention', by which he meant getting to young people before the radicalizing 'bad influences' – ideally, when they were still schoolchildren – with the goal of teaching them to be 'proper' Muslims.

'No suicide bomber has ever had a proper grounding in Islam, which prohibits the killing of innocents,' he insisted.

It was in Britain's madrassahs and primary schools, he was convinced, that the war on terror would eventually be won.

But that was mostly a prescription for the future. The reality of the present was that a great many young London Somalis had turned not to Allah for their salvation, but to the gangs.

The violence and tenacity with which the Somalis fought

to defend 'their' postcode had long been notorious. Like red squirrels chased by grey ones, existing gangs of other ethnicities were frequently driven off their traditional territories. According to a Special Branch officer I later interviewed, two Punjabi gangs in Southall, the Holy Smokes and the Tooti Nungs, had been 'wiped out' by the Somalis, a new generation of gangs whose aggression was often explicit even in their names, such as MDP (which stood for Murder Dem Pussies) and GFL (Gunz Fully Loaded). In Bristol, according to a study published in 2008, the Somali newcomers were so feared that two long-established rival gangs, one white and one Afro-Caribbean, formed an unprecedented alliance in order to oppose them.[4]

The reason for the Somali gangs' extreme viciousness, according to 'a number of senior police officers' spoken to during the same study, was 'the level of violence experienced in Somalia, coupled with the level of alienation Somali communities experience in Britain'. Were they right to infer that Somali gang violence was partly learned behaviour, copied from the mayhem witnessed in the homeland? If so, then here was another reason for Britain to involve itself in the search for a political settlement in Somalia – because the effect of the gangs is arguably even more pernicious than the threat of exported terrorism.

There is no question that religious extremism, and the implicit threat of terrorism that goes with it, undermines the Western way of life. Britain has been forced to live with the possibility of a spectacular terrorist attack for over a decade. And yet the tally of people actually killed by Muslim extremists on British soil since 9/11 stands at just fifty-six, all of them in the 7/7 bombings of 2005. The danger of terrorism is mostly in the mind, unlike the threat to personal safety posed by street gangs. Between 2009 and 2011, there were ninety-two gang-related murders in London alone.[5]

The petty crime and violence they trade in are banal compared to 9/11 or the prospect of a nuclear dirty bomb. Yet these things eat away at the urban social fabric on a daily basis, spreading fear and misery (and drugs) in the inner cities, blighting lives, and trashing the country's reputation internationally. Britain locks up more of its young people than any country in the Western world apart from the US, and its prisons are bursting, yet the gangs are still not under control. The mindless violence and lawlessness they espouse was well expressed by a four-day riot that broke out in several English cities in August 2011. The catalyst for the riots, which cost the taxpayer at least £133m in policing and compensation bills, was the police shooting in Tottenham of 'Starrish Mark' Duggan, a founder member of the Star Gang. Analysis of the nearly 2,000 people later brought before the courts revealed that 13 per cent were involved in gangs, a figure that rose to 19 per cent in the capital.[6]

Gang violence seemed almost glorified by some sectors of the Somali community. *Shank*, a knife crime drama released in 2010, was the debut film of the London-Somali music video director, Mo Ali. It followed characters with names like Tugz, Kickz, Craze and Rager through a futuristic urban dystopia (but actually filmed in the south London borough of Walworth) when 'the gangs have taken over'. The film was not well received by the critics. It received a rating of 0 per cent on the cinema review aggregator website, rottentomatoes.com. *Empire* magazine said it 'looks like it was informed by a generation raised on *Grand Theft Auto* for any sort of cinematic aesthetic . . . If this is the future of film then we're all doomed.'

Less laughable was the experience of Jane, a tough, no-nonsense teacher I knew, who spoke to me on condition that I neither gave her real name nor identified the secondary state school in south-east London that employed her. As many as a third of her school's 1,500 pupils were Somali-born, easily the largest ethnic group in a school where only 28 per cent of the pupils were born in the UK. The behaviour of a small minority of these Somalis, Jane said, could be 'feral'. A fierce rivalry between two local gangs, the Woolwich Boys and the Thamesmead 'T-Block', was played out constantly in the school. The former gang ran a cadet organization called the Younger Woolwich Boys, some of whom were as young as seven. Beyond the school gates they were all in the drug-selling business; the seven- and eight-year-olds, according to Jane, were often employed as runners because the police would never think to stop and search someone so young.

'I'm not racist, but the behaviour of some of the Somalis is so impossible that the system just can't cope,' Jane said. 'I'd have fewer of them in the school if I had a choice.'

One night in October 2009, three former pupils of Jane's, all Somalis between the ages of seventeen and eighteen, were among a group of five Woolwich Boys who travelled by taxi to Thamesmead, intent on avenging an earlier incident in which one of their number had been chased by a pack of T-Blockers. As they later explained to police, they had 'gone hunting'. On a footbridge, the gang fell upon

22-year-old Moses Nteyoho, a random pedestrian who had nothing to do with the T-Block, and stabbed and bludgeoned him to death using knives and a hammer. Pathologists later calculated that Nteyoho had taken less than ninety seconds to die. Far from turning them in, the killers' female relatives then helped the boys to flee to Nairobi, a truly depressing indication of how poorly integrated into British society certain segments of the Somali community still were. Happily for the cause of justice, the killers made the mistake of returning to Britain after two months, when they were caught and jailed, as were the relatives when their role in the Kenyan flit was discovered.

Many of Jane's Somali pupils were appalled by the senseless savagery of Nteyoho's death.

'Some of my Somali kids say privately that the situation is worsening for a whole generation of Somalis in the 16-year-old-plus bracket,' she said. 'They are worried that the Somali community is increasingly being perceived as a danger to society as a whole.'

It wasn't fair, because most of Jane's Somali pupils had nothing to do with the gangs, and many of them were excellent students. She had noticed, however, that the success stories were almost exclusively from what she called 'the middle-class families'.

'I've got one Somali at the top of Year 11 . . . his dad's a doctor,' she said. 'Education is obviously the key.'

At Jane's school, clever or studious pupils were known as 'bods', who did not mix with the 'losers' who were more likely to be gang members or to be in trouble with the law. This division reflected a polarization in the community generally. Successful, 'middle-class' British Somalis tended to be descended from an earlier generation of refugees, often northerners from Somaliland, who had had time to establish themselves in Britain. Assimilated Somalis were sometimes disparaged by their more traditionally oriented countrymen as 'fish 'n' chips Somalis'. They made a stark contrast to the more recent arrivals who had flooded in during the early 1990s following the Siad Barre collapse. The newer refugees tended to be from the south where the civil war had raged most fiercely. Thus it was that the bitter north–south clan divide that had wracked Somali society for so long at home was perpetuated in another form in exile on the streets of London.

For Jane, the number-one problem was that so many of her Somali pupils were chronic underachievers. Some seemed genuinely unable to stop themselves from performing and behaving badly, as though there was something deep in the nomad psyche that responded negatively to the constraints and rules of school. The problem was replicated across London. Sharmarke Yusuf said that between 2009 and 2010 in Ealing, as many as 280 Somali pupils, some of them as young as five, were 'permanently excluded' from the state education system: one of the highest expulsion rates in the entire country.

The causes were complex, the explanations varied. The traditional authority figure in a Somali boy's upbringing, Sharmarke explained, was the father. But this source of discipline was often absent from families living in Britain, either because the father had been killed previously in Somalia, or else because he was 'out working in factories, or doing a 12-hour shift as a taxi driver'. For whatever reason, the job of disciplining teenage boys tended to be left to the mothers, who were spectacularly failing to fill the gap. Somali families were often large. Broods of five, six or more children were common, and as recent refugees they were often very poor. Depression, anxiety, and other debilitating mental disorders associated with displacement and the trauma of war were also alarmingly widespread, further affecting many families' ability to cope.

Language, according to Jane, was another 'huge issue'. The mothers were often unable to speak, let alone read, English, so they depended on their sons to communicate not just with the school but with all representatives of official-dom. The results were predictable – for what wayward teenager would choose to read out a headmaster's letter of reprimand addressed to their mum? Jane thought that Somali mothers were in any case unusually deaf to criticism of their sons, whom they appeared culturally predisposed to spoil.

'In our culture, if a boy does something wrong, we discipline him. But if a Somali boy does something wrong, the mother frequently buys him a present – trainers, the latest gadget – as though to control him through bribery. Whatever he has done wrong is forgotten about, and no shame attached . . . It is the opposite for girls, for whom the shame is apparently permanent. This is very weird parenting.'

I asked Jane if Islamic extremism was an issue, either within the school or beyond its gates. As an occasional teacher of Religious Education, with a mandate to instruct her pupils in the basics of all the world's religions including Islam, she was perhaps in a position to know.

'Somalis are always being marginalized as potential extremists,' she replied, 'yet I'm constantly struck by how little they know about their own religion. Then again, they know amazingly little about anything . . . But the younger ones don't even know what the main parts of a mosque are called. My impression is that a lot of them go to mosque once or twice a year at most.'

Her answer tended to support Sharmarke Yusuf's conviction that it was ignorance of Islam rather than a surfeit of it that put young Muslims on the path to violent radicalism. I asked her, rather tactlessly, if she had heard of Gary Smith, the head of Religious Education at the Central Foundation Girls' School in Bow in east London, and she stopped me, horrified, before I could go any further. Smith had been walking to work one morning in July 2010 when he was attacked and severely injured by four heavily bearded Muslim men armed with a brick, a Stanley knife and a metal bar. One of them, Azad Hussein, 26, had a niece at the school, and disapproved of her being taught by Smith.

'He's mocking us and he's putting thoughts in people's minds,' Hussein was heard to say. 'How can somebody take a job to teach Islam when he's not even a Muslim himself?'[7]

Hussein showed how short the distance could be between gang crime and religious extremism. The journey from one to the other was explored in detail in a Channel 4 documentary first aired in 2008, *From Jail to Jihad*, in which the ex-Reuters Middle East correspondent Amil Khan interviewed a member of a gang called the Soldiers of Allah. This gangman – evidently a recent convert to Islam – saw himself as a kind of Muslim vigilante.

'We are all soldiers of Islam, all slaves of Allah,' he mumbled through the mask he wore to preserve his anonymity. 'We no criminals, you get me? We just people dat fix da environment.'

It was a highly distorted, street version of the faith that could be used to justify violence against other, non-Muslim criminals, or as Khan's interviewee put it: 'Kuffars, you can take what they have, cos they don't worship in the ways of Allah.' Part of the proceeds of crime could even be paid to charity as *zakat*, the third pillar of Islam. A track by a long-disbanded gang-cum-rap group called SMS – the South Muslim Soldiers – confirmed that London gangland had effectively come up with its own version of jihad:

> For the cause
> We kick down doors and break laws
> We don't care about police we live by Allah's laws
> For the cause I clap down niggaz that test me
> I'm a Muslim, I can't let nothing oppress me
> For the cause I won't stop until I reach my garden
> I beg your pardon, I ride with bin Laden.

Times had changed and bin Laden was dead, but the 'al-Qaida chic' which underpinned gangs like SMS was as strong as ever; and as the police realized, it was a very short hop indeed from belonging to a gang like the Soldiers of Allah to signing up with an actual terrorist organization.

'It's just another form of belonging,' said Abid Raja of the Muslim Contact Unit, a part of SO15, the Metropolitan Police's Counter Terrorism Command. 'Radicalization is a subtle progression. The kids sometimes don't notice the massive steps they're taking. And Somalia is such a cause célèbre now . . . Certainly, some of them aspire to go there.'

Raja and his colleague, Detective Sergeant Paul Birch, worked from a semi-fortified office block in Earl's Court. They took me for a coffee in their canteen on the thirtieth floor, from where there was a stupendous easterly view across central London to the cranes and offices of the City, rising like a crystal bar-chart through the urban haze. Five minutes after we had sat down, I glanced back through the window to find that the city had vanished, and that the horizon's centre point was now Windsor Castle, 18 miles to the west. The policemen had neglected to mention that the entire thirtieth floor was slowly revolving – an apt metaphor, no doubt, for those critics who thought the government's Prevent strategy was also going round in circles.

The Muslim Contact Unit was set up in 2002 by Bob Lambert, a former professor of Islamic Studies at Exeter University, with the aim of forging partnerships with Muslim community groups in order to fight extremist ideologies from the inside. His idea was to recruit the relative moderates among the Islamist community because they were best placed to understand, and thus counter, the twisted Salafist theology deployed by al-Qaida.

'Lambertism', as the MCU's doctrine was known, had many early successes, notably in helping to turn the community of Finsbury Mosque against the country's most infamous radical preacher, the hook-handed Abu Hamza.

The doctrine had since fallen out of political fashion, however. Critics charged that some of the MCU's local partners were too close, ideologically speaking, to the very radicalism that SO15 was supposed to be countering. When the Prevent programme was relaunched in 2011, dozens of the MCU's former partners found themselves reclassified as 'non-violent extremists', and their funding was withdrawn on the grounds that they were opposed to 'fundamental and universal' British values. Lambert himself remained a right-wing hate figure, even though he retired from the MCU in 2007. One blogger recently called him 'the last beacon of hope for Islamists in the remnants of Londonistan'.[8] These were difficult times, therefore, for the MCU.

'The political agenda has slid to the right, and the funding cuts are interfering with practical solutions,' Abid Raja said.

And yet in its quiet way, the MCU remained at the spear-tip of the fight against radicalization. Birch and Raja insisted they still had the support of London's communities, and had little time for the vicissitudes of Whitehall and its unhelpful 'labels'. Meaningful community relations depended on trust that took years to build up. Raja, who had been in the Met for seventeen years, explained that the MCU's 'street cred' was crucial. This was partly why six of its eleven most senior officers were Muslim, including the Pakistan-born Abid, who wore a turban and a very substantial beard. 'To be frank, it's taken years to get to where I am now,' he smiled.

He explained how as a younger man he had been a non-practising Muslim, a 'Jack-the-Lad Londoner into girls and nightclubbing', but that a personal tragedy, the death of a daughter, had turned him towards Islam. He flirted with fundamentalism, but 9/11 forced him to question the direction of his faith. Eventually, under the tutelage of a religious scholar called Shafi Malik, he evolved his own Muslim *modus vivendi* based on tolerance of others.

'It was a very personal, individualized journey, as I think it has to be for all Muslims. But I am convinced that it *is* possible to live by Sharia and to live in the West.'

It was easy to see how the MCU had been misunderstood in its work. Abid Raja the Pakistani philosopher-copper did not fit the public's image of counter-terrorism authorities, and nor did his Lambertist prescriptions.

'Give 'em Islam: conservative Islam,' he said at one point with a stroke of his beard when I asked what he thought should be done about the Somali gangs. 'The *Daily Mail* doesn't like it, but Sharia is the saviour of law and order. It is the opposite of an attack on Western values.'

The Home Office did in fact try to 'give Islam' to Muslim miscreants, notably through its network of prison imams. But these individuals went through such a strict government vetting procedure before they were appointed that, as Amil Khan pointed out, they often lacked vital credibility with the hardliner prisoners that the government most needed to reach – for who among them was going to listen to an imam bearing a stamp marked 'UK government-approved'?

The MCU's task, according to Raja, had not changed in ten years: they were on constant lookout for people with religious credibility who enjoyed the respect of their community, and who might work alongside the MCU as 'local partners'. Such relationships, however, had to be handled 'incredibly carefully' if the credibility of the partner was not to be tainted by association. Paul Birch admitted that the MCU was 'still playing catch-up' with the Somali community in this regard.

'There are some Somali imams out there with the right level of credibility, but they are very low profile. The only way they can reach an audience of any size is to use the media, but if they do that, then their credibility is destroyed . . . It's catch-22.'

The media organization most deeply involved in the Somali community fight against extremism, and which continues to enjoy Home Office funding for their vital hearts and minds work, is the privately owned Universal TV, a Somali television channel that has broadcast from London since 2004. I went to meet one of UTV's star producer-presenters, Abdi Jama, at the Jump in Jack café near his home in Acton Town. Until recently, he explained, UTV was the only UK-based Somali broadcaster, although these days there were as many as seven. It sounded a lot for one ethnic minority, but UTV's audience was genuinely global, and its ratings appeared not to have been dented at all: Abdi Jama said that his Saturday night show, *Social Issues*, was regularly watched by 2.7 million viewers. As the *New York Times*'s veteran Somalia correspondent Jeffrey Gettleman pointed out, UTV plays a unique role in the wider community, like a guardian of nationhood in exile: 'If there is any nucleus of the Somali diaspora, any glue holding together a people who have been scattered by war and settled everywhere from Sydney to Minneapolis, it is Universal TV.'⁹

Jama saw the battle against religious extremism as a 'moral obligation', and a lot of UTV's programming, such as Sunday night's *Young Perspective* or *YP Show*, was overtly organized around this principle and directly aimed at Somali youth.

'We can't afford another 7/7,' he said. 'It could have been my own kids on that bus.'

His speciality was the phone-in programme. He employed a roster of seven imams who answered questions from young viewers seeking guidance on how to live as good Muslims in the West. The resultant discussions covered everything from the reporting of crime to female circumcision and the age of consent.

'The imams get a lot of abuse from people accusing them of working for MI5 and stuff, and we don't pay them, but they still do it.'

Jama recalled a debate on wearing the jilbab, where an imam patiently explained to a young female viewer that wearing the veil was not, in fact, an obligation under the Koran.

'And this girl says, "Oooh! So you're with the kuffars!" It was an outrageous way to speak to a sheikh. But that is what we are up against.'

Jama's method of dealing with al-Shabaab was not to demonize them, as the West tended to do, but to engage with their arguments, including through textual exegesis if necessary. He had recently hosted a debate in which not one but two imams agreed that nowhere in the Koran did it say that suicide bombing was ever justified. The viewer phone lines rang hot after that, followed by an al-Shabaab declaration of a fatwa on all things UTV, forcing the temporary closure of the channel's Mogadishu office for the safety of its staff.

The danger from extremists was not confined to

Somalia. On Ealing Common in 2010, where an estimated 50,000 Somalis gathered to celebrate Eid, the Muslim holiday that marks the end of Ramadan, Jama was threatened by a group of young Somalis simply for filming.

'They had this attitude that television was an infidel thing; one of them accused me of working for the CIA, and said it was haram even to watch TV. I was shocked.'

The source of this antediluvian thinking, he discovered, was a well-known maverick called Mohamed Mahmoud, a self-styled sheikh unaffiliated to any mosque but who preached regularly anyway, mainly in the Southall area.

'This guy has fifteen young Somalis among his followers, they've all failed their GCSEs, yet he tells them that university is haram because British students have to pay interest on their loans ... It's a disgrace! And I think Tony Blair was right when he said the government's three top priorities should be education, education and education.'

He told the story of Mohamed, a 24-year-old Somali he had interviewed on his show recently, who had been brought up in a care home, began drinking at twelve, had been in prison twice by the age of fifteen, and had grown up with no qualifications at all. He had straightened himself out by attaching himself to a mosque in Shepherd's Bush. There was, however, a problem with this mosque, which propagated a potent ideological blend of Salafism and Wahhabism.

'The people there won't even say salaam to me because I don't have short trousers and a beard. And now Mohamed thinks everyone else is a "bad" Muslim, including me. He says it's haram to look at women, but really that's just an excuse for not looking for work. Western society is not segregated. It is not possible to function as a citizen here without mingling with the opposite sex.'

In Whitehall-speak, Mohamed's group at the Shepherd's Bush mosque were 'non-violent extremists' whose faith was already far beyond the reach of UTV's voice of moderation. As Detective Sergeant Birch understood, the fact that the channel's counter-radicalization programming was funded by the British government automatically made its message suspect in the eyes of many conservative Muslims, and damaged its credibility on the street. He was convinced that the better way to influence people like Mohamed – perhaps the only way – was through their ideological peers.

For jihadist street cred, it was hard to beat the founder of the Active Change Foundation, a youth outreach pro-gramme in the north-east London borough of Waltham Forest. Hanif Qadir, a middle-aged Pakistani born in the North Yorkshire town of Thornaby, had not just sym-pathized with the jihad as a younger man. In 2002, after the American invasion of Afghanistan, he had actually travelled there and volunteered to fight for the Taliban. What happened next turned him into one of the most valuable assets that the Met's Counter Terrorism Command has ever had.

'My perceptions of jihad were shattered the moment I arrived,' he explained in his bluff Teesside accent. 'I went there with this vision of standing shoulder to shoulder against the infidel with my brother Muslims, but I quickly discovered that if you weren't Arab or Afghan, you were nobody. What I saw was a lot of poor, humble people being manipulated. It was made quite clear that we had no hope for the future except martyrdom. We were cannon fodder.

The volunteers had noble Islamic motives, but the Talibs had no respect for that. They wouldn't give me the time of day when I challenged them on this, and when I insisted, they became aggressive.'

By the time he had travelled through the Khyber Pass and reached the Afghan border town of Torkham, he was so thoroughly disillusioned that he turned round and came straight back to Britain. He set up the Active Change Foundation soon afterwards, and had spent most of the last decade warning young Muslims that the path to paradise in Afghanistan was a dud.

'Looking back, I'm glad God guided me in the way he did,' he said. 'He helped me escape death, or Guantanamo . . . who knows.'

He had set up his headquarters in a youth centre on the Lea Bridge Road next door to the Jamia Masjid Ghosia, the largest mosque in Waltham Forest. His chosen area was one of the most multicultural in the city, with a populace very different from the Victorian and Edwardian office workers for whom it was first built. The mock-Tudor gables above the shops around the mosque recalled Olde Englande, but the goods and services on offer were all about travel and escape: the Grill 'n' Spice takeaway, a travel agency specializing in Hajj and Umrah package tours, a hairdressing salon called Paradise. It was hard to avoid a feeling that the Lea Bridge Road, with its chip shops and betting shops and buses whizzing too fast along the route between Clapton and Whipp's Cross, was a neighbourhood tolerated rather than loved by its inhabitants.

Stocky and avuncular, Hanif exuded a kind of calm wisdom that reminded me immediately of the beard-stroking

SO15 officer Abid Raja. They were two British Pakistanis of the same sort of age, who had embarked on very similar journeys of Islamic self-discovery as young men. The routes they had taken were certainly different, but they had arrived at the same destination in the end. Hanif explained how he had been brought up a moderate Barelvi Muslim, as the majority of British Pakistanis were, but had been drawn to the more conservative Deobandis when he moved to London. The untimely death of a sister deepened his interest in Islam, just as the loss of a daughter had for Abid Raja. He experimented with Sufi mysticism, Wahhabism and Salafism, but eventually rejected all of these in favour of a bespoke faith rooted, as the SO15 man's was, in tolerance of others.

'My nephew became a Salafist. All of a sudden it was "their way" or "no way". I banned him from my house,' he said, with a faint smile that acknowledged the paradox. 'I understand kids who go from Barelvism to Salafism because I did the same journey; I understand how that misinterpretation works.'

The purpose of his foundation, he said, was to show young Muslims a shortcut to enlightenment, although he insisted that religious guidance was only a part of the solution.

'A lot of them have legitimate grievances, which we try to address. Everyone is different. Engagement is the key. You have to look at the person and try to get where they are coming from.'

This was in sharp contrast to the approach usually taken by government which, he said, was driven by 'performance indicators ... They are not interested in the emotional stuff, and that neglect just plays into the narrative of oppression that radicalization begins with.'

He was a believer in the 'hug a hoodie' philosophy once embraced by David Cameron in his bid to rebrand his Conservative Party, a controversial approach to youth crime that the Tories had quietly dropped once they returned to government. It was intriguing to meet someone who both practised the technique and swore that it worked.

Hanif had had a great deal to do with young Somalis over the years. He had seen several would be Somali jihadis in Islamabad and Rawalpindi on his way to Afghanistan in 2002, and saw a strong similarity between the Taliban and al-Shabaab in the way that the latter manipulated the idealism of its young foreign recruits. He had coaxed several Somalis away from the path that led to terrorism, and offered the example of 'Blade', an ex-street gangster whom he had met during a four-day Outward Bound course in the Surrey countryside near Guildford in 2010. Instead of scolding Blade when he was caught skiving off smoking a joint in the woods, Hanif had made a point of befriending him. He was clearly a natural mentor with a knack for winning the trust of a certain type of confused young person. Blade, he learned, had joined an Afro-Caribbean gang 'for the authority', and had slid into a life of 'severe violence' from which he was struggling to escape.

'We drilled down,' said Hanif. 'His mother was devout and she had thrown him out for smelling of weed, so all he had was the gangs. There was no father or father-figure in his life.'

Amil Khan, the documentary maker, had described to me 'a particular poor UK urban shittiness that the middle-class world hardly ever sees', and Blade's story sounded a good example of that. Khan thought that the poverty, although real enough, was almost incidental to the main problem, which he identified as 'a lack of opportunity, or a perception of not having opportunities . . . At the same time there's a youth culture that quickly coalesces around social problems to make dysfunction a badge of pride.'

Back in Waltham Forest, Hanif persuaded Blade to attend one of his 'gang workshops' that were designed to give people like him a chance to vent their grievances. It was in the course of one of these sessions that he revealed he had recently downloaded some bomb-making instructions from the internet.

'His life was a mess and he blamed "the West" for that,' shrugged Hanif, 'and so he wanted to bomb some non-Muslims.'

It was possible, or even likely, that Blade would never have acted on his bomb-making impulse. Terrorism – or as Hanif described it, 'disastrous action' – was no more than a form of desperate self-expression born of frustration and anger, with only the very loosest connection to political Islam, let alone to al-Qaida or al-Shabaab. The same could not be said, though, of the Active Change Foundation's most celebrated deradicalized Somali, Kader Ahmed, who had specifically wanted to be associated with the cause of al-Shabaab.

Kader had been so close to the London suicide bombers of July 2005 that he phoned each of the 21/7 gang, one by one, to wish them luck on their mission shortly before they set off. He was also among the group of Muslims photographed, notoriously, on a terrorist training weekend at Baysbrown Farm in the Lake District in 2004 run by Mohammed Hamid, an East African Indian Muslim preacher and

In 1920, when British Somaliland was threatened by the Dervish leader Sayyid Hassan (*left*), the RAF's Z Force (*above*) attacked his fort headquarters at Taleh (*below*), whose modern inhabitants are still demanding compensation.

The bombing of civilian areas remains controversial, a point made by the cartoonist Amin Amir in this sketch (*right*) of the Kenyan airforce in action over Kismayo in 2012.

Top: A humanitarian mission to relieve a famine in 1992, Operation Restore Hope, began with a farcical Mogadishu beach landing by US Marines. It ended two years later after two US helicopters were shot down following a botched night raid (*above*), and their injured crewmen were lynched and dragged through the streets (*left*).

The grim reality of Sharia law, as applied by some extremists. Mohamed Abukar Ibrahim, 48, was stoned to death for adultery in 2009. These photographs were later used by the Kenyan Army as propaganda against al-Shabaab.

Siad Barre, Somalia's dictator president from 1969 to 1991 (*left*); US-born Islamist Abu Mansoor al-Amriki (*centre, right*) with al-Shabaab's deputy, Sheikh Mukhtar Robow; al-Shabaab's hardline leader Ali 'Godane' Zubeyr (*bottom left*); the 'spiritual leader' Sheikh Hassan Aweys (*bottom right*).

Clockwise from top left: Mohamed Farole, the president of Puntland; former TFG President Sheikh Sharif; President Hassan Sheikh Mohamud, elected in September 2012 following the first genuine presidential poll in a generation.

Suspected pirates are intercepted by the French Navy in 2009. But what will happen to the captives? Prison places in Somalia are in short supply. Here a pirate suspect sits in chains.

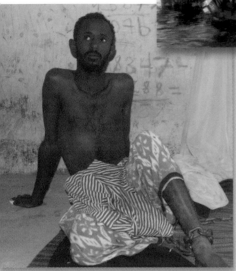

EUNAVFOR, which has a fleet of 25 warships at its disposal (*above*), insists that a sustainable solution will only be found on land. But counter-piracy measures such as the new Puntland Marine Force (*below*) have proved controversial.

Somali terrorism arrived in the UK with the London Transport attacks of 21/7, 2005: key perpetrators Muktar Said Ibrahim (*above left*), and Somalia-born Ramzi Mohamed during their arrest. Police had earlier filmed their gang on a training exercise in the Lake District (*left*). The reformed jihadist Hanif Qadir (*below*) has made it his mission to dissuade other young Muslims from copying them, through his Active Change Foundation in East London.

YOUTH, GET OUT FROM AL-SHABAB BEFORE IT IS TOO LATE
IMPLEMENTED BY C.C.D

LET US BE UNITED TO FIGHT OUR ENEMY. AL-QAEDA
Implemented by C.C.D

AYMAN AL-ZAWAHRI AND GODANE YOU WILL END LIKE USAMA BIN LADEN

WE FOUGHT AL-SHABAB, IT'S EASY TO FIGHT AL-QAEDA TOO
Implemented by C.C.D

ALL MOTHERS TEARS ARE THE SAME

BOOKS NOT GUNS

The diaspora have played a key role in resistance to al-Shabaab, as regular demonstrations across the world have shown.

Below: The London Conference of 2012 – the twentieth peace conference since 1991 – was judged a success. But will the international community keep up the pressure on Mogadishu?

LONDON CONFERENCE ON SOMALIA 23 FEBRUARY 2012

reformed crack addict known as Osama bin London. Kader was only seventeen in 2004 when he first came under the spell of Hamid, at a rally at Speaker's Corner in Hyde Park. He was sent to Belmarsh Prison's high security unit for his involvement in the terror cell, but had come under Hanif's influence on his release, and was now on the same deradical-izing mission. He was famous for touring the worst housing estates on his bike, and stopping to tell his cautionary tale to any youths he found hanging about there.

The story of Kader's progression from confused refugee street kid to Islamist terrorist was like a version of Hogarth's *Rake's Progress*, updated for the twenty-first century. His parents had fled the civil war in the 1990s in the usual way, and begun a new life in a council flat in Plaistow, a short bus-ride south of the Lea Bridge Road. But his father left when Kader was twelve, and his devout mother took him out of secondary school at fourteen, apparently intent on educating him at home. Hanif described Kader as an 'emotional, compassionate person' and a natural 'seeker'. He was also young and lonely; and so when he fell in with Mohammed Hamid's group of fellow seekers, his mother, disastrously, encouraged him. Kader quickly rose up the ranks of the group, becoming the favoured protégé of its leader, and growing close, too, to its number two, a 'very aggressive Turkish Cypriot' called Atilla Ahmet.*

* Ahmet, according to Hanif, was the model for Barry, the crazed white extremist character in Chris Morris's 2010 movie *Four Lions*, a 'jihad satire' that British counter-terrorism officials referred to almost constantly in the course of my research. Barry's plan to bomb a local mosque in order to 'radicalize the moderates' provides one of the film's best black-comedy moments.

'It was just the wrong crowd,' said Hanif. 'All his desires and grievances were massaged. He was taught to hate, and all his cultural norms were stripped away . . . I would call it abuse, brainwashing.'

It took the grim reality of the London Transport attacks, and then a spell in Belmarsh, to make Kader see the mistake he had made.

Despite his successes, Hanif was far from sanguine about London's young Somalis. He, too, thought that the violence and lawlessness of a section of that community were getting worse, and he agreed that there was a Somali crime 'time-bomb' in Britain, waiting to go off.

'Somalis are harder to engage with than any of the others,' he said. 'They never change, no matter what you do for them. They are much harder to crack than the Algerians, the Afghans . . . you can be six months into a programme with one of them, and you think you're making some progress, and then, boom! Something happens, and it's back to square one. It takes a lot of money and patience, and, to be honest with you, I've used a lot of my patience up now.'

Somalis, he had concluded, were often 'special' in their disrespect for authority, the ease with which they could be manipulated, and the speed with which they resorted to extreme violence.

'Life is cheaper to them even than it is to the Afghans,' he said, 'and they seem to have no code of conduct, even among themselves.'

A lot of Somalis he worked with, furthermore, could be 'very thick', with an inability to think for themselves that was uniquely self-destructive. For instance, the foundation's bike shed had been vandalized recently by one of Hanif's regulars, a Somali whose street name was Fester; his crime had been caught on one of the centre's four CCTV security cameras. Hanif confronted Fester, who apologized with a cheery 'Sorry, Uncle!'. But a few days later he returned, and was filmed trying – and failing – to destroy the cameras that had betrayed him the first time. A month or two later came the Tottenham riots, which showed that Fester had still not learned his lesson. Hanif recalled watching the television news one night and immediately spotting Fester, the only youth in a huge crowd of law-breakers not wearing a mask or hood.

The danger was that young men like Fester seemed capable of almost any atrocity, any imbecility – including, no doubt, going back to Somalia to be trained by or to fight for al-Shabaab. You didn't need many brains to do that, as was proved by a bizarre episode at Mogadishu airport in March 2012, when a black Briton arriving from London via Nairobi was stopped with hundreds of CDs and a quantity of mysterious powder in his luggage. When questioned he said he was trying to get to Kismayo 'to help the Muslims' – at which point, AMISOM security personnel arrested him. The hapless would-be jihadi, later identified as Jamaican-born Clive Everton Dennis, had failed to do his homework about who controlled the Somali capital.

Dennis was deported, but Britain's security services knew that many British Muslims like him had made it through, and that others were continuing to try. The more usual way to reach al-Shabaab territory was simply to walk over the poorly guarded Kenyan border. Two 18-year-olds from Cardiff, Mohamed Abdulrahman Mohamed, a

Somali, and his Pakistani friend Iqbal Shahzad, were arrested trying to do just that in October 2011.

'He was brainwashed and taken away from us and he was told that he was going to fight a holy war in Somalia,' said Mohamed's father, Abdirahman Haji Abdallah, who flew to Kenya to raise the alarm.

Mohamed and Shahzad were classic examples of the misguided teenager recruit identified by SO15's Abid Raja. After questioning back in London, counter-terrorist police released the pair back to their relieved families in Cardiff. The threat posed by other British Muslims was much graver, however. In May 2012, for instance, Kenyan police were reportedly still searching for Samantha Lewthwaite, a Muslim convert and the widow of the 7/7 London bomber Germaine Lindsay, whom they suspected of organizing the finances of the Jermaine Grant bomb plot in Mombasa.

A report by the Royal United Services Institute in February 2012 said that as many as a quarter of the estimated two hundred hardcore foreign fighters in al-Shabaab's ranks were British. Many of them were of non-Somali origin. Bilal al-Berjawi from west London, for example, who was killed near Mogadishu in January 2012 by an American drone strike, was Lebanese. With perhaps 2.8 million Muslims resident in the UK – as well as a British expatriate community of around 30,000 living in Kenya – it was no wonder that British security services were worried. Somalia, according to one unnamed intelligence official, was 'regarded as a dog which has barked but not yet bitten ... These people are no mugs. Somalia is awash with weapons and there are some very tasty fighters out there.' Al-Shabaab, this official thought, had the potential to become a 'very accomplished' international terrorist organization.[10]

'Those who survive tend to return [to Britain] in a matter of months or perhaps a year,' said RUSI's director general, Professor Michael Clarke, adding: 'It is only a question of time before their commitment to the cause, and their newly acquired expertise, are likely to be seen on British streets.'[11]

Clarke's assertion was based in part on what had happened in recent years in the US, where as many as forty-eight Somali-Americans were known to have travelled back in secret to Somalia in order to receive terrorist 'training' from Islamist extremists. On the tenth anniversary of 9/11, the American Congressman Peter King, the chairman of the US House of Representatives Committee on Homeland Security, came to London to warn British MPs that there was 'increasing evidence' of terrorist-trained Somali-Americans attempting to come back to the US, where the danger of radicalization had grown 'much worse'.

Tightened security in the West, King argued, meant that it was now 'very difficult [for al-Qaida] to attack on a large scale from the outside'. As a consequence, al-Qaida – and the congressman made little distinction between that organization and al-Shabaab – had changed tactics. Even President Obama's Deputy National Security Advisor, Denis McDonough, agreed that al-Qaida was now 'definitely recruiting within the Muslim American community'.[12]

The enemy within: it was the West's greatest nightmare, as the success of the 2012 TV drama series *Homeland* perhaps demonstrated. Audiences on both sides of the Atlantic were gripped by the series' atmosphere of moody paranoia, and its plot revolving around a CIA agent's pursuit of a US marine who, rescued after years in al-Qaida captivity, had been 'turned' by his former captors and was now plotting against the Washington government. It seemed to say something about the closeness of Britain and America in the War on Terror that Damian Lewis, the actor chosen to play the US marine, was British.

The SO15 detective Paul Birch thought that Britain ought to be paying more attention to the American experience, if only on the grounds that 'what happens over there always happens over here eventually'. I was particularly intrigued by the Upper Midwest's 'Twin Cities', Minneapolis and St Paul, the home of the largest Somali community in the US, from where at least twenty young Somali men had vanished since 2007, only to reappear soon afterwards in Somalia as fighters for al-Shabaab. In some cases, they had become suicide bombers. Most of the twenty had been in their mid-twenties, but at least two of them were still at high school when they left, aged just seventeen. In proportion to its size, the Twin Cities had exported far more Somali jihadis than London, or anywhere else in the Western world. How had that happened? And what could be done to stop the same from happening in Britain? In the autumn of 2011 I went to America to try to find out.

13

The missing of Minneapolis

Twin Cities, Minnesota, September 2011

Ten years had passed since the attacks of 9/11, but it was as though they had only just happened at New York's Newark airport, where I stopped to change planes for Minneapolis. A soldier in full combat gear was stationed at the main terminal entrance, his legs apart and his rifle cradled in his arms, an alert and aggressive reminder from the government to the people that America remained a country at war. The New Jersey Port Authority, apparently fearful that al-Qaida would mark the 9/11 anniversary with another Twin Towers-type strike, had plastered the terminals with posters exhorting the public to be vigilant. One of these depicted a hooded figure with a rucksack over his shoulder, slipping into a door marked AUTHORIZED PERSONNEL ONLY, above the shouted headline 'What's wrong with this picture?' and a phone number to call.

There seemed, at least to my European eyes, to be quite a lot wrong with the picture. Wasn't there enough paranoia in America's airports already, without encouraging its citizens to spy on one another in this Orwellian way? It felt like an affront to civil liberties in this supposed Land of the Free. The Port Authority's determination to avoid any accusation of racial profiling was also laughable. The figure in the poster's foreground conscientiously phoning the cops was an indeterminate brown, while the suspect in the background was white. He looked to me less like a terrorist than a naughty teenager looking for somewhere to smoke an illicit cigarette.

But however exaggerated the reasons for fear and suspicion might have been, I knew they were not groundless. Support for al-Qaida – or for its affiliates, such as al-Shabaab – was real enough in the US, above all in the city to which I was headed. A Minneapolis Somali called Omer Abdi Mohamed had only recently pleaded guilty to a federal charge of conspiring to recruit fighters for the insurgency.[1] The case of 'Brother Omer' had been cited by Congressman Peter King – who was fresh back in Washington from his address to British MPs, and about to chair another Homeland Security Committee hearing into extremism among American Muslims – as evidence that 'jihadi sympathizers' were still active in the Minneapolis community.

'With al-Shabaab's large cadre of American jihadis and unquestionable ties to al-Qaida, we must face the reality that al-Shabaab is a growing threat to our homeland,' he said.[2]

In 2008 when the FBI launched Operation Rhino, as they called their investigation in the Twin Cities, they quickly discovered that many of the young men who had gone missing in Somalia had known each other, either because they had once been friends at the same school, or else because they had prayed together at the same south central mosque, the Abubakar as-Saddique Islamic Center. It was this last detail that really alarmed the FBI. Were the young men recruited by militant Muslims preaching at the Abubakar? If so, how had these preachers managed to operate in the heartland of America for so long, wholly undetected by the DHS, the vast, multi-agency Department of Homeland Security, which had been set up after 9/11 specifically to ensure that such a catastrophe could never be repeated? In the Twin Cities, it seemed, America's worst nightmare was in danger of coming true.

Between 75,000 and 100,000 Somalis live in Minneapolis and St Paul, comfortably the largest concentration in the States, although it is not immediately obvious why. Minnesota's legendary winters, where temperatures routinely drop to minus 15°C and snowfalls of eight feet have been known, are the planetary opposite of the desert heat of the Horn of Africa. It was, as the locals joke, a very cold place for a hotbed.

Their presence, I eventually discovered, was down to the Lutherans. Minnesota's first settlers were farmers from Germany and Scandinavia, and Lutherans still run the state's social services with an efficiency and generosity of spirit of which the Great Reformer himself would have approved. A number of economic migrants from Somalia, mostly professionals with ambitions to study or to set up businesses, had been drawn to the Twin Cities even before the civil war by the abundance of jobs and social housing on offer, at a time when the local economy was conspicuously booming. Word soon spread of the good life to be had in

Minnesota, making the state the destination of choice when the main refugee exodus began in the early 1990s. The US Immigration Department had a policy of distributing new arrivals evenly around the country, but the Somalis, with their long nomadic tradition of scouting out the greenest pastures, seldom stayed put in a place that didn't suit them, and a wave of secondary migration took place.*

There was no shortage of work for the newcomers, even when they didn't speak English. Many of them began their life abroad on an assembly line at companies like 3M, a manufacturing conglomerate headquartered on the edge of St Paul, or at the IBM computer plant at Rochester, 90 miles to the south. Many others did as the first wave of Somalis had done, and set up their own businesses. By 2008 there were some six hundred Somali-run businesses in operation in the Twin Cities. It seemed, on the face of it, to be a remarkably successful immigration story. Where had it gone wrong?

I caught a cab from Minneapolis airport to the Holiday Inn, a hotel I'd chosen for its proximity to Cedar-Riverside, a district where so many Somalis lived that it was known as Little Somalia. My room overlooked the Riverside Plaza, a

---

* In their excellent account of the Somali-American experience, *The Somali Diaspora: A Journey Away* (University of Minnesota Press, 2008), Doug Rutledge and Abdi Roble recount a story told to them by Mariam Mohamed, the wife of Ali Khalif Galaydh, the former prime minister of Somalia (and founder of Khatumo state). Mariam's mother-in-law came to visit them in upstate New York, where her husband was teaching at Syracuse University. One morning, she looked out of the window to find the ground covered in snow. Turning to her daughter-in-law she asked, sharply: 'So who scouted Syracuse?'

multi-coloured complex of six high-rise apartment blocks built in a 1970s brutalist style, and home to the densest concentration of Somalis in the US. The Plaza had a poor reputation among white locals, who nicknamed it Little Mogadishu, the Ghetto in the Sky or, worse, the Crack Stacks. Yet I saw nothing to fear on an exploratory stroll down Cedar Avenue. There was no change of atmosphere as I approached the Plaza, no sense that I had strayed over some invisible line. The precise boundaries of this ghetto were strangely hard to discern.

It was a warm Sunday evening and the local football team, the Minnesota Vikings, had just lost a home match to their old rivals, the Detroit Lions. Their pasty-skinned and purple-shirted fans, many of them noisily drunk, had spilled on to the pavement from a cluster of bars and restaurants where rock music blared at the junction of Cedar and Washington. Barely a hundred yards further on, a strip began that was dotted with Somali-run snack bars, hawala offices, a grocery called Afrik and a restaurant called Masha'allah. Somalis sunned themselves outside coffee shops or passed up and down the pavement, laughing into their mobile phones. It all looked and felt far more relaxed – more *Americanized* – than I had been led to expect. The proximity of the drinkers up the street apparently presented no cultural difficulty at all. Directly opposite the Plaza there was even a 'world pub' called the Nomad. Could such a city really be the West's leading exporter of Somali jihadis?

The following morning I went to the de facto parliament of the Somali community: a Starbucks, fifteen minutes' walk away at the bottom of Riverside Avenue. This was where older men came to discuss clan politics and the war back home. Their banter was often so impassioned that the staff were said to have bought a decibel meter to ensure the noise they made remained within the legal limit.[3] It was still early in the morning when I arrived, so the noise from inside was not yet ear-splitting, although it was easy to imagine how it might become so. I was later told that fifty-six of the estimated 140 clans, sub-clans and sub-sub-clans were registered as resident in the Twin Cities.[4] Several dozen middle-aged Somali men were already congregated at Starbucks, with more joining them all the time, greeting each other with hugs and jolly slaps on the back. It was the nearest thing to a Mogadishu coffee shop that one could hope to find in America.

I had come to meet Abdirizak Bihi, whose 17-year-old nephew, Burhan Hassan, was one of the al-Shabaab recruits who never came back. Burhan was not the first to vanish from Minneapolis, but he was the youngest – and it was his disappearance, in November 2008, that first awoke the Somali community to the scale of the problem in their midst.

Bihi was one of those who were convinced that the leadership of the Abubakar mosque, where Burhan had once worshipped, was complicit in the tragedy in some way. At an earlier round of Congressman King's hearings into Muslim extremism, in Washington in March 2011, he had insisted that his nephew had been 'lured, brainwashed, radicalized' in Minneapolis – and he continued to repeat the allegation in the media whenever he could. Securing an interview with him had not been difficult, therefore. Over the years he had emerged as a kind of spokesman for the local families of al-Shabaab recruits, although no one had elected him to that role, and not everyone liked or agreed with him. He was so vociferous, and some of his allegations were so outlandish, that some people thought Burhan's death had affected his sanity. But although he conceded his nephew's death had come at great cost to him personally – 'I never thought my life would go in this direction,' he told me – I found him sane enough.

He was a slight man with a sensitive face, a salt-and-pepper moustache, and natty, black-top glasses that he repeatedly pushed up on to his forehead as he spoke. I wondered privately if his campaigning was driven as much by guilt as by anger at what had happened. Did he secretly blame himself for not having been a better uncle, who might have spotted the signs of trouble and intervened before it was too late?

Burhan's story was certainly tragic. A quiet, bespectacled boy nicknamed 'Little Bashir', he was to outward appearances the most unlikely candidate for violent jihadism. He lived with his widowed mother Zienab, Abdirizak Bihi's sister, in an apartment on the nineteenth floor of a Riverside Plaza tower block. He was a diligent student at Roosevelt High School, a short bus ride away, where he earned As for the calculus and advanced chemistry courses he took. He dreamed of studying medicine at Harvard.

But one day, Burhan did not come home from school. When Zienab searched his room, she found that his clothes, laptop and passport were missing. There was also a receipt from a local travel agency for an $1,800 air ticket to Nairobi. Burhan had no job, so could not possibly have afforded this. Who had paid for it? Three days after his disappearance, Burhan phoned home to say he was in Somalia and was safe, although he kept the phone call short and refused to give any further details. But it soon became clear that he had not travelled alone from Minneapolis. The word around town was that four other young Somali men, including two promising students at the University of Minnesota, had gone with him. Burhan's family went to the police.

The week before Burhan left, five suicide car-bombers blew themselves up in a coordinated attack across northern Somalia that killed twenty-eight and injured dozens. One of the bombers, who ploughed into an office of the Puntland Intelligence Service in Bossasso, was identified as Shirwa Ahmed, 26, a graduate from Roosevelt High who had been among the first wave of Minnesotans who left for Somalia in December 2007. It was the first ever suicide bomb attack to be carried out by an American citizen. An investigation was already under way in Minneapolis because of Shirwa, but the news that a further five young Somalis had absconded from there sent the FBI into over-drive. Somali-Americans everywhere began to be stopped and questioned at airports, shopping malls, or in their homes. Former classmates of the missing boys were subpoenaed to appear before a federal grand jury. For the first time, the Minneapolis community came under national and then international media scrutiny.

At first, many of the young men in Somalia kept in touch with their friends back home. Burhan, however, rang his mother. On one occasion he told her that, while travelling on a boat to an al-Shabaab base somewhere in southern Somalia, he had been so violently sick that his glasses had flown overboard. His mother sweetly fetched his prescription and read it out to him, in the faint hope that he could find an optician to replace them.[5] Burhan was not the only one struggling in the warzone. Others complained to their friends about the heat, and the malaria. They missed things like McDonald's, and coffee. They were soft, city boys, lost in a land far harsher than they had expected it to be.[6]

In early May, Burhan rang home and asked: 'If I come back to America, will they arrest me and put me in Guantanamo?' Sensing he had had enough, his family wired money to a relative in Nairobi, who agreed to meet him at the border, take him to the US embassy and try to get him home. By now, however, Burhan was famous – and al-Shabaab, according to Bihi, had much to lose if he were allowed to return to the US. He would undoubtedly spoil their recruiting efforts abroad by telling the world how unhappy he had been in Somalia. He could also reveal names and other important details about the mechanics of transporting young men half way around the world in secret.

The precise circumstances of his death in June 2009, seven months after he left home, have never been made clear. According to one report, he was killed in Mogadishu by a random bullet. His uncle Bihi, on the other hand, was convinced that he was executed with a shot to the head when his al-Shabaab commanders learned that he intended to quit. However he died, the militants publicly described him as a 'martyr'. The news came in an anonymous call to his mother, who threw her phone against a wall in her grief. Burhan died just two weeks before he was due to try to come home.

Bihi dismissed as 'nonsense' the idea that Burhan and the

others had joined the al-Shabaab cause out of anti-Ethiopian nationalism. He said that more young Minnesota Somalis had gone back to fight after the Ethiopian withdrawal, in January 2009, than before it. Burhan and the others, he was sure, had gone to fight purely as jihadis. He was equally sure that they had absorbed the ideology necessary to do that in Minneapolis's mosques.

'Ninety per cent of the kids who have gone back to fight came from single mother homes,' he said. 'Without a father figure to guide him, Burhan was *raised* by imams. And they say they are not responsible? That's baloney.'

His feud with the Abubakar mosque was as bitter as ever. In 2009, he claimed, the imam had preached a sermon suggesting that if any of the congregation had the chance, they should run Bihi over with their car. Then Bihi alleged that Hassan Jama, the mosque's director, had personally met Burhan and the other new recruits at Nairobi airport when they first arrived from Minneapolis in 2008, and driven them to the Abubakar's sister mosque in Eastleigh, Nairobi's teeming Somali suburb, for onward transportation to the war.

This incendiary accusation was curiously detailed. If correct, it implied that the Abubakar, one of the largest mosques in the US, was a thinly veiled front for al-Shabaab – which, I almost had to remind myself, had been formally designated a Foreign Terrorist Organization by the US State Department since February 2008. Could it possibly be true?

'Everyone in Minneapolis knows the truth about Hassan Jama,' said Bihi, leaning back and pushing up his glasses. 'Ask anyone. It's an open secret in our community.'

'But if it's true, why haven't the FBI investigated?'

'Ah ... the FBI,' he said. 'They have their own reasons. And they never tell you anything.'

I went to test this assertion a few days later at the FBI's Minnesota headquarters, a striking glass and steel block on the edge of the downtown business district. Supervisory special agent E. K. Wilson was a short, sharp-faced man in a white shirt and dark tie. The previous evening, when I had told my contact on the local *Star Tribune* newspaper, Paul McEnroe, who I was going to see, he said: 'Oh my God! It's the Burnsville Flash!'

Minneapolis, I was learning, was the sort of town where everyone knew each other. Paul and E.K. had once played hockey together in and around Burnsville, a southern suburb where E.K. was brought up. The nickname was a playful tease. E.K. was a determined player, according to Paul, and quick on his feet, yet he was somehow always being flattened by the other kids who were taller and heavier than him.

E.K. and I sat across a table from each other in a windowless interview room, where he explained how he had led the charge on Operation Rhino for the last three years. He sighed when I relayed what Bihi had said about Hassan Jama and the Abubakar mosque: he had clearly heard it often before.

'There is no evidence that the Abubakar or any other mosque was responsible for the recruitment or radicalization of any of the kids,' he said carefully. 'That is not to say the recruiters didn't use the mosque – they clearly did. And there was some level of organization – but not at the level of the mosque leadership.'

'And Jama? Bihi says he is immune from prosecution because he's providing you with information on extremists.'

'Any supporter of a terror organization would be indicted whether or not they were providing us with information.'

It was plain enough that he thought Bihi's allegation was nonsense. What was interesting was the care he took to avoid saying so specifically. In fact, his responses to all my questions seemed unusually diplomatic for a law enforcement officer.

'There is always rumour in this very . . . *communicative* culture,' he said at one point. 'Rumours and allegations are constantly in motion. The challenge is to see beyond the misconceptions.'

In a sense, of course, E.K. *was* a diplomat – an envoy of America in Little Somalia – and like a regular ambassador abroad, he couldn't afford to be seen to be taking sides. When the first wave of al-Shabaab recruits left, he recalled, none of their friends or family reported what had happened to the police, for fear they would end up in Guantanamo. It had taken his team years of difficult 'outreach' work, involving dozens of public meetings in conference centres, youth forums and, eventually, mosques, to persuade the community that the FBI was not anti-Somali or anti-Muslim, but anti-terrorist. The FBI's mandate was to protect all US citizens – '*including* Somali-Americans,' E.K. emphasized – and he had worked out that the best and probably only way to do this was to win, and maintain, the trust and cooperation of all parts of the Somali community, regardless of their views. It was a delicate task and, as he acknowledged, still far from complete.

'Operation Rhino will still be going long after I'm gone,' he shrugged, philosophically.

He also frankly doubted that young American Muslims had stopped travelling back to fight.

'I think we've slowed the flow down some, but it hasn't stopped. It's likely more underground now.'

E.K. was comfortable that the FBI's response was proportionate to the reality of the terrorist threat. Although they had 'no credible information' about any al-Shabaab plot to attack America, he insisted this remained a possibility they couldn't afford to overlook.

'There are ten Minneapolis Somalis that we know about who are still fighting for al-Shabaab, an organization that has pledged allegiance to al-Qaida,' he said. 'The camp training they receive includes instruction on handling explosives. That is a threat to US interests – and it *is* illegal for a US citizen to provide material support to a terror organization.'

This last remark was a reference to the ongoing trial of two local Somali women, Amina Farah Ali and Hawo Mohamed Hassan, who were accused of fundraising for al-Shabaab. The women had participated in interstate teleconferences dedicated to the Islamist cause, as well as going door-to-door in Minneapolis while pretending to be collecting for the poor. The sums involved were not great: at the end of one teleconference, the pair had recorded pledges totalling just $2,100. For this they faced a maximum penalty of fifteen years in prison for conspiracy.[7]

At their trial, Amina, the younger woman, distinguished herself by repeatedly refusing to stand for the judge, a gesture of defiance that earned her an additional fifty days in jail for contempt of court. It was classic Somali behaviour, the sort of self-destructive obstinacy I had seen for myself in Galkacyo, where the aunt-biting teenager Kafiyo preferred to go to jail rather than apologize. I remarked to E.K. by email that such behaviour was 'hard to love, yet at the same time, impossible not to admire somehow' – a paraphrase of Gerald Hanley – but E.K. was having none of it.

'I'll save my admiration for the persistence and tenacity of other community leaders,' he shot back.

Amina and Hawo were far from the only American Somalis accused of fundraising for terrorists. The FBI had been investigating the phenomenon for more than two years, and were in the process of bringing to court twenty similar cases. The Burnsville Flash, it seemed, was as dogged on the trail of al-Shabaab as he had once been in pursuit of a suburban hockey puck.

The FBI had concluded that the al-Shabaab recruitment process in Minneapolis had no 'mastermind' but was, as E.K. put it, 'a very lateral, peer-to-peer organization' – which was another way of saying that the recruits had talked each other into it. This might have happened at the Abubakar mosque, but that did not mean the mosque was complicit. In fact, the Abubakar's leadership was closely focused these days on reaching out to young people to keep them on the right path and away from al-Shabaab. Indeed, the mosque worked so closely with the FBI that some Minnesota Somalis felt an ill-defined sense of betrayal.

Two months previously, a young Somali attending Friday prayers disagreed so vehemently with the peace-inclined sermon of a visiting scholar that he attacked the mosque director, Hassan Jama. The episode made the local papers, and had been cited by Congressman King in Washington as yet more evidence of radicalism in the Minneapolis community. The attack was defended afterwards by a website called Somali Midnimo – 'Somalis United' – which was run by Abdiwali Warsame, a student and part-time cab-driver. He was at the wheel of his cab when I interviewed him.

'Some people think I am ... controversial,' Warsame acknowledged, with a hint of pride he could not quite conceal.

Warsame's attacks on the Abubakar's leadership had become so virulent recently that he had been banned from the mosque's premises. Somali Midnimo had quite a high profile online, so it was a surprise to discover that the website had a staff of one – him – and that it didn't have a business address of any kind.

'People think I run my operation out of a big office somewhere, but actually – this is it,' he laughed, nodding at the laptop sitting on the grimy front passenger seat of his cab.

The thrust of Warsame's complaint was that the leaders of the Abubakar mosque were hypocrites. Back in 2007, he asserted, they had collectively sung a different tune, preaching against America for its backing of the Ethiopian invasion of Somalia. He said that many young Somalis, Burhan Hassan and Shirwa Ahmed among them, had been encouraged by this to return to Somalia to fight the invaders. The Minneapolis community was understandably confused now: why had the mosque leaders abandoned their previous position? This, he explained, was what the attack at the mosque two months previously had been all about.

As Warsame described what had actually happened, however, I began to see that the 'attack' on the mosque director was not so much an expression of radicalism as an outbreak of hot-tempered fisticuffs. The visiting scholar, Mohamed Idris Ahmed, had used his Friday address to urge worshippers to focus on their lives in Minneapolis, and not to be distracted by the destruction and fighting back in Somalia, which he blamed equally on the TFG and al-Shabaab. At one point he asked: 'Who destroyed Mogadishu?'

'Gaalo!' called out a young man in the crowd. 'Foreigners!'

Two other young men in the congregation murmured their agreement, but Ahmed tutted and shook his head.

'Tell me: who destroyed it?' he repeated, before answering himself: 'Somalis destroyed Mogadishu.'

The first young man was agitated by this and wanted to argue the point. But this is not done during a Friday address, any more than it is acceptable in the West to interrupt the vicar in the middle of a sermon on a Sunday. The mosque director asked the young man to pipe down and to put his question in writing, at which point the young man lost his temper and tried to punch him. The confusion was heightened when someone turned the lights out: the act of an 'accomplice', according to some reports. Amid shouts and catcalls, the trouble-makers were ejected from the building.

The significance of all this had been wildly exaggerated. Disagreeing with a visiting cleric about who was responsible for the destruction of Mogadishu was hardly evidence of jihadism, as Congressman King claimed. Nobody was hurt, apart from the mosque director who sustained a slight cut to his lip. Warsame, furthermore, was no jihadi. I told him some of the stories I had heard, about mutilations and beheadings and death threats towards foreigners, and he conceded them all.

'Shabaab ideology is all bullshit,' Warsame said. 'They are confused. It is not Islamic to kill innocent people – journalists, aid workers trying to help. Al-Shabaab say they are spies. Maybe it was justified in the nineteenth century, but not now.'

What he liked about al-Shabaab was that they had defended the homeland and successfully resisted the infidel Ethiopian invaders.

'But the Ethiopians have left Somalia now, haven't they?' I asked.

'Physically, yes. But they are still very influential in Somalia – and we are still under foreign occupation. I am against the African Union. Their foreign troops kill Somalis all the time with their rockets and shells. They should get out of our country.'

'But if they weren't there, al-Shabaab would be running the government now,' I said. 'You wouldn't want that, would you?'

'Maybe al-Shabaab are better than occupation by the African Union. The areas they control are all peaceful. Anyway . . . what's your book going to be called?'

He frowned when I told him, and fell silent, looking out at the traffic-clogged freeway with a disapproving air.

'I don't think your title is true,' he said eventually.

'Well you're not living there, are you?' I observed.

'That's true. But I could if I wanted to.'

Warsame had lived in Minneapolis for eight years, and hadn't been in Somalia since he was child. He looked at me wide-eyed when I told him I'd been in Mogadishu the previous month, and immediately asked if he could interview me for his website. He was typical of other diaspora Somalis I had met, in that his knowledge of current affairs back home was often second-hand. In Minneapolis, it was evidently so rare to come across anyone with recent experience of Mogadishu that even a gaalo's impressions had value.

He was, in the end, an armchair nationalist, whose patriotism seemed badly misplaced. His view of the homeland had been sentimentalized and distorted by time, distance and the internet; perhaps especially by the internet. I suspected he would quickly change his mind about al-Shabaab if he ever went back to Somalia and saw for himself how they operated. He reminded me, rather, of NORAID, and all those green-spectacled Irish-Americans in the 1980s who outraged British public opinion by putting money in a bucket for the IRA during St Patrick's Day parades in New York. It was highly ironic that one of the best-known IRA supporters in those days was none other than the Irish-American congressman Peter King. The self-appointed champion of homeland security had rather more in common with the likes of Hassan Warsame than he perhaps realized. I glanced again at the laptop on the passenger seat next to Warsame, and was struck by the absurdity of taking anything he said too seriously. It seemed another measure of America's paranoia that anyone did.

E.K. Wilson thought that Minneapolis's al-Shabaab volunteers had recruited each other. In order to understand what was going on in their minds at the time, therefore, it followed that all I needed to do was to ask their old school friends. The friends, however, turned out to be as mystified as everyone else.

Nimco Ahmed attended Roosevelt High with several of the volunteers. Shirwa Ahmed, the first suicide bomber, was one of her best friends.

'He was the most quiet, humble kid you could meet – clever and responsible, not troubled at all. He loved to live life to the full. I was devastated when I heard . . . I never thought he'd hurt a fly.'

Nimco was the personification of Somali diaspora success: 28, demurely beautiful, and a career Democrat party worker, whose office walls were plastered with photographs of her arm-in-arm with Barack Obama. She worked downtown at City Hall as a policy advisor to a senior councillor, Robert Lilligren, a liberal politician with a flamboyant ponytail who liked to boast that his aide had the president on speed-dial.

She took me to a coffee shop in a nearby mall where the barista – young, female, white – shyly told Nimco that she liked her headscarf. It was difficult to tell if she understood that the scarf was not, or at least not primarily, a fashion item. Nimco in any case accepted the compliment with a filmstar's grace. Once we had sat down she revealed that she had only been wearing it for a year.

'I only used to cover my head during Ramadan, but after the New York mosque affair,* I wanted to show that I'm

* The plan of the American-Egyptian imam, Feisal Abdul Rauf, to build a Sufi Community Center two blocks from Ground Zero ran into intense opposition in New York in 2010.

not afraid of letting people know that I'm Muslim ... I am very political,' she added with a smile.

She said there had been nothing Muslim at all about Shirwa's appearance when they graduated from Roosevelt High together in 2000.

'He wore cool clothes in those days: sneakers, saggy jeans, you know ... He was big into basketball. He was just a regular dude.'

They both got their first jobs out at the airport: she worked in a gift shop, he as a wheelchair pusher for NorthWest Airlines.

Sometimes he made the girls laugh, at work, by flipping up the collar of his porter's uniform and affecting a goofy swagger.[8]

'We used to leave work early on Fridays and go for a movie at the Mall of America, or eat dinner, or just hang out together,' said Nimco. 'He was fun to be around.'

For a moment I felt almost sorry for the people responsible for security in the city's public places. Shirwa went on to become the first American suicide bomber, but no amount of profiling would have picked him out back then.

Soon after graduating, though, Shirwa began to change. He started to pray regularly, five times a day, including at the Abubakar mosque. He grew a beard and wore a kufi cap. The sagging jeans were replaced by shalwar, the baggy, pyjama-like trousers worn in Pakistan and Afghanistan. Shirwa wore his shalwar short, above the ankle, the style favoured by traditionalists because, it was said, that was how the Prophet had worn them. He didn't hang out at the mall with Nimco any more. Sometimes she saw him on the street, preaching to other Somalis and encouraging them to pray. Had someone radicalized him?

'Radicalized?' said Nimco. 'The Feds are always asking that for their profiles. I still don't know what the word means.' She paused, thinking about it. 'What I would say is that Shirwa found God, and that he was in a good place. The hugs stopped; he wouldn't even shake hands with a girl any more. But he always acknowledged me when I saw him, even without my headscarf. And he never preached to me.'

Nimco was still struggling to bridge the gap between the friend she had known – including the later, Islamicized version – and the Shirwa who blew himself up in Bossasso.

'Someone must have told him some gibberish to make him do that,' she said.

But she also remarked, as Abdirizak Bihi had done, that the majority of the Minneapolis recruits had been raised without a father, an upbringing that she thought ultimately made young men more vulnerable to manipulation.

'Men have egos, so they won't go looking for help or advice when they need it. But they will respond if a mentor approaches. Girls are different.'

A 'mentor' didn't have to be someone they actually knew. Online jihadist propaganda, she was sure, had played a crucial role. The sermons of the Yemeni-American cleric Anwar Al-Awlaki were 'legendary ... And Al-Amriki – that half-Lebanese guy from Mississippi? He's clever. Everyone has seen his videos. He's one of the guys who *made* al-Shabaab.'

Abu Mansoor Al-Amriki, the nom-de-guerre of Omar Shafik Hammami – actually half-Syrian, and from Alabama, not Mississippi – had joined al-Shabaab not long before Shirwa, and had risen through the ranks to become one of the insurgency's best-known commanders. He was famous for the rap lyrics of his recruitment videos which were aimed directly at all young American Muslims, not just Somali ones.

> You can't find someone more happy than a shaheed
> He got everything but one thing he requests and pleads
> To come back and fight, and fight and be killed
> And keep coming back and getting killed if only Allah
>   willed
> But we don't need that, the youth are coming and bold
> Every martyr being replaced by a hundred fold

I was already familiar with the narrative of Shirwa's short life, from 'regular dude' to suicide bomber. Counter-terrorist experts had analysed every detail of it, hunting for the shove that pushed him down the slippery slope towards Islamic martyrdom. The clues to the tragic outcome were all discernible in the beginnings of the story. Fatherlessness was a clue. A youthful attachment to rap music, and the gang culture it celebrated, was another. Both spoke to a deep-seated crisis of identity caused by the trauma and dislocation of war.

Zuhur Ahmed, another twenty-something graduate of Roosevelt High, was a specialist in the psychology of young Somalis. For the last four years she had presented a local radio show called Somali Community Link,[9] which had emerged as one of the most important forums for the discussion of youth issues. Her recording studio was almost across the street from the Riverside Plaza.

'In Somalia, the parenting style is to rely a lot on the extended family, but that doesn't work so well in America,' she said. 'A lot of kids end up with guardians or very loose foster parents, and eventually get kicked out and, often, made homeless. There's a lot of neglect out there – a lot of depression and mental illness. I talk to them all the time on my show.'

Like Nimco, whom she knew well, Zuhur had been at school with many of the al-Shabaab recruits. One of them, Abdillahi Farah, was still fighting for al-Shabaab. She recounted how she had gone on holiday that summer to Burao, Somaliland's second city, to stay with relatives, and had been astonished to receive a Facebook message from Farah the moment she arrived.

'I was freaked,' said Zuhur. 'I was like: how did he know I was there? I didn't tell anyone I was going.'

She added, rather primly, that she had since 'defriended' him from her list of Facebook friends.

She was naturally more in touch than Nimco with the darker side of the Somali youth community, a seedy world of drugs and gangs and violent crime. In her experience, the line between joining a street gang and signing up with al-Shabaab was a fine one: a conclusion that the rap-recruiter Al-Amriki had obviously drawn too.

'They're just street boys who want to belong some-where,' she said. 'Of course al-Shabaab looks attractive to some of them.'

This was also almost exactly what Abid Raja, the SO15 officer, had told me in London.

Zuhur had the facts to back her theory. In October 2007, she had interviewed Zakaria Maruf who, in the 1990s, had dropped out of college to become a founding member of a Somali gang called the Hot Boyz. But then he found God, repented, became a shelf-stacker at Walmart and, eventually, a youth leader at the Abubakar mosque. Like Shirwa Ahmed, he was often seen in the streets around Riverside Plaza, preaching to other young Somalis, offering himself as an example of redemption. Zuhur still had a recording of Maruf describing the neglect he once suffered at home, and how Allah had saved him from sin and a life of crime. Two months after this interview he vanished, along with Shirwa: part of the first wave of al-Shabaab recruits from the city. He later became notorious for his attempts to persuade others to join him in the jihad by telephone from Kismayo. He particularly targeted young Somalis who prayed at the Abubakar, many of whom he used to drive to weekly football practice. He was reported killed in July 2009.

Zuhur had watched Minneapolis's gang culture mutate over the years. At Roosevelt High in the 1990s, she explained, the prevailing culture was 'African-American: all saggy pants and "wassup" slang'. The Somali boys tried to copy them, but the African-Americans couldn't stand that, and there was constant fighting. The first Somali gangs such as Maruf's Hot Boyz were, she said, formed for self-protection against the African-Americans. Like other street gangs, the early Somali groups were often involved in petty crime and drug-dealing. By 2006, however, some of them had developed into serious and often violent criminal enterprises. Indeed, Zuhur had set up her radio show in response to the FBI's busting of a thirty-strong Somali sex-trafficking ring. Girls as young as thirteen were being abducted from mosques and schools, and sold to Somali men in Columbus, Ohio and as far away as Nashville, Tennessee.

'This was something very shocking for us . . . it was such a very un-Somali thing to do,' Zuhur said.

Street gangs were obviously as central to the Somali story in the Twin Cities as they were in London, a critical part of the radicalization jigsaw. And so a few days later I was pleased when I met Abdulkadir Sharif, who had been a gang leader for twelve years. Fortunately for me, no doubt, he had turned his back on street crime when he found God in 2007. These days he helped out at the Islamic Da'wah Center in St Paul, sandwiched between a Cash-'n'-Pawn shop and an auto-repair business on one of the city's main arterial routes. I found him marshalling traffic in the mosque parking lot which, it being a Friday, was filling fast with cars full of Somalis come to attend the Jumu'ah prayer service.

'Zakaria Maruf? Yeah, I remember Zak,' he rasped, when I asked. 'He was a pussy, man.'

Sharif's nickname was Chino, on account of his high cheekbones and narrow eyes. His Damascene moment had come when he was stabbed in the neck during a street fight and almost killed. The damage to his voice box meant that he would for ever speak in a hoarse whisper.

'If I'd known he was planning to go and fight for al-Shabaab, I'd have tried to stop him. Those guys are just so lost . . . What Shabaab are doing? That ain't Islam.'

I had been directed to Chino by the imam at the center, Sheikh Hassan Mohamud, who liked to hold him up as proof of the redemptive power of Islam. He was an exceptionally tall man of thirty-two, who moved about the car park with a rolling, loose-limbed swagger. There was a raw, barely suppressed energy about him, like a coiled spring. His hands moved ceaselessly as he described his former life.

'I was a top dog,' he said. 'The Feds couldn't catch me. No one could stop me. Only God did that – know what I'm saying?'

He pushed back the hood of his anorak, revealing a grubby kufi cap, and tilted his head, inviting me to look more closely at the scar that curved around the side of his neck to his throat.

'Give me some skin!' he said suddenly.

I gave him some skin; and he grinned at me with his mouth full of bad Somali teeth.

'You from London,' he said. 'They have gangs in London?'

'Sure.'

'An' they got guns, or knives?'

'Mainly knives, I think.'

'Yeah that's what I heard!' he said, flicking his fingers in delight. 'Here, we got guns. I got me a rack of them: Uzi, M-16, AK, nine mil – everything. You come to my place, I could show you. I keep them in a special closet.'

'You've still got them?' I said, confused. 'Don't you think you should . . . hand them in or something?'

'Um, yeah . . . I have been meaning to.'

Chino looked around contemptuously as a pair of police cruisers howled past on University Avenue. His rehabilitation suddenly seemed an uncertain thing. This ex-gangster top dog reminded me of a rescue greyhound my family once owned, a graceful but mercurial animal that we never quite managed to house-train. Years of unknowable abuse had damaged the puppy's psyche so deeply that the risk of recidivism in the adult had become permanent.

I had been in the Twin Cities interviewing Somalis for a week now, long enough that I recognized one or two of them as they arrived for the Friday service. I said hello to Omar Jamal, in his trademark tweed fishing hat. He had two small children in tow, with hair combed and braided, their clothes clean and pressed for mosque. Jamal was, incongruously, the First Secretary of the Somali Mission to the United Nations. I nodded, too, at Mohammed Hassan, a planning official at Hennepin County Council, who held the interesting theory that it was not just the youth in exile but the Somali nation as a whole that was suffering an identity crisis. Traditional Somali culture, he had observed to me, was steadily being subsumed by an Arab one. It was a source of private regret to him that his father had named him Mohammed rather than giving him a traditional Somali name, like Warsame or Diblawe or Roble, as he was sure he would have been in his grandfather's time.

'At least Mohammed is a Muslim name,' he said. 'A lot of Somali girls these days are named after Saudi pop stars like Aseel or Waed, names that have nothing at all to do with our culture.'

Chino had certainly split with Somali tradition. Zuhur had described how some of her contemporaries tried to copy the black street gangs. Chino had gone a step further and actually joined one of them. He was originally from Beledweyne in central Somalia. His father had sent him and one of his sisters to America in 1996, when Chino was seventeen; his mother, he said, was dead. The Immigration Department settled him and his sister, unusually, in North Dakota, but the two fell out, and he left soon afterwards for the bright lights of Minneapolis, where he lived on the street. One night he was attacked by an African-American gang known as the Vice Lords.* Chino fought back with a tenacity that so impressed its leader, 'Mr Rico', that he was recruited on the spot.

'By 1997 I was one of their gunmen,' he said, miming a pistol with his hands. 'I went to war for them in Chicago: bam! Bam!'

What I had at first taken as a blemish on Chino's cheek was, I now saw, a teardrop tattoo: an indication, in America, that the wearer has killed someone, although it can also be a sign of mourning for a slain gang comrade. I doubted whether one teardrop was enough in Chino's case. He was quite open about killing people, something he claimed to have first done not for Mr Rico, but back in Beledweyne when he was just fourteen. He told his story with startling brevity.

'This clan militia broke into our house and raped my two sisters, right in front of me. I knew who they were. So I borrowed a gun from a soldier in the market and killed all five of them. I killed one a day for, like, a week.'

By 1998 in Minneapolis, this boy killer had set up his own Somali-dominated faction known as the Conservative Vice Lords. He rolled up a sleeve to prove it: 'CVL', in large

* This was the local franchise of a US-wide African-American gang network, originally called the Almighty Vice Lord Nation, that was established in Chicago as long ago as the 1950s.

medieval script, was tattooed all down the length of one arm. What began as a neighbourhood cocaine- and heroin-dealing operation quickly grew into a business with Colombian and Mexican connections in New York. As it expanded, it split into half a dozen sub-gangs with names like the Riverside Rs and Murda Squad. But Chino remained the boss of all of them, feared by everyone and known as Lord Chino.

'I'm not a god. God's above me,' he explained, his face hard and serious again, 'but I am a leader of people.'

The gangs were organized like an army: every member was given a rank. He had private doctors and nurses on his books – 'I ain't never been to hospital in my life,' he said and even, he claimed, three policemen, to whom he slipped $10,000 a month.

'I was rich, man. I had a Mercedes, a BMW. I made $200,000 a month, easy. I once made $50,000 in one day.'

He said he didn't miss the money because he served God these days, not Mammon; although not, apparently, to the point where he wished to be martyred for his faith. He said he had no wish ever to go back to Somalia. If he did, he thought, he would certainly be hunted down by the vengeful relatives of the Beledweyne rapists he had killed. The threat of this, he said, was one of the reasons he had to leave Somalia in the first place.

I wondered how much of Chino's story was really true. What he said happened in Beledweyne seemed almost too vivid to be real, like the blood-thirstiest scenes from a Quentin Tarantino movie. A little later, in a small office off the Da'wah Center prayer hall, I repeated what Chino had told me to the man responsible for keeping him on the path of righteousness: the orange-bearded imam, Sheikh Hassan Mohamud.

'Yes, well . . . A lot of bad things happened during the civil war,' was all he would say about Chino's childhood.

The Da'wah Center served both as a mosque for the general public and as a religious school for around 150 college and high school students, to whom he offered classes on how to be a good Muslim in America. From the way that members of his flock kept popping in to ask his advice or simply to kiss his hand hello, it was obvious that Sheikh Hassan was a dedicated and popular leader of his community. He was a trained lawyer who went by the nickname Jaamici ('the Educated'): an articulate, cerebral conservative, and the kind of man who tended to speak his mind. In the past he had apparently argued that suicide bombing was justified (albeit only in Palestine). He had also spoken in a fundraising video of 'the hell of living in America', and had publicly defended the right of Somali taxi-drivers to refuse to accept passengers carrying alcohol or dogs.[10] These views had made him something of a target for the right-wing media, where he had been identified by some as a potentially dangerous radicalizing influence, so he was wary of me to begin with, insisting that our interview be recorded. But he relaxed soon enough; and when he was called away to officiate at the Jumu'ah, he invited me to come back afterwards for a further chat. I found him clever, honest and thoughtful, and ended up spending much of the day there.

As an imam, he saw himself as a kind of social lightning conductor.

'I absorb a lot of anger in the community, and try to

neutralize it through engagement and debate,' he said. 'I sit on the police advisory board. I do whatever I can to reduce violence in the Twin Cities.'

But he was also a political operator, evidently still deeply involved in the affairs of his homeland. He blamed the social anger he had to deal with in Minneapolis squarely on US policy in Somalia, especially Washington's decision to back the Ethiopian invasion of 2006.

'Mogadishu has been destroyed as a result. Thousands have been killed, two million people displaced, yet no government has yet mentioned human rights violations . . . the young are angry at the silence of the world.'

He had little time for the 'untrustworthy' TFG, or for the African Union troops who supported them. The Ethiopians might have left physically, but their influence was still felt in Mogadishu: 'No president or prime minister can be appointed without Ethiopian approval.'

The answer, he thought, was fresh elections. He described himself as 'democratic by nature', and was convinced that genuinely 'free and fair' new elections would produce a moderate Islamic government with a constitution based on Sharia law. Such a regime, he insisted, would pose no security threat to the West.

'Al-Shabaab would never be elected now. The vast majority of Somalis are moderate by nature,' he said.

The problem, in his view, was America's inability to see that a preference for Sharia and support for al-Shabaab were entirely different things. He cited a recent debate on Universal TV, which he said showed 95 per cent support among Somalis for a constitution based on Sharia.

'The Constitution of Medina and the UN Charter are

80 per cent the same document. But how do I explain to the US that Sharia is workable? I want to form a bridge between the two worlds I live in, but I can't!'*

The news that morning had been dominated by a sensational development in Yemen: the killing, by an American drone-launched missile, of the famous al-Qaida ideologue (and US citizen), Anwar Al-Awlaki. Sheikh Jaamici, however, had been too busy that morning to listen to the news, and his eyes widened when I asked what he thought about it. He was genuinely shocked.

'Well,' he said eventually. 'I think – and I don't care if you *are* recording this – I think that is very sad. Many Muslims here love Awlaki. His scholarship was extraordinary. Ask anyone. Haqim, have you heard this news?'

His portly young assistant, who had appeared in the doorway, affirmed that he had. I had spoken to Haqim earlier and learned that he had been a student in Birmingham, that he still had a sister living in Chingford in east London, and that his favourite food in the world was fish and chips.

'And what do you think of Awlaki?' said Jaamici.

'He recorded the *best* series of talks on the life of the Prophet,' said Haqim.

'You see?' Jaamici said. 'This is a big loss to America. Awlaki was misunderstood. He was never the problem: it is like shooting the messenger! And killing him will do no

---

* The Constitution of Medina, drawn up by the Prophet Mohammed in 622, was the basis of the future Caliphate and effectively founded the first Islamic state. Like the UN Charter, ratified in 1945, the Medina Constitution was specifically intended 'to save succeeding generations from the scourge of war'.

good. It will only create more anger and more radicalism. You will see.'

He had to break off then, to lead the Jumu'ah in the carpeted prayer hall across from his office. The shoe rack by the entrance was already overflowing. In the corridor I swam upstream against an incoming tide of worshippers, a couple of hundred of them at least, and went out to the parking lot to talk to Chino again. By the time Jaamici and I resumed our conversation, the corridor was empty once more apart from the warm smell of breath and old socks.

'I had to say something about Awlaki,' he confided as soon as we sat down. 'Two people came up to me just now, and said, "We are so angry about this" . . . As their imam, I had to give a statement. I told them that his killing won't help. You are not Fox News – but they would *turn* this!'

The gap between his world and Washington's had just yawned wider. Obama had been on television all morning, explaining how Awlaki had taken the lead in 'planning and directing efforts to murder innocent Americans' and boasting that his death was 'another significant milestone in the broader effort to defeat al-Qaida and its affiliates'. Sheikh Jaamici, by contrast, thought Awlaki 'one of the most moderate imams in the world . . . Based on his teachings, I don't think he's even al-Qaida.' Awlaki, he pointed out, had unequivocally condemned the attacks of 9/11 soon after they happened.* The Yemeni-American's eloquence and

---

* In an interview with Brian Handwerk and Zain Habboo for National Geographic News, 28 September 2001, he said: 'There is no way that the people who [attacked the Twin Towers] could be Muslim, and if they claim to be Muslim, then they have perverted their religion.'

ability to reach out to young Muslims via the internet, Jaamici implied, could and should have been Washington's most powerful weapon against radicalism. It was tragic that instead, in the intervening decade, Alawki had turned into America's *Public Enemy No. 1.*

Jaamici returned to his theme that American foreign policy was responsible.

'The US targets those who are angry with them, but it never stops to try to find out *why* they are angry.'

What was desperately needed, he thought, was more civil and less military engagement, or as he put it, 'more debate, fewer drones'. US strategy, disastrously, was under the control of military 'extremists' who were unwilling, or unable, to countenance an alternative approach.

'Obama may be in office, but Bush is still in power. America is still cowboy country! But there *are* moderate imams in Somalia. There are even relative moderates within al-Shabaab.'

The US had failed to recognize that al-Shabaab's decision to embrace al-Qaida and its goals had not been taken unanimously. Obama had instead lumped the moderates and hardliners together, the Robows with the Godanes, and seemed intent on expanding his drone war rather than exploring paths towards reconciliation.* If Obama didn't reverse that strategy, Jaamici added, then Somalia risked 'turning into another Pakistan'.

---

* The first US drone strike in Somalia came in June 2011 near Kismayo. The target was thought to have been the al-Shabaab leader Ibrahim al-Afghani, although his death was still unconfirmed at the time of writing.

He was unequivocal in his message that al-Shabaab's interpretation of Sharia was wrong, and had even led a demonstration against the movement in Minneapolis in 2009, footage of which was still viewable on YouTube.

'Al-Shabaab do not like me,' he said.

And yet his condemnation of the movement was not total.

'The fact is that al-Shabaab's areas *are* more peaceful than the government areas. They are more organized, and corruption is never reported there. This must be put into the balance.'

His brother, he said, had chosen to return to live in al-Shabaab-controlled Elesha Biyaha, just west of Mogadishu, because he felt his family were safer there than in the capital. Jaamici compared the situation to Kabul in 1996 when the Taliban, despite the harsh social restrictions they imposed, were welcomed because of the security they brought to the streets. To a populace as tired of violence and lawlessness as the Afghans then were, security counted more than anything – and peace was just as much a priority now for Somalis.

Jaamici knew how ambivalent he sounded. His voice was lower, telling me things I was sure he would never say to Fox News.

'I still send $50 each month to my brother in Elesha. I send it the same way everyone else does – by Amaana, one of the hawala money transfer companies. But Amaana are taxed by al-Shabaab. Such taxes form a big part of their income. It means that, technically, the US could accuse me of providing material support to a terrorist organization. But what am I to do? There is no other way to send money, and I cannot let my brother starve.'*

It was, to say the least, not easy being a Somali in America, where the lead weight of suspicion had dropped over them all. Their case wasn't helped by a national public awareness campaign launched in 2011 by the Department of Homeland Security called 'If you see something, say something'. At Minneapolis's privately owned Mall of America – the largest shopping mall in the US and, as the Twin Towers once were, a conspicuous symbol of the country's economic might – security guards had responded to the DHS campaign with frightening zeal. According to the guards' own 'suspicious activity reports', hundreds of customers had been confronted for the tiniest aberrations in what they considered 'normal' behaviour.

One man was stopped – and detained, and questioned in the basement for two hours – because he 'wasn't holding his video camera "like a typical tourist would do"'. Another customer was accosted by a guard who thought he was looking at him 'oddly' and walking 'nervously'. He turned out to be an insurance company manager looking for a SpongeBob SquarePants watch for his son.

No Somali was immune from suspicion in so fevered an

---

* In December 2011, the US government briefly outlawed money transfers to Somalia under anti-terrorism legislation, but later lifted the ban following lobbying by aid agencies. 'Through remittances, American Somalis provide a lifeline to hundreds of thousands of people,' said Daniel Wordsworth, president of the American Refugee Committee. 'With famine and drought already impacting families throughout Somalia, the cessation of bank transfers [would] be devastating on a national scale.'[11]

atmosphere, where racial profiling had become the norm. Minnesota Public Radio, who broke the Mall of America story, found that nearly two-thirds of the shoppers stopped were 'people of color', in a state that was 85 per cent white. And yet the mall's management felt little need to apologize.

'Unfortunately the world has changed,' said Maureen Bausch, the mall's vice president. 'We assume you'd want your family and friends to be safe if they are in the building. And we simply noticed something that we didn't think was right.'[12]

Every Somali I spoke to had their story. Sheikh Jaamici recalled how a group of imams had once been arrested at a gas station simply for praying; they had earlier been attending a counter-terrorism conference in Minneapolis dedicated to improving community relations. Laura Yuen, a Minnesota Public Radio reporter, told me how a Somali policeman, Mohamed Abdullahi – 'one of only two Somali beat cops in the whole state' – was once detained for two hours at the airport where he was repeatedly asked if he was a Muslim. Yuen added that the affront to his badge hurt him so much that he cried. Nimco Ahmed told me that she too had been detained recently as she returned through the airport from Nairobi. Not only was she well known locally: this was a woman who sat on the DHS advisory panel that actually initiated the 'If you see something, say something' campaign.

'The security guards knew exactly who I was.' Nimco shrugged. 'Sometimes the US is a very weird place.'

Nimco was phlegmatic about Somalis' place in American society, but the despondency of Yousef Firin, a 31-year-old limo driver with a boyish face and a tufty beard who plied his trade outside the Holiday Inn, struck me as rather more typical of the mood in Minneapolis. Yousef's family had escaped Mogadishu in 1992 when he was eight. They settled in Washington, but moved to Minneapolis in 2001 on the recommendation of friends: a classic example of secondary migration. Minnesota had been very kind to them: 'Like a love affair,' he said, although the love affair was over now. The recession meant that many Somalis could no longer find work. He knew of several families who, like the nomads they were, had recently packed up and left in search of pastures new. Minnesotans, he feared, were out of patience with their Somali guests. The 'missing kids' story had damaged the state's reputation, and Somali-related gang crime was perceived to have made the city unsafe.

He told me the sorry story of Ali Omar, the teenage nephew of a close friend, who the previous month had been stabbed to death in a fight in north-east Minneapolis. Yousef had had to identify the body at the coroner's office, an experience from which he had yet to recover.

'I told him, two weeks before he was killed, that he should do something with his life, get off the streets, maybe join the army, or he'd get into trouble – and look what happened. I had to bury the poor kid. It was really sad.'

The police's unwillingness to investigate the murder was, he claimed, all too typical these days.

'He was in a flat with three other Somalis when he was killed. Everyone in the community knows who did it, but the police just say they have no suspect. Their attitude is, "If you're killing each other and you can't sort it out yourselves, why should we get involved?" People just don't want to know any more.'

Reading the comment thread beneath an online news story about the murder later on, it was hard to disagree.[13]

'It's not good old Nordeast anymore down there,' wrote one contributor. 'Drive near Central and Lowry just about any time of the day. It is sad to see.'

'Fightin over that last crack hit at 2am,' wrote another.

'Cut me another big ol' piece of that diversity pie!!!!' remarked a third.

Minnesota, it seemed, was beginning to regret its reputation for charity. For all the community work done by the imams, a significant number of Somali youth still felt lost and alienated in their adopted country, and they were angrier than ever. Despite three years of painstaking investigation, the FBI, by their own admission, had failed to dismantle the underground railway that led young Somalis into terrorism.

In October 2011, a month after I left America, another young Somali-American blew himself up in Somalia. He was the third suicide bomber from the Twin Cities since Shirwa Ahmed in October 2008. Abdisalam Ali, 22, had gone missing from his home in north-east Minneapolis the previous month. He had lived in America since he was a baby, and had become a promising student at Thomas Edison High School (motto: 'Belong, Believe, Become') where he had lifted weights and sold shoes out of his locker in order to support his family. His friends called him Bullethead.[14]

At least ten people died during his attack on an AU outpost in Mogadishu. Shortly before the operation, Bullethead

– or his al-Shabaab handlers – uploaded a recorded message that once again urged Somalis in exile to take up the jihadist cause, a message that sounded all the more persuasive for being unscripted.

'My brothers and sisters, do jihad in America, do jihad in Canada, do jihad in England, anywhere in Europe,' he said. 'It is not important that you, you know, you become a doctor or you become, you know, uh, some sort of engineer. We have to believe in Allah and die as Muslims ... Brainstorm, don't just sit around and, you know, be a couch potato and you know, you know, just like, you know, just chill all day, you know. It doesn't, it doesn't, it will not benefit you, it will not benefit yourself, or the Muslims.'

In the Twin Cities, the long war against Islamic extremism was not about to end any time soon.

14

'Clanism is a disease like AIDS'

London, February 2012

The FBI's remit to protect America from terrorism is mainly a domestic one, but that does not stop the Bureau from keeping a close eye on London, a city with a Somali community that is bigger, more diffuse, more complex, and therefore much more difficult to engage with than any of the communities living in the US. One of the most obvious differences from the Somali viewpoint is that in the UK it is still legal to chew qat. Around the world, the leaves are consumed by an estimated 10 million people every day.[1] Qat is illegal in the US, however; and in January 2012, when even the Dutch voted to ban it, Britain became the last country in the Western world where it is still permitted.

This anomaly troubles the FBI, which sees a link between qat, organized crime and terrorism. In April 2012, seven people in London, Coventry and Cardiff were arrested following a tip-off from the Americans, who suspected they were involved in smuggling qat to the US and Canada in order to raise money for al-Shabaab. The news followed a startling claim by CNN that Britain's qat-chewing dens had become an al-Shabaab recruiting ground.

'Young [qat users] become vulnerable, not clearly think-ing, and the paranoia kicks in and that's when they start to hate the British public – especially the police,' said Abubakr Awale, a British-Somali anti-qat campaigner. 'They are thinking everybody is out to get them, and that's exactly the kind of individual that the likes of al-Shabaab are targeting.'[2]

I needed to know more about qat, a drug that I had never got around to trying despite its centrality to Somali culture. To plug this shameful gap in my knowledge, I went back to Southall. The location of my chosen chewing den, or *marfish*, was hard to beat for atmosphere: a grubby room overlooking the station, above an industrial unit that housed a freight-forwarding business specializing in imports from East Africa. The adventure began the moment I stepped off my train, when a cry of 'Stop, thief!' went up and a hooded figure was seen to jump down from the platform and run doggedly away across the railway lines, stumbling in the track ballast. The victim, a Japanese student whose iPhone had been pickpocketed, tried to give chase, but gave up as an Intercity train came blasting through with its two-tone horn blaring, only narrowly missing the pickpocket, who quickly vanished through a hole in a fence. Southall was fifteen minutes but a world away from central London. Even the welcome sign above the ticket office was written in the Punjabi Gurmukhi script.

The marfish was in the middle of a row of brick

buildings to the end of which was affixed a giant Conservative Party billboard, a leftover from the 2010 election campaign, displaying a bearded and blue-turbaned Sikh, Gurcharan Singh, with David Cameron's face floating ethereally over his right shoulder. The accompanying slogan, VOTE FOR CHANGE, sounded a hollow note now. When polling day came, the constituents of Ealing, Southall had voted exactly as they had done at every election since World War Two, for Labour. It was doubtful, however, whether a change of party here would have made any difference so far as qat was concerned. Parliament first debated whether or not to ban the drug in 1996, but had always decided against. The argument for inaction seldom varied. Evidence of harm resulting from qat use was judged 'insufficient to merit its control'; its use in any case was confined to a minority community from East Africa; the issue was therefore 'culturally sensitive', and best left alone.[3]

It is true that the habit is ingrained in the culture of East Africa, where qat has been consumed in one form or another for hundreds if not thousands of years. Richard Burton reported that it produced in the locals 'a manner of dreamy enjoyment, which, exaggerated by time and distance, may have given rise to that splendid myth the Lotos, and the Lotophagi'. These lotus-eaters, he went on, were 'like opium-eaters, they cannot live without the excitement . . . It is held by the ulema here as in Arabia, "Akl el Salikin", or the Food of the Pious, and literati remark that it has the singular properties of enlivening the imagination, clearing the ideas, cheering the heart, diminishing sleep, and taking the place of food.'[4]

In 2012, qat was more popular than ever among Somalis,

between 60 and 75 per cent of whom are thought to be users or sellers of the drug. Because qat cultivation requires more water than is available in most of Somalia, the majority of it is imported from Kenya, with smaller amounts arriving from Ethiopia and Yemen. The Kenyan qat trade alone is said to be worth $250 million a year.[5] Somalia is hooked – although not yet as badly as Yemen, where an estimated 90 per cent of men are regular chewers. The habit certainly isn't doing them any good. Some 40 per cent of Yemen's scant water resources are used in the irrigation of up to half a billion qat plants, prompting experts to warn that Sana'a, Yemen's ancient capital, could literally run out of water by 2017, the first major city to suffer such a fate in modern times.[6] Yemen offers a terrible illustration of what can happen if the chewing habit is left unchecked, and yet the government in London has so far shown little appetite for controlling it in Britain. In 2011, an astonishing ten tonnes of qat was permitted to pass through Heathrow from Nairobi every week.[7]

There was no sign showing the way to the marfish above the Southall industrial unit: you had to know it was there. On the other hand, there was nothing to prevent anyone from walking in off the street and up the dark staircase to the entrance, a blue swing door with a smudged glass panel covered with peeling stickers, one of which read DON'T DO DRUGS: *Curiosity Will Kill U*. I pushed on inside. The room resembled a working man's social club, with utilitarian strip-lighting and plastic chairs and round Formica tables scattered about on a cheap wood laminate floor. It was none too clean and smelled faintly of wet football socks. A small bar area with a fridge stood in one corner. A television opposite relayed the latest BBC news from the Middle East, although no one seemed to be watching. At the far end was a fire escape that doubled as the smoking area, which overlooked the train tracks along which the pickpocket had run away.

There were a dozen or so Somalis present, all men, all middle-aged, some sitting alone in silence, others locked in noisy conversation, and one man laughing like a hyena. None of them seemed to object to the presence among them of a gaalo. The man behind the counter merely giggled when I explained what I was there for.

'It's three pounds with a Coke,' he said, nodding for me to help myself from a small, damp crate on the counter next to him. 'You want a bag?'

The crate contained perhaps twenty-five tightly bound bunches of qat, twenty stems to a bunch. Their bushy fronds were wilting slightly, and their reddish-green stalks resembled loops of electrical flex. I made a selection and watched as the qat-seller searched on the shelf behind him with slow and fumbling hands. It was obvious from his glassy eyes and his rictus grin that he was very stoned indeed.

'Sorry,' he said, as he at last produced one of the thin blue bags that I had seen snagged everywhere on the desert thorns of Somalia, and put my purchase into it. 'I really need to go home and sleep. It's been a long night.'

It was eleven o'clock in the morning, although it seemed best to let that pass. The bar, I now saw, doubled as the main switchboard for a minicab service of, I suspected, questionable reliability. The qat-seller had been chewing to keep himself awake through the nightshift. He explained that he had been about to go home some time ago, when a new consignment of qat arrived – fresh in from Nairobi, he said – and he had stayed behind to test the wares, and that one thing had led to another. But the main thing was that he could vouch for the consignment's freshness. He said a full crate contained about a hundred pounds' worth of leaves, and that this marfish got through four to five such crates every day.

I copied the others and settled down to chew. There seemed little technique to it. I picked off the tenderest leaves one by one in the manner of a snacking gorilla, and mulched them into a ball in one cheek until the juices trickled down my throat. I soon discovered what the Coke was for because the taste was appalling: sharp and astringent. Some of the customers had drilled a small hole through the plastic cap of the Coke bottle to regulate their sips and to keep in the fizz, a modern take on the traditional cold water sipped from a smoked gourd.

When a stalk was stripped of leaves I did as the others did and tossed it on the floor, which was already strewn with discarded foliage, for there was no bin in the room. And then I selected another stalk and began the gorilla thing again, wondering if I should spit or swallow the slimy green bolus in my cheek.

'Your first time chewing, huh?' said a kindly customer at the counter who had seen my dilemma. 'Mm. The first time can be . . . difficult. But it's OK to swallow.'

He turned out to be a bus driver on the suburban 105 route, Greenford down to Heathrow. He said he was an ex-driver, but that he 'could work again whenever he wanted to', a remark that caused the smiley-stupid barman, who showed no sign of going home yet, to laugh out loud. I deduced that the driver was really just skiving off work. He said he was from Hargeisa originally, like most of the other customers present. That, he explained, was the way it worked in the London marfishes: their clienteles tended to break down along clan lines.

'And why do you chew qat?' I asked.

'It passes the time,' he replied.

That attribute explained why a good supply of qat was considered an essential rather than a luxury by the pirate kidnappers along the Indian Ocean coast, whose tedious job it was to guard docile foreigners for months or years while their ransoms were being negotiated. The author Jay Bahadur described how pirate qat-chewing sessions often lasted for 24 hours or more, because the drug took away any need to break off to eat or to sleep. Time lost meaning for the dedicated qat-chewer in the same way that it did for the addicted gambler. The Southall marfish reminded me of Las Vegas's casinos where there were never any clocks on the walls or even windows to remind their patrons that it was high time they stopped.

I had no wish to fall into such a temporal black hole; and after about half an hour, by when I had consumed most of my bag without any noticeable effect, I made my excuses and headed back out to the sunlight. Burton wrote that Europeans 'perceived but little effect' from qat, an observation that I took for an example of the lazy genetic racism of his imperial times when I read it. Now I began to wonder if he had been right. My disappointment was brief, however, because back at the station while waiting for the return train to London, my teeth started to grind, one leg began to jiggle, and I felt an unmistakable euphoric glow. I suddenly had so much energy that it seemed a shame, a crime even, to remain sitting down. I did not doubt that I could easily have walked the eight miles back to Paddington; possibly on my hands. It was an unlikely place, but Platform 4 at Southall station was where I finally got the point of qat.

I could also see why many Somali community leaders wanted it banned. Qat's defenders tended to argue that it was a harmless social activity on a par with drinking a pot of strong coffee, an argument that I now understood could only work with those who had never tried it themselves.

'Those people in the marfish? Most of them haven't got a life,' said Sharmarke Yusuf, the chairman of the Association of Mosques and Islamic Centres.

Because chewing was traditionally a man's habit, many of qat's most vociferous critics were women, who complained that it made their husbands spend time and money in the marfish rather than at home with their families, and that it also killed their will to work. After what I had just observed, I was sure they had a point. Furthermore, everyone from Jane, the state-school teacher in south-east London, to Hanif Qadir in Waltham Forest, asserted that qat was a major contributor to the specific Somali problem of paternal absenteeism. How many of the customers in the marfish I visited were the fathers of wayward teenage sons?

The damage qat caused to family life was difficult to prove, and naturally hotly disputed by many Somali men. Yet the serious medical harm that overconsumption could cause was not in doubt. In Hargeisa I had been accosted in the street by a ranting, shoeless madman with cud like puréed spinach dribbling from one corner of his mouth, his breath reeking of silage, his pupils as big as chocolate buttons. Mania and psychosis were classic signs of qat abuse, while even moderate long-term use was associated with depression, aggression, irritability, paranoia, insomnia, lethargy, heart problems, tremors, impotence and mouth cancer, not to mention the risk of teeth being stained permanently green.

Cathinone, qat's active ingredient, was a naturally occurring substance that was nevertheless classified as a 'Schedule 1' drug under the UN Convention on Psychotropic Substances, the same classification as LSD and Ecstasy. In its chemical structure it was closely related to the once-fashionable Western designer drug mephedrone, also known as miaow-miaow, which was linked to so many deaths in the UK in 2010 that the government introduced emergency legislation outlawing it. My Ealing friend Ayaan – who thought qat-chewing 'absolutely revolting', and the government's failure to ban it a disgrace – said the miaow-miaow ban proved that parliament could move quickly against drugs when it wanted to. For all the soothing talk that qat was a benign socializing drug, I very much doubted it would be so popular if it didn't have cathinone in it. The chemical was highly unstable, with a tendency to break down and lose potency as the leaves dried out. This was why qat was flown into London from Nairobi four times every week. If you wanted to get high, the leaves had to be fresh.

Ayaan was convinced that the government would regret it if they did not ban qat soon, because the argument that the habit was confined to middle-aged Somali men, and therefore not worth legislating over, was no longer true.

'I've seen school kids in uniform aged fourteen, fifteen, white ones, black ones, Indian ones, chewing qat on the way to school,' she said. 'An English guy asked me just the other day where he could buy qat. I misunderstood him. I thought he wanted to buy a cat.'

She reckoned the habit was increasingly popular with Somali women, too, although they didn't frequent the marfishes but tended to chew at home, in secret. Ayaan knew of an Ealing woman who chewed when she was pregnant, and gave birth to an underweight baby as a result. She knew of another, a childhood friend, who had progressed from qat to crack cocaine, an almost unprecedented development among Somali women.

'The long-term use of qat leads to mental illness, no question,' she said. 'It's just as bad as cocaine for that.'

She wasn't alone in worrying about its effect on the young. Paul Birch, the SO15 officer, recalled how as a policeman on the street in Wood Green in north London, he would occasionally come across a car-load of young Somali men 'looking hard and nasty with these blazing red eyes from the qat – and there wasn't a damn thing we could do about it'.

In January 2012 the Conservative MP Mark Lancaster, the sponsor of the latest parliamentary debate on qat, pointed out that no fewer than three Conservative shadow cabinet ministers had pledged to ban the drug while in opposition, and expressed his frustration that, a year and a half after election victory, no government action had been taken beyond the commissioning of a fresh review by the Advisory Council on the Misuse of Drugs.

'Kicking this issue into the long grass with further

"monitoring" is simply unacceptable,' said Lancaster. 'After years of talk on qat, if my Government wish to retain the trust of the East African community, the time has come to follow the rest of the Western world and act.'[8]

His opinion was echoed by the UK ambassador in Nairobi, Matt Baugh, who described qat as a 'festering' social issue in Britain. Officialdom's inertia, Baugh thought, was 'symptomatic that we've kind of forgotten' about Somalia and its problems: an example of the old policy of containment rather than the new one of engagement that the government was supposed to be pursuing.

Ayaan put it more forthrightly. 'Of course it should be illegal,' she said, 'but why would the government give a toss?'

It was perhaps fortunate that, despite the experiment-ation of a minority, the great majority of young diaspora Somalis felt as Ayaan did, and had rejected qat without the encouragement of officialdom. Chewing was a pastime associated with their parents' generation, not theirs, most of whom had grown up in the West, and thus had little or no nostalgia for the old café culture of Somalia. I thought it significant that none of the customers in the marfish in Southall was under thirty. But there was another and more important reason why many young London Somalis con-sidered marfishes uncool. As the route 105 bus driver had explained, the chewing dens were patronized according to clan affiliation. They thus perpetuated in exile the political system that had pushed Somalia into civil war. I later heard of a stretch of road in Kentish Town in north London where there were five marfishes in a row, one for each of Somalia's main ethnic groups. It was a street version of the

4.5 clan power-sharing formula espoused by the TFG in Mogadishu – and as I was still discovering, there were a great many young diaspora Somalis who had nothing but scorn for that.

'I think clanism is a disease, like AIDS,' said Ayaan. 'I hate it. When people ask me what clan I'm from I never tell them, ever. It makes some of the older Somalis really mad, but I just laugh at them.'

Her attitude was not unusual among London Somalis. She was in fact one of a new breed that was determined to challenge tradition and break with the disastrous prejudices of the past, the first and worst of which, she believed, was clanism. I had a lot of sympathy for this view. Not long previously I had received another heart-breaking email from Aden Ibrahim in Mogadishu, who against the odds had found a job at last, but was now about to lose it again in the cruellest way.

> I think our contact became a low on these months, because I am busy in a job working in 9 hours in a day and an internet café is not near to my residence in the night going a far away from the village is danger.
>
> I was really happy having this job but now things are changing, I have to train a person who will take my job in 30 days time and that will left me a jobless!!!!
>
> The one that I am teaching a job his uncle belongs to the company which I work for, Tribalism is common problem across the country!

Perhaps the purest expression of Ayaan's impatience with clanism – or tribalism – was an organization of which she wholeheartedly approved called the Anti-Tribalism Movement. From its base in Acton, west London, the ATM had accrued more than 67,000 online members since its launch in 2010, the great majority of them between the ages of sixteen and thirty. I went to meet the ATM's director, Adam Matan, in a hotel café near Paddington station.

He was a 25-year-old business management graduate from Roehampton University who had gone on to work as a 'community engagement officer' for Hounslow Council.

'We are not against the tribes, which are an important part of who and what we are,' he said, 'but we are against tribalism, a system that fragments and diminishes us.'

The ATM's supporters were by no means all from the diaspora. Some 27,000 people had signed up from within Somalia itself, including nearly 4,000 in Galkacyo.

'Why?' said Matan. 'Because Galkacyo is the *home* of tribalism . . . The Darod and the Hawiye who live there think of each other as animals.'

The movement's 'three visions', according to Matan, were the eradication of tribalism, the unification of Somali hearts and minds, and the promotion and preparation of the future leaders of the country. Some supporters of the ATM, which described itself as a 'revolutionary youth-led non-profit social reform movement', hoped it might even herald an Arab Spring for Somalia.

As Matan well knew, he was not the first Somali to attempt to abolish the clan mindset. Others had tried and failed in the past. The country's first political party, the Somali Youth Club, was founded in 1943 by thirteen activists who refused on principle to reveal their clan lineage. Siad Barre also identified tribalism as the greatest obstacle to scientific socialist progress. In 1970 he held a huge public rally at which a Guy Fawkes-style effigy of *qabyalad*, tribalism, was symbolically burned and buried. The regime's official maxim became *maxaa taqaan* rather than *ayaa taqaan* – it was not 'who you knew' but 'what you knew' that mattered.[9] Siad Barre's prescription for Somalia failed, but that did not mean it was wrong. The problem was that he refused to swallow his own medicine. Even in his first cabinet, appointed in 1969, half of the fourteen ministers were from the dictator's own Darod Marehan clan; bias and this only grew more pronounced as his rule progressed.

Tribalism and the violence it engendered, Matan argued, were not natural to Somalia but were a foreign construct of the nineteenth century, 'an aid to colonial control'. He explained that at the Berlin Conference of 1884 the imperial powers, having carved up Somalia between them on a map, agreed to keep order in their respective dominions by creating enmities between clans that had previously co-existed in peace.

'Somalis are the classic victims of divide and rule,' he said.

The Green Line in Galkacyo was the direct legacy of this manipulation. So was the ongoing border dispute between Puntland and Somaliland. Matan explained that he himself came from an aristocratic Darod Dolbahante family who had once followed the Mad Mullah, and that every one of his great-grandparents had been killed at Taleh in 1920.

'I used to believe that it was the British with their aircraft who had killed them, but no: it was co-opted tribesmen, armed by the British, who followed on. They were responsible for the massacre.'

On a recent visit to Mogadishu – his first time back in Somalia since he had left as a child – Matan was briefly detained and questioned for taking photographs at the airport by jittery South African SKE security men, an experience that explicitly reminded him of the famous foundation myth of the Dervishes, the arrest of the Sayyid in Berbera in 1895.

'I thought to myself: "I'm Somali: how dare you stop me at my own airport?"'

He had gone to Mogadishu to deliver a consignment of food aid raised through the ATM for famine victims in the city, enough to feed 220 families for three months. At one distribution point, however, his team was surrounded by forty gunmen who demanded dollars and a substantial chunk of the aid consignment, and who underlined their claim by firing their weapons into the air. Matan had not previously appreciated that the graft in Mogadishu could be so crude.

'It was horrible, shocking, what I witnessed,' he said.

The gunmen answered to Yusuf Mohamed Siad, a notorious former Islamist warlord known as Inda-Ade ('White Eyes'), who had briefly served as Minister of Defence in the TFG, although he had resigned over a year previously to start up his own faction. What Matan found most amazing was that Inda-Ade's men, who were really no more than onshore pirates, were nevertheless still dressed in government army uniforms.

Matan, unsurprisingly, had no more time for the 4.5 clan formula than Ayaan did – 'I can't understand it. How can anyone be half a person?' he joked – while noting, with sudden earnestness, that the TFG's rules were at present scandalously unfair towards the young.

'There is a rule at the moment that an MP must be married, must be well known in their constituency, and that they must be over thirty-five. That rule must not remain in the constitution.'

He had written to the TFG urging this and several other constitutional changes, notably for a solid commitment to the principle of One Man, One Vote, although lobbying in this way was only a small part of the ATM's programme.

Matan was planning to send over 150 diaspora Somalis, all Western-trained, local authority officials like him, to work as unpaid interns in the home country's various administrations, in order to 'teach them how to operate, and to show them how corruption is killing Somalia'.

The ATM wanted to send doctors to Mogadishu, and was organizing further famine relief. They had already begun work on a 'Building of Hope' on the Green Line in Galkacyo, and were seeking funds from DfID, UNDP, Somali business leaders, local London councils, and the National Lottery to establish a national 'Peace Day' across Somalia, an event that would be organized by a 'liberty leader' appointed in each of the country's eighteen regions, and which would coincide with a series of 'reconciliation sessions' around the diaspora.

'When that day comes, we will show the older generation that it is our time now,' he said.

Some of Matan's ideas, such as a plan to set up an 'alternative youth parliament' in Mogadishu, sounded impossibly ambitious, particularly to older Somalis who remembered the failure of past attempts to eradicate tribalism. But the ATM could not easily be dismissed as naive, because both the American and the British governments took such diaspora youth organizations seriously. There was a belated but growing realization among politicians as well as Western counter-terrorism officials that it was essential to engage with the younger generation, because it was from them that the threat to Western security principally emanated. This was why, in the run-up to the London Conference on Somalia in February 2012, a major international event attended by senior representatives of forty governments and organizations, Matan was included in a group of diaspora representatives invited to Downing Street for a consultation with the prime minister.

The ATM was not the only pioneering, cross-clan Somali-British youth organization. Andy Pring, a coordinator on the government's Prevent counter-radicalization programme, knew of at least seven comparable groups in London alone, including the one that he was most closely involved with, the south-London-based Elays Network (slogan: 'Youth empowering their peers for a safer today and a better tomorrow'). I went to meet Pring and a dozen or so young Somalis at the Network's Battersea Park Road headquarters, a long, thin room on the ground floor of a high-rise block on the enormous Doddington housing estate, in an area of London infamous for muggings and drug-related crime. A Somali, 20-year-old Mahad Mohammed, had been knifed to death on the nearby Winstanley Estate in July 2010.

Pring, who had spent time in Quetta and the West Bank, spoke 'rusty' Arabic, and had once briefly considered converting to Islam, explained that Elays did not tackle radicalism directly. It was more about building the self-esteem of young Somalis through sport and other activities, particularly film-making, that took them off the streets and away from crime; although, as the Pakistani London MP Sadiq Khan had remarked to him recently, the progression from there to radicalism was 'the path well trodden'. *Elays* meant 'light' in the sense of a lighthouse, a beacon to guide travellers on the right path.

The organization was unusual in that it was almost entirely youth-led: another good example of young diaspora Somalis who were willing and had learned to help themselves. There was only one Somali adult involved, a quietly spoken volunteer 'project manager' called Mohamed Ali, who thought the risk of radicalization had been badly hyped by the media.

'I promise you, the last thing on any of these kids' minds when they come in here is religion,' he said.

Nevertheless, he ran an evening Koran class that had proved popular with the Network members.

'Somali Londoners are trying to mix cultures, and there are a lot of crazies out there. We do need to teach kids the real meaning of the Koran, and to correct any wrong impressions they may have about, for instance, the concept of jihad. And I do teach them that Islam doesn't endorse suicide bombing. But most of all, the Koran is a life guide . . . if you get to the student young enough, it prevents social problems later.'

In the manner of Ayaan or Adam Matan or the Somali Youth Club of the 1940s, he never allowed any discussion of the clans in his classes.

For a small local youth organization, Elays had support in some surprisingly high places. The Battersea Somalis were the darlings of the US embassy, which had encouraged them to set up a public relations campaign under the banner 'That's not our Jihad'. Two of their number had travelled to Washington recently to help set up a State Department-funded counter-radicalism website. A larger group, including Andy Pring, had just been asked to the US ambassador's annual Eid celebration garden party at Winfield House, his official residence in Regent's Park. And in 2011 when Elays launched a film – a drama called *Pentagon*, about the racial stereotypes faced by five London Somali brothers – an embassy press attaché was sent down to Battersea to teach them how to write a press release. The Americans' overt engagement with London Somali youth was the polar opposite of the softly-softly approach through local partnerships advocated by SO15. Elays, however, didn't seem to mind being associated with the US embassy one bit.

Their unlikely relationship dated from 2008 when Quintan Wiktorowicz, a former professor of international studies at Rhodes College in Memphis, Tennessee, spent several months attached to the London embassy, studying British Islamism and its link to terrorism. He went on to join the White House National Security Council where he was put in charge of the US version of Prevent. Wiktorowicz, who interviewed hundreds of young London Muslims (and who concluded, not uncontroversially, that it was the most religious among them who were the least likely to end up being radicalized), had apparently singled out the Elays Network as one of the best counter-radicalization youth projects in London. To the US, it seemed, the doctrine of 'early intervention' meant countering radicalism by whatever means and wherever possible, including abroad if that lessened the chance of terrorism reaching America's shores. It was hard to imagine the British embassy in Washington taking this level of interest in a Somali youth organization in Ohio or Minnesota.

The diaspora experience was a double-edged sword. It could lead Somali youth into a crisis of isolation and despair, and from there towards drugs, criminal gangs, extremism and terrorism. But other young Somalis had understood and exploited what the West had to offer, and emerged from their often difficult childhoods as rounded, educated, employable citizens who had forged a new kind of identity for themselves. The money they earned and remitted back home dwarfed the sums that the international community was able to muster, and was responsible for small miracles of post-war reconstruction and famine relief. They had learned the technical expertise and taken on board the liberal Western values that their broken country needed if it was ever to be fixed – and a great many of them were impressively, movingly, prepared to go back and apply the lessons they had learned. In fact, the further into the Somali diaspora I travelled, the more certain I became that the salvation of their homeland rested in the hands of the young.

Mohamed 'Tarzan' Nur, the Mayor of Mogadishu and a one-time Labour candidate for Camden Council, whom I had met under fire at the Villa Somalia in Mogadishu, was regularly portrayed in the British press as a model returnee: brave, selfless, determined to use his skills to help rebuild his country. Early one summer evening I went to meet Shamis, Tarzan's wife, and three of their six, twenty-something children, at the family's council flat on an estate near Queen's Crescent in Kentish Town, and found them to be no less convincing examples of the new diaspora breed. Shamis was a kindly, effusive woman who fed me hot samosas, cheesecake and raspberry juice, and whose mothering instinct was so strong that before the evening was out she had declared that I was like another son to her.

'I hate the tribes,' she said. 'I never taught my kids their lineage. Somalis are just Somalis.'

'The 4.5 formula is just a child's mentality,' added her 25-year-old daughter, another Ayaan, squashed up on the sofa next to her. 'Of course ministers should be appointed on merit, not according to clan.'

The flat was small but tidy, with plush leather furniture, gold tassels on the curtains and an Islamic homily in Arabic hanging on one wall, although what the visitor was supposed to notice were the framed photographs of the Nur children, each of them wearing a gown and mortarboard on the day that they graduated. In Mogadishu I had spotted a public information poster with the caption 'Our best chance for happiness is education', a slogan that might have been coined in the Siad Barre era. It was a principle that the Nur family had evidently taken to heart. Shamis had worked as a teacher in London for fourteen years. She was also a former community link worker for Sure Start, the government programme dedicated to improving children's early education.

Her faith in the power of schooling was, perhaps, characteristic of the Somalis. When Gerald Hanley visited

Mogadishu in 1962, he found the newly independent populace gripped by a 'madness about education', a passion for learning so strong that the captain of the barge that took him ashore complained that 'they would eat a book if you gave it to them, some of the young men nowadays'. Hanley observed: 'There cannot be anywhere in Africa with such ready and hungry people, with such swift minds, waiting to read their way out of a thousand years of dependence on the camel, and the spears that had ensured its possession ... When the education factories start work among them they should surprise Africa, and themselves.'[10]

The education factories, however, were destroyed by the civil war; it was partly in order to find new ones for their children that the Nurs had moved to Britain in the early 1990s. And now Ayaan had a degree in criminology from Middlesex University and was hoping for a job with the police. Abdullah, 21, the youngest, was studying digital media studies at London Metropolitan. His older sister Mona had a post-graduate qualification in sexual health and was working at the Whittington Hospital in Islington. A third sister, Maryan, was hoping for a university internship in New York.

The family had moved to London so long ago that the younger children had little or no memory of their native country, and considered themselves almost more British than Somali. Both Ayaan and Abdullah spoke fluent estuarine English, their accents coarse and glottal.

'My Somali is terrible,' Ayaan confessed. 'Some of the newer arrivals can't believe it when they hear me.'

At the same time, the children were close followers of what was happening back in Mogadishu and intensely proud of what their father was doing there, although concerned for his safety.

'Dheere is out of prison now,' said Ayaan. 'We're worried what he might do to Dad in revenge.'*

Shamis, although not her children, had been back to Mogadishu briefly in 2010 to visit her husband, and found it deeply dispiriting.

'Everything is so ugly there now, and nothing works. We were once the cleanest country in Africa, but now even the shower water is salty.'

She made an interesting, if sweeping, observation about the difference between her 'old' generation and the younger one.

'The old Somalis are mostly good people, but you can't trust the new ones. They are too traumatized. They have seen so much killing and blood . . . I couldn't sleep when I went back to Mogadishu, but those people don't notice the gunfire any more.'

It was clear that she was not the only one who thought the Somalis left behind had been almost literally dehumanized by exposure to so much violence.

'When Mohamed became mayor, my Somali neighbours here said, "Ask him to come back! Those people will hunt him like an animal!"'

Later in the evening she began to describe how Mogadishu had been when she was young. She remembered listening to James Brown records, watching the latest Fellini films at the cinema, and reading magazines with names like *Photo-Romanca*.

* For an explanation, see Chapter 5, pages 113–14.

'We were a developing country then. We could have been like South Africa. But everything went backwards because of the war.'

Shamis produced a photograph of her and Tarzan taken in 1980 which made her children hoot with laughter. Tarzan wore the platform shoes and flares of the high disco period; Shamis was wearing a miniskirt and long, pretty earrings beneath an immense Afro hairdo, in striking contrast to the abaya and scarf that now enveloped her.

'I never wore a scarf before 1989,' she said. 'Hardly anyone in Mogadishu did.'

I asked what she thought had prompted that sartorial revolution and she shrugged, as though she had never given it much thought.

'We were still Muslims inside when we wore miniskirts, but it wasn't a big thing,' she said. 'It was the war that turned us religious. Maybe the war was our punishment for being bad Muslims.'

The family all hated qat. Nur senior, indeed, had organized a local campaign against it, following a savage murder in a Kentish Town marfish one Saturday night in 2003. A 33-year-old supermarket shelf stacker, Hassan Abdullahi, had been watching *Match of the Day* with some friends when another Somali, Abdi Aziz Warsame, thirty-one, attacked and killed him with an eight-inch kitchen knife.

'There were a dozen other people in the marfish,' Abdullah added, 'but they were all too stoned to do anything.'

Warsame claimed, bizarrely, that he had killed Abdullahi in self-defence. At his trial, though, he also admitted to feelings of paranoia, which no Somali doubted had been caused by anything other than too much qat.[11]

The Nur children had grown up in a rough neighbour-hood. The nearby Queen's Crescent was once so notorious for gang violence that it was nicknamed 'the Murder Mile'. The district's drug dealers delineated their territories by tying a pair of sneakers together and slinging them over one of the telegraph wires that crisscrossed the streets. There were several local Somali gangs with names like the Money Squad, the African Nation Crew and the Centrics. They fought the black and Asian gangs for supremacy, and also rival Somali gangs from Tottenham, sometimes with fatal results.

'The Somalis got the upper hand in Queen's Crescent cos they're more men'al,' said Abdullah. 'They don't give me any trouble. I knew a lot of them at school. They were the ones who were always smoking weed, skipping classes.'

'You would be under more pressure if you mixed with Somalis more,' said his mother.

'It's worse in Toron'o,' Abdullah shrugged. 'There are some guns here but not like over there. A friend of mine got shot there.'

It was simply good parenting, and the ethos of achievement and self-improvement that the grown-ups had instilled in the family, that had kept Abdullah on the right path and away from the gangs. Islam played a role, although not an overbearing one. When I asked Abdullah when he'd last been to mosque he said on Friday – which drew a sarcastic 'Yeah, right' from Ayaan, followed by a disapproving cluck from their mother, and then an angry look from Abdullah at his sister for betraying him. It was clear enough that he was more interested in nightclubbing than attending Friday prayers. He said that he had attended a traditional Sufi mosque in Tottenham, once, but he found their mysticism too much to take and he hadn't been back.

'It was all music and drums and stuff,' he said. 'I got quite scared.'

By strange coincidence, the teenaged Abdullah had been passing through King's Cross tube station on 7 July 2005 when Germaine Lindsay detonated his bomb that killed twenty-six people.

'I had my iPod plugs in but I still heard the bang. Then I saw smoke and I started running.'

There seemed little danger of him being radicalized.

His sister Ayaan's religious stance was more enigmatic. On the one hand she had no time for extremism, either in Britain or in Somalia.

'Some Somalis do go back to fight for al-Shabaab, but their star is waning. People talk about them all the time on Universal TV. It's madness what they are doing. Proper explicit!'

On the other hand, it emerged that she had only recently begun to wear an abaya like her mother. She also kept her head tightly covered throughout our interview. Her conservatism was not quite as it appeared, however.

'I put an abaya on during Ramadan last year and I've been wearing one ever since,' she said. 'I like wearing it. It's comfortable and easy to wear.'

One of the advantages of a scarf, she admitted, was that it allowed her to go out when her hair was in a mess. The nose-stud she wore also suggested that her abaya was at least partly to do with fashion. She said she would never wear a full veil, as did her genuinely conservative sister-in-law, whom she disparaged as 'a ninja'. And yet she understood that the headscarf was a 'badge of Islam', and had thought through the implications of wearing one of those. In this she was very like Nimco Ahmed in Minneapolis, who at some quite deep level also wanted people to know she was a Muslim. Both women understood that the traditional outward appearance of their religion had been stolen by the extremists, and were quietly intent on reclaiming it for themselves. Shamis, backtracking on what she had said earlier about the headscarf, recalled how some young Somali women in Mogadishu in the 1980s had covered their heads as an act of rebellion against Siad Barre and his aggressively secular scientific socialism.

'Wearing a scarf is like being an ambassador for Islam,' Ayaan added. 'You can't choose your destiny, but maybe you can choose your identity.'

Taken together, the Nur family presented an impressive riposte to those who claimed that multiculturalism in Britain wasn't working. They were not the Islamist ghetto dwellers of popular imagination but almost model citizens of the world: ambitious, forward- and outward-looking young people who would undoubtedly end up as net contributors to the society that had taken them in as refugees.

'I don't even have any Somali friends,' said Abdullah. 'My mates are Bosnian, Bengali, Turkish, English.'

If multiculturalism meant knowing how to adapt to a new host environment – an essential part of nomadism, after all – then these Somalis were naturals.

This was not to say the family always found it easy. The children had been brought up to feel gratitude towards a state that had given them housing and benefit and education, but now, according to Abdullah, the London Somali community was 'confused . . . people *are* very grateful, but they are feeling a bit persecuted these days. They can't understand why the system is starting to turn against them.'

This was not paranoia. Shamis explained how in 2008, her eldest son, Mohamed, a youth worker for the Kentish Town Somali Welfare Association – a body that his father had in fact set up through the local community organization – had been so badly harassed by MI5 that he complained to his MP about it, and eventually went to the newspapers with his story. Shamis was able to produce the relevant cutting from the *Independent*. 'Exclusive,' I read. 'How MI5 blackmails British Muslims.'[12]

Mohamed, now twenty-nine, had been eight years old when he came to Britain, and had always been more religiously inclined than his siblings. In 2003, aged twenty, he went to Egypt for a while to study Islam and Arabic.

'He never smoked or did anything wrong when he was young,' Shamis said. 'He wore a beard and he always went to mosque.'

One morning at 6 a.m. in August 2008, Mohamed opened the door of his Camden flat to a postman carrying a red Royal Mail bag. He turned out to be an MI5 agent in disguise, who accused him, first, of being an Islamic extremist. When Mohamed denied this, the agent revealed the true purpose of his approach, which was to coerce him into working for British intelligence.

'The agent said, "Mohamed, if you do not work for us we will tell any foreign country you try to travel to that you are a suspected terrorist."'

MI5 were obviously desperate to infiltrate the Kentish Town community organization, for they approached five other Somali workers there in much the same heavy-breathing way. None of the six complied.

Shamis still felt genuinely hurt by what had happened to Mohamed, as well as baffled that anyone could think that any of *her* children could become a terrorist.

'This country has been like a mother to us,' she said. 'I love this country, I don't have another. And my kids don't know any other home. Why would they burn their own house?'

It was a fair question. According to Shamis, MI5 had even briefly taken away Mohamed Jnr's mobile phone and iPod. It was a stupid as well as a shabby way to treat an immigrant Muslim family as blameless as the Nurs, and if it was as typical as Abdullah claimed, it was no wonder if London's Somalis felt 'a bit confused'.

The previous November, David Cameron had described Somalia as 'a failed state that directly threatens British interests', citing the radicalization of young Somali Britons, attacks on British tourists, and the impunity with which the pirates apparently continued to operate.[13] Among the victims he had in mind were the retired yachting couple from Tunbridge Wells, Paul and Rachel Chandler, who were released alive in November 2010 after hundreds of thousands of pounds of ransom money had been paid, 388 days after their yacht, the *Lynn Rival*, was boarded off the Seychelles.

Perhaps the most extraordinary aspect of the Chandlers' long ordeal was that the public campaign to rescue them was led not by the British government, or even by the

British, but principally by London Somalis appalled at the way the couple had been treated by their countrymen. According to the SO15 officer Paul Birch, mainstream Britain tended to look on Somalis as part of the 'feral underclass' that the justice secretary, Kenneth Clarke, identified as being responsible for the 2011 summer riots, a characterization that Birch thought profoundly unfair. He had recently attended a Somali famine relief rally in Regent's Park, where he had seen for himself how astonishingly public-spirited the Somali community could be: 'Not feral at all,' as he put it.

The Chandler campaign's rallying point was an earnest music video called *Sii Daaya Lamaanaha* – 'Release the Couple' – a performance of which was recorded by Universal TV and became a modest hit on YouTube.[14] With exquisite irony, the performance and its recording were organized by Tarzan Nur's Kentish Town Somali Welfare Association, a part of the very body that MI5 once considered such a threat to British security that they had tried to infiltrate it.

'We started that campaign!' said Ayaan Nur. 'The video galvanized Somali public opinion. There was a lot of shame here about the way that old couple were treated. They weren't rich, and they hadn't done anyone any harm.'

Somali donations to the Save the Chandlers fighting fund reportedly reached £150,000, some of which may have been used to pay the pirates' ransom. This was in marked contrast to the British government which, in line with long-established ransom policy, contributed nothing.

The Chandlers' release was negotiated on the ground by Dahir Kadiye, 56, a former minicab driver from Leyton in east London, who was born in the noted pirate town of Adado and belonged to the same Hawiye Saleban sub-clan as the pirates. His involvement was said to have begun when his 17-year-old son, Yussuf, saw television footage of the Chandlers in captivity and urged his father to do something about it. Kadiye then spent nine months shuttling back and forth to Adado urging the Saleban elders to pressurize the pirates to negotiate a deal.

The whole story seemed an example of the diaspora operating at its very best, and turned the usual media narrative about Muslim immigrants dramatically on its head. When the Chandlers were released, even the *Sun* – a newspaper that had long positioned itself as a bulwark against what it called Britain's immigrant 'tidal wave' – took Kadiye to its heart, describing him as 'a brave ex-London cabbie' who had heroically saved the Chandlers from the 'blood-thirsty pirates'.[15] Britain's collective imagination was so gripped by this stirring triumph of good over evil that Kadiye was taken on to the books of Max Clifford, the celebrity publicist. Hollywood was also rumoured to be interested.

And yet Kadiye seemed unlikely filmstar material, as I found out when I went to meet him in his Leyton council flat. He was, in the first place, not nearly as anglicized as the 'London cabbie' description suggested, but a Somali of the old school, who spoke English poorly for someone who had lived here for twenty years. He entertained me with tea and cakes in the formal style of his homeland while his wife, unequivocally veiled, hovered dutifully in the background. At one point he broke off our conversation to scold her for not serving me properly. I was reminded of an old

Somali saying: *Caado la gooyaa car alle ayey leedahay* ('the abandonment of tradition calls forth the wrath of Allah').[16] I was unsurprised to discover that he had never heard of Adam Matan's Anti-Tribalism Movement.

Neither Kadiye nor his role in the release of the Chandlers was quite as reported. The morality of his tale was not black and white as Hollywood and the tabloids liked it, but an ambivalent shade of grey. Although it was true that he had driven a minicab when he first arrived in London in 1991, and indeed had risen to become a director of a company called Delta Chauffeurs in the Euston Road, Kadiye was more of a wheeler-dealing entrepreneur than a cabbie. He had small-time, family business connections all over Somalia, with interests in the import and export of everything from construction materials to bananas, fish and livestock. He had in any case cashed in his shares in Delta Chauffeurs by 2009, and used the money to set up the Somali branch of Tacforce International, a Dubai-based private security firm that specialized in hostage crisis management. In early 2009, well before the Chandlers' kidnap, Kadiye had visited Adado, Harardheere and Hobyo to carry out what he called a 'field assessment' of the piracy problem. Whatever else it might have been, therefore, helping the Chandlers was also a savvy business move, an opportunity cannily grasped to advertise Tacforce's services while gaining a foothold in a lucrative but notoriously crowded market sector.

'In my heart I am a businessman,' he told me. 'My dream for the future is for TIS [Tacforce International Somalia] to launch and to operate and to make a profit.'

It was never entirely clear how much ransom money was

eventually paid out (although Kadiye said that it totalled $400,000), or, precisely, to whom. Nor was it certain where all the money came from. According to one report – hotly denied by Kadiye – 'a rich Somali woman living in the Persian Gulf' had contributed $100,000 to the final ransom pot to ensure that the deal went through.[17]

I asked the Chandlers by telephone in early 2012 – by when they had published a book about their experience and were back in Southampton, preparing for another world cruise on the *Lynn Rival* – but not even they were sure.

None of this meant that Kadiye was insincere about helping the Chandlers. On the contrary, he explained with convincing passion how the couple's kidnap was 'to the shame of *all* Somalis; it was maybe the only thing we have all agreed on since 1991'. The British Somali role in the Chandlers' release had put his community in the best possible light, and he was proud of that, as well as pleased that it had given others something to be proud about.

'My goal is to help people, and to create a bridge between my two communities,' he said.

He had approached Waltham Forest Council to help him to go on a lecture tour, although the council, to his disappointment, had declined.

'The lack of communication: that is our greatest problem,' he said. 'My right hand is Somali but my left hand is British. I have to find a bridge . . . There are so many in the Somali community who want to do good, but they don't have the access.'

His campaign against the pirates was certainly well pitched. Armed with Universal TV footage of demonstrations and the music video from north London, Kadiye spent much of 2010 crisscrossing central Somalia where he met with 'maybe 80 per cent' of the Saleban's clan elders, to whom he argued that releasing the Chandlers was more than just a moral duty – it was also an obligation according to *magan*,* a pillar of the traditional, pre-Islamic nomadic honour code.

'If you walk from Galkacyo to Mogadishu, nomads will feed and shelter you. But the tradition is that you must return the favour whenever you can . . . I explained to the elders that 300,000 Somalis had been given food and shelter in Britain, and that this was paid for by British taxpayers like the Chandlers. I made them see that we owed them.'

The same point had been made in the lyrics of the music video from Camden:

> Our people fled their homes
> The host countries did not look at the colour of our skins
> We need to show our debt to them,
> For it is the donkey who does not acknowledge the debt

Appealing to the Saleban elders' sense of clan honour was not the only line of Kadiye's attack.

'I tried every argument in the book,' he said. 'I told them that if they pressurized the pirates, they would benefit directly through an increase in foreign aid – although they have not seen any benefit yet.'

There was one argument that he did not try, however,

---

* *Magan* is similar to the Afghan Pashtun custom of *nanawatai*, the obligation to grant sanctuary to anyone who asks for it, even an enemy; and is closely related to the Bedouin tradition of offering hospitality to travellers known as *diyafa*.

and that was old-fashioned moral censure. He was, in truth, in no position to condemn the kidnappers on those grounds, because as the Saleban clan elders well knew, some of Kadiye's own extended family were in the piracy business too – a detail that might have caused the *Sun* to report his story rather differently had they known of it. And yet Kadiye himself was disconcertingly open about it. He explained how a cousin, a respected elder who lived in Hobyo, had six sons. This family, he said, were relatively well-to-do, with a flock of a hundred sheep and goats, although none of the sons had ever worked as a herdsman. The two eldest sons were in fact dead: killed in clan fighting after joining the local militia. Of the remaining four, two had gone to sea to try their luck as pirates, where the youngest two would soon be joining them. The family had been forced into piracy, Kadiye argued, by simple economics.

'A five-year-old sheep is worth $48: enough money to feed the family for three weeks. But there is no market for the sheep, because the nearest port is 600 kilometres away at Bossasso – and there is no possibility of reaching Bossasso because of clan problems. The family could kill and eat the sheep, which would feed them for 24 hours, but if they did that the herd would be gone in three months, and the family would be destitute. Now, my cousin says to me: "If one of my sons goes to sea, and survives, we get a million dollars, and no one ever has to be a pirate again" . . . Tell me, what else can they do?'

'Have they tried fishing?' I suggested. But Kadiye, increasingly agitated, shook his head.

'If a boy does that he ends up being stopped by your navy

and put in jail. And they have no boats, no freezers, no training, no healthcare. Meanwhile the West spends $2 billion a year on anti-piracy patrols . . . It's crazy! We *have* to make a better life for these people. Sometimes it makes me cry.'

I looked up to find that Kadiye's face had crumpled and that he was, indeed, sniffing back tears.

'I'm sorry,' he said when he had regained his composure, 'but my people are dying very easily.'

Dahir Kadiye's story in some ways epitomized Somalia's tragedy. I thought he was essentially a good man, not a bad or callous one, who knew that piracy was cruel and wrong. And yet he refused entirely to condemn it, because in his eyes the crime could be justified by the imperative of survival. The complexity of this moral conundrum was enough to make anyone cry.

The paradox was that he understood very well what lay at the root of Somalia's troubles: the unending clan violence that had killed his cousin's two eldest sons and prevented the rest from trading or travelling, thus forcing the family into piracy and robbing them all of the chance of a decent life. Clanism had almost destroyed Somalia and was ultimately responsible for the death and displacement of millions of his countrymen, including Kadiye himself. And yet, even after twenty years in Britain, he was unable – or stubbornly unwilling – to consider any alternative.

In Kadiye's view, it was not clanism that was to blame for Somalia's troubles but that amorphous entity 'the West' for failing to intervene as they should have done. The West was also culpable for the misbehaviour of the diaspora young, because they had failed to understand the importance of the

parental discipline inherent to a traditional Somali upbringing. He typified an older, conservative kind of Somali
whose faith in the old ways of doing things was
unshakeable.

'We Somalis had our own culture when we arrived here
in London in 1991,' he said, 'but the West forced us to
follow their culture, and it was too strong for us. Fathers
have lost control of their sons because they are not allowed
to beat or shout at them. The government has to stand
shoulder-to-shoulder with the parents, otherwise the
Somalis will become the worst people in the world!'

In the spring of 2012 I had begun to prepare for another
trip to East Africa, where the battle for the soul of Somali
youth had entered a dangerous new phase. Although the
war appeared to be over in Mogadishu, al-Shabaab's
campaign of terror there decidedly was not. The conventional fighting, meanwhile, had shifted away as the
insurgents retreated on their stronghold, the far southern
port of Kismayo. And it was to the troubled south that I was
hoping to go, for it was here that the future of Islamism in
East Africa would surely be decided.

'Al-Shabaab?' said Kadiye when I mentioned this. 'They
are not proper Muslims. I think some of them are
Christians, even . . . It's just business for the leadership. I
know some of them. My wife is Marehan, the same as al-
Shabaab's Commanding Officer in Kismayo. In fact, I
called Kismayo last night.'

For some Somalis, it seemed, the bonds of clan would
never truly be broken, even by an ideology as dangerous as
al-Shabaab's.

15

Operation Linda Nchi:
The end for al-Shabaab?

Besançon to Nairobi, March–June 2012

The civil war had scattered Somalis to some unlikely places around the world, although few were stranger than where Mohamed Mohamed Abdi had ended up. For almost thirty years this former Minister of Defence, who at sixty-three was still a senior MP in the Mogadishu parliament, had lived in the suburbs of Besançon, the capital of Franche-Compté, a sub-Alpine region of eastern France world-renowned for its cheese.

It was early March 2012, and snow was piled high on either side of the road from Geneva airport. The two-hour drive to Besançon was skiddy and mountainous, and I wondered briefly if the effort was worth it. Mohamed Abdi was interesting, though, for he was no ordinary Somali politician in exile. A holder of PhDs in geology and anthropology, and the author of eight books that dealt with such subjects as the importance of phallic symbolism in the Horn of Africa's prehistoric stelae, he was universally known as

Gandhi because, as he liked to explain, he was 'against violence'.

A year previously, Professor Gandhi had announced the establishment of a large new semi-autonomous region in Somalia, with himself as its president. This federal statelet, he said, would comprise the three southern provinces abutting Kenya: Gedo and Lower and Middle Juba, an area inhabited by 1.3 million people. His project did not look likely to succeed at first, for these areas were still firmly under the control of al-Shabaab in 2011. Many Somalis rolled their eyes at what they perceived as Gandhi's over-weening ambition. This was the tenth region to declare semi-autonomy in the last seven years. But Gandhi was supported from the outset by Kenya, who liked the idea of a stable buffer state along their lawless and porous eastern border; and in October 2011, when Kenyan troops suddenly invaded Somalia in an operation codenamed Linda Nchi ('Protect the Country' in Swahili), everything changed for Gandhi.

I was greeted at the door of his house by his wife Christine, a former industrial chemist from northern France. The couple had met at Besançon University, where she was studying and he had been sent on a scholarship by the Somali Ministry of Education. They eventually married and settled where their relationship started, and now had three student-age children of their own. With his round, bald head and eyes that twinkled behind glasses, Gandhi did faintly resemble his Indian namesake, although tonight he was not wearing the homespun cloth favoured by Mahatma but a comfy-looking black and white jumper. He led me through to the dining area while Christine prepared supper in the kitchen – spaghetti Bolognese, still the *de facto* national dish of Somalia – and, in a mixture of French and English, began to explain his semi-autonomizing plans.

His new polity, fantastically, was to be called Azania. The name turned out to have nothing to do with the fictional nation in Evelyn Waugh's 1930s comic novel, *Black Mischief*, of which Gandhi had never heard. Azania, he explained with the enthusiasm of a true anthropologist, was what the Romans had called this part of the East African coast, a place mentioned by both Pliny and Ptolemy in the first century. The boundaries of ancient Azania were unclear – some scholars thought it extended as far south as Tanzania – although what mattered to Gandhi was his belief that the word derived from *ajam*, the Arabic word for a non-Arab, a foreigner.

'I wanted something that would reflect the Somali identity,' he explained. 'We are not Arabs, as some people say. Azania means "the country of non-Arabs". This is very important to us in the south.'

Gandhi explained how, at a conference at Limuru near Nairobi in March 2010, over four hundred regional delegates had agreed on a draft constitution for Azania, drawn up with reference to all three of Somalia's legal traditions: the secular law once applied by the Italians, Sharia law, and xeer. The delegates had agreed on a bi-cameral parliament in which all thirty-seven sub-clans living in the region would be represented. The 4.5 clan formula adhered to elsewhere was specifically rejected. Azania's clan-inclusiveness, Gandhi insisted, would make his statelet quite unlike the other autonomous or semi-autonomous regions, all of which were fundamentally mono-clan entities.

'The south of Somalia has a greater mix of clans than anywhere else,' he said. 'Azania has Bantu people, Sheekhaal people, Marehan, Hawiye, Biamal ... All these groups are fighting against al-Shabaab *côte à côte*, with the Kenyans behind. If we can get peace here, Azania could be a model for the whole country to follow.'

His new government, he added, was ready to start administrating right away. They had divided Azania into fifteen districts, and even agreed where the capital should be, at Bu'ale on the river in Middle Juba. There was only one obstacle – a considerable one, I thought – which was that Bu'ale was still occupied by al-Shabaab. I wondered why he had picked such an obscure town as his future capital. Did he perhaps have in mind a particular building his government could occupy?

'No,' he grinned, 'there is nothing at Bu'ale. We will use someone's ordinary house. Or we could meet like the elders, under a tree.'

There were, it seemed to me, many worse models for Somalia to follow. I found Gandhi inspiring: a rare example of an older generation Somali whose rejection of clanism was both sincere and closely reasoned. He insisted, for instance, that the Western stereotype of violent Somalia was unfair. Inter-clan aggression, he thought, was a kind of default position for people with 'empty' heads, who were in no way representative of his countrymen.

'The West interprets clanism as *un fléau* – a scourge, a national curse. But it is not the Somali norm. Clanism is new. It is just the legacy of a terrible civil war.'

His worldview was close to that I had heard from many young diaspora Somalis, and the precise opposite of the likes of Dahir Kadiye in Leyton. Like Ayaan in Ealing, he stoutly refused to reveal his clan lineage when I asked (although it was actually no secret that he was one of the Ogadeni Darod, and therefore among the majority in the Azania region).

He seemed, in fact, to have consciously embraced the West's liberal values when he settled in France all those years ago. This was a man, after all, who had married an infidel, a Frenchwoman who had not converted to Islam. After the spaghetti, the First Lady of Azania stayed listening to her husband talk, occasionally interjecting that Somalis were all *foux*, or else commenting on the antics of the family cat, Schubert. She translated the odd difficult French word for her husband, and plied me with the alcoholic speciality of the region, a sherry-like *vin jaune*. Gandhi, teetotal, looked on benignly.

'I am not a very good Muslim,' he shrugged, 'but I am a Muslim nevertheless.'

Their two sons who were present had evidently been raised in the Western tradition, and were still busy forging their own complicated, transnational identities. Rageh, the older boy, came in just before suppertime. He was ostentatiously draped around his defiantly Asian girlfriend, with whom he was about to go out on the town, this being a Saturday evening. The younger son Sami, who was staying in, had long hair tied back in a trendy bun, and wore a T-shirt that read *Citoyen du Monde*.

Gandhi's stout defence of the Somali national character reminded me strongly of Nuruddin Farah, the novelist, who had taken the same line with me over dinner in Minneapolis. Farah's friend Shuke, the revered head of the

Puntland Development and Research Center in Garowe, and even Mohamed Omaar, the Foreign Minister in Mogadishu, had been equally impatient with my suggestion that the Somalis' capacity for violence was innate. I was not particularly surprised to discover that Gandhi knew all these men well. They belonged to the same class and generation, and were all prominent in public life. At the same time, the faith they shared in the underlying goodness of their countrymen was striking, for it was not a view commonly held in Somalia.

The explanation, I assumed, lay in their upbringing. As children born in the 1950s, they were fortunate to have benefitted from Siad Barre's state-sponsored educational revolution in the 1960s and '70s. It meant that they were members of the last Somali generation to have received, collectively, any peacetime, university-level training. Gandhi and his peers were thus ageing but unique showcases for their country's immense potential: impressive and eloquent flag-bearers for the Somalia that might once have been, and perhaps could be again one day.

For now, though, Azania remained a pipedream. Its success was entirely dependent on the continuing support of Kenya, and it was by no means certain that Gandhi could rely on that, for he was not the only regional player with plans for southern Somalia. The KDF, the Kenyan Defence Force, had other local allies, notably the Raskamboni Movement, a militia led by the former governor of Kismayo (and former ally of al-Shabaab), Sheikh Ahmed Madobe; and Nairobi was bound to back whoever looked likeliest to succeed militarily against their enemies.

This was because the implications of Operation Linda

Nchi were existential for Kenya, and not just because it was that country's first ever foreign military venture. The brain-child of the Internal Security Minister, George Saitoti, the invasion followed a spate of al-Shabaab-linked kidnaps and murders of Western aid workers and tourists on Kenyan territory, which Saitoti quickly announced 'would not be tolerated'. It was certainly true that tourism was, and remains, vital to the Kenyan economy. But it was also true that the murder of tourists provided a welcome justificatory figleaf for an otherwise unprovoked invasion of someone else's country. The abduction in September 2011 of David and Judith Tebbutt, a British couple who had been staying at the Kiwayu Safari Village beach resort close to the Somali border, had generated some particularly lurid, and useful, international headlines.*

As Gandhi now confirmed, Operation Linda Nchi was not spontaneous but had been in preparation for years. Somalia's unrest had threatened Kenyan security for half a century. Mohamed Omaar, the former Somali Foreign Minister, was not the only one who worried that Kenya's Muslim Swahili coast was the 'soft underbelly' of East Africa, ripe for exploitation by Islamic extremists. But it was not until 2011 that the political establishment in Nairobi felt confident enough to try to deal once and for all with the country's most troublesome neighbour.

Kenya's Somali population was estimated in 2009 at 2.3

---

* David Tebbutt, a 58-year-old publishing director from Bishop's Stortford in Hertfordshire, was shot dead as he tried to resist his assailants. His wife Judith was released six months later following payment of a reported $1m ransom.

million, about 6 per cent of the national total. The country's North Eastern Province, an area the size of England, had long been dominated by ethnic Somalis. Somali nationalists, indeed, historically regarded it as a part of Greater Somalia. In 1963, the year Kenya gained independence from Britain, Somalia fought an unsuccessful campaign to annex the province, the so-called Shifta War, which did not end until 1967. The nationalists may have lost, yet this swathe of sovereign Kenya is still represented on the Somali national flag as one of the five points of the white 'Star of Unity'.

The North Eastern Province is also home to the world's largest refugee camp, at Dadaab, which in August 2012 contained more than 450,000 Somali refugees,[1] making it by some margin the third largest population centre in Kenya after Nairobi and Mombasa. Dadaab was a permanent source of insecurity for the Kenyan state, an easy place for al-Shabaab both to hide in and to recruit new fighters. No wonder the Kenyans were so keen on a Somali buffer zone, which could only improve security in the border areas, and might even one day encourage Dadaab's refugees to start returning home. Gandhi said that Nairobi had been conniving at the creation of Azania since 2008 when, at his instigation, the Kenyan government began to arm and train 2,000 Azanian troops.

The strategy carried obvious risks for Kenya, the greatest of which was that the presence of their soldiers in Somalia proper was bound to inflame a section of Somali opinion locally, especially if the KDF lingered for any length of time, and began to resemble an occupying force rather than an expeditionary one. It was also risky for Gandhi, who could easily end up looking like an opportunist puppet of Nairobi rather than the nationalist visionary he claimed to be. This, however, was not the greatest threat to Gandhi's well-being, for it was common knowledge – and Christine whispered confirmation of the fact when Gandhi went out of the room for something – that the would-be president of Azania had a serious heart condition, and was often extremely unwell. The reason he spent as much time in France as he did – and he had inevitably been criticized for this – was his need to stay close to his cardiologists. The stakes in southern Somalia were as high as they could be, and the rules of the game were rough. Was Gandhi physically up to the challenge of playing it?

'I worry about him all the time,' Christine muttered. 'He's not a young man any more.'

Like so many Somali politicians, her husband had survived more than one assassination attempt in recent years. He was obliged to travel about with an imposing security detail in Somalia, and to vary his routine constantly. Even in Nairobi, a radical imam had placed him under a fatwa. He had been forced to change his accommodation there many times as a result, and never took the same route to work if he could help it. Survival required constant vigilance. Although Christine followed Somali politics closely, and understood and supported what her husband was trying to do, it emerged that in all the years she had been with him she had never once been to Somalia, or even to Kenya.

'It is too dangerous,' she said. 'I live a completely separate life here.'

It was another three months before I made it back to Nairobi, where I hoped to meet up with Gandhi and travel up to southern Somalia with him on an inspection tour of the war. By June 2012, al-Shabaab had their backs to the sea. The Kenyans were no longer alone in their incursion: at the beginning of 2012, and for the second time since 2006, Ethiopian troops had also crossed into Somalia. By February they had ousted al-Shabaab from the symbolically crucial town of Baidoa, and now they, the Kenyans, AMI-SOM and the TFG, were all closing in for the kill. When another key al-Shabaab town, Afmadow, fell to the Kenyans in late May, the head of the KDF, General Julius Karangi, was prompted to announce that the insurgency's last stronghold, the port of Kismayo, would be in Kenyan hands by August.

'It will not be difficult to capture Kismayo,' boasted Sheikh Madobe, leader of the Raskamboni Movement. 'Al-Shabaab's fighters are on the run, morale is low and it is only a matter of time before they are completely expelled from southern Somalia.'[2]

There was no doubt that Kismayo was a game-changer. The port lay close to the mouth of the river Juba, the only permanent river in Somalia. As the commercial centre of the nation's breadbasket, Kismayo had been the key to control of the south since medieval times. These days there were also thought to be large reserves of oil just offshore, which only added to the port's allure and legendary richesse. Al-Shabaab's dependence on it as a source of revenue was almost total. Without it, the alternative admin-istration they claimed to provide was doomed.

Yet for all the triumphalist talk, and despite the Kenyans' lengthy period of preparation, there were concerns in some foreign quarters that the KDF lacked the experience to handle such a complex campaign. Their advance in 2012 was snail-like, and their efforts to consolidate captured ground less than convincing. Eight months into Operation Linda Nchi, the KDF's eastbound supply convoys were still being ambushed on an almost daily basis, even on the Kenyan side of the border. The generals chose to launch their invasion in October, in the middle of the lush Juba valley's main rainy season when many roads become impassable. Foreign military advisors had warned them to delay the start of the campaign, but the advice was ignored and, as predicted, the KDF's heavy vehicles almost immediately became bogged down. Kenya's generals might profitably have paid more attention to the name of the Somali border town, Dhobley, that they had earmarked as their forward base of operations. Dhobley derived from the Somali word for mud.

The KDF's amateurism was soon exposed again by the clumsiness of their propaganda operation. An army spokesman, Major Emmanuel Chirchir, made an international fool of himself when he posted on Twitter a photograph of a man being stoned to death, claiming that the victim was from Nairobi and that the picture had been taken the previous day in Kismayo. (See picture section two.) A war of words then erupted which the major decisively lost. A disturbingly Anglophone spokesman for al-Shabaab pointed out that the stoning had taken place in 2009, that the victim wasn't Kenyan, that it hadn't taken place in Kismayo, and that it wasn't al-Shabaab who perpetrated it. The photograph had in fact been doing the rounds on the internet for so long – ever since the set of pictures it was taken from was sold to the news agency Associated Press – that even I had seen it before.

'KDF must employ a new PR strategy to save face,' tweeted @HSMPress, al-Shabaab's tech-savvy press office. '@MajorEChirchir's half-witted Twitter Psyops have made him a laughing stock.'

'I strongly disagree!' responded a tweeter in America. 'He's looking for a new job: official KDF comedian. He aims to make all and sundry laugh.'

The KDF ran regular supply flights up to Dhobley, but securing a place on one of them proved much harder than I expected. My plan to exploit Gandhi's influence with the Kenyans was thwarted by the discovery that he was unwell again, and had gone back to Besançon almost as I arrived in Nairobi. Left to approach the KDF alone, I was quickly stymied by officialdom. I spent an entire fortnight lobbying three colonels, each of whom insisted that it was not they but only one of their colleagues who could authorize my visit, without ever revealing which. It obviously did not help that the Internal Security Minister George Saitoti, the 'architect' of Operation Linda Nchi, had just been killed in a mysterious helicopter crash, an event that al-Shabaab called 'a droplet of justice', and which led to the temporary grounding of all official aircraft. Yet even this did not quite explain the colonels' strange inertia.

Eventually I realized that they were deliberately stonewalling, and that I was the victim of a classic East African feud. Kenya had just formally joined AMISOM. But the KDF were reluctant to cooperate with that organization's press office – through which I was obliged to communicate – because AMISOM was dominated by Uganda, whose President Museveni had recently insulted the KDF by referring to it publicly as a 'barracks army'. This spat did not augur well for the newly expanded AMISOM, at a moment when close cooperation between the allies was likely to be essential. There was no escape from the colonels' Mobius loop of red tape, and with Gandhi still incommunicado, I eventually gave up and decided to appeal instead to Sheikh Madobe's Raskamboni Movement, Gandhi's main rival for control of southern Somalia.

Named after Ras Kamboni, the southernmost Somali border town where it originated, Sheikh Madobe's militia was said to have replaced Gandhi's Azanians as the KDF's favourite local partners. His fighters ran regular convoys from the eastern Kenyan city of Garissa to Dhobley, bumping along 90 miles of dusty roads in 4×4s with technicals front and back for protection; perhaps I would be able to hitch a ride with them.

I went to meet Sheikh Moalim Mohamed, Sheikh Madobe's number two, at an address I had been given in Eastleigh, the main Somali suburb in Nairobi. Eastleigh was a place that I had heard much about but never visited before. As the diaspora's principal international gateway to the homeland, it shone very brightly in the constellation of communities abroad. It was much more than a mere travellers' staging post. Eastleigh was where the weightiest decisions about the future of Somalia tended to be taken. All the country's political, religious and financial elites had offices in Eastleigh, which since the 1990s had also evolved into a major commercial centre in its own right. It was often described as Mogadishu's Bakara Market in exile, an immense entrepôt where reputedly anything and everything could be bought or sold, including, it was often said, guns.

After a taxi ride that took almost two hours, thanks to Nairobi's legendarily awful traffic, I found Eastleigh's main roads to be even more flooded and potholed than was normal in the rest of the city. Jostling herds of *matatu* minibuses filled the air with their aggressive tooting. The rough and dirty pavements seethed with shoppers threading their way between stalls, hawking everything from shoes and shaving foam to qat and jerry cans of camel milk. This much I expected. But I was taken aback by the size and number of tall new buildings housing luxury hotels, all-night shopping malls, even a Barclays Bank, whose hoardings offered Sharia-compliant, *la riba* interest-free loans. Eastleigh was known, predictably, as Little Mogadishu, but for once the nickname was not an exaggeration, because it really did feel like a city within a city, with an economy and atmosphere entirely distinct from the rest of Nairobi. I later read that Somali businessmen had invested some $1.5bn in the suburb in recent years,[3] and it showed, because business was evidently booming here.

Native Kenyans viewed this enclave with a mixture of suspicion and affection. It was accused of many things: it was a hotbed of extremism, a centre for the laundering of the profits of piracy. Yet to my eye, Eastleigh's spirit did not seem criminal or ideological, but hard-working and commercial. In 2011, high-end property prices in Nairobi rose by 25 per cent, the fastest growth rate in any city in the world, a boom widely attributed to the phenomenon of Somalis in exile.[4]

Sheikh Moalim and his entourage were staying at one of the enclave's brash new glass and marble hotels called the Nomad Palace. Security was remarkably light – just one armed policeman on the front door, and none of the usual sinister men with tell-tale bulges beneath their jackets hanging about the busy lobby – which seemed a good indication of how little feared the insurgents were here.

The Somali flair for commerce, it occurred to me with sudden clarity, was the most powerful antidote imaginable to the reductive and impoverishing ideology of al-Shabaab, whose Islamist project could not succeed without the moral and financial support of Eastleigh's big business interests. It seemed inconceivable, for instance, that those interests would ever allow al-Shabaab to continue their tenure of a port as profitable as Kismayo. The Sheikh was unquestionably Eastleigh's man; I very much doubted that he paid his own bills in this hotel. He ushered me towards a group of purple, cuboid armchairs in the middle of the lobby as though we were in the living room of his home.

He was a big, broad-chested man, a former judge in the Islamic Courts Union who still exuded the confidence and authority of a respected religious scholar. He wore tinted rectangular glasses and a large, fuzzy beard, as well as loafers and Argyle socks and a grey-green cotton suit. Although the buttons of his jacket carried the words MEN'S FASHION, its breast pocket was done up with a zip, which lent him a faint but distinct paramilitary air. He later joked that he had spent so long fighting and sleeping in the bush that whenever he saw a tree in Eastleigh, he felt an impulse to lie down in its shade.

He told me almost immediately that I was welcome to come and inspect his war. He even thanked me for taking an interest, and said that I could join one of Raskamboni's eastbound convoys whenever I liked.

'To us, Sharia has never been about slaughtering people, as it seems to be for al-Shabaab,' he said when I asked him what he was fighting for. 'We want to replace them with a system that is fair to everybody. War has caused enough suffering already.'

His movement was militarily effective, he explained, because its members knew their enemy so well.

'I know many al-Shabaab fighters personally,' he continued, with an eloquent twist of his hand. 'I even taught some of them when they were young. And now they say I am an infidel! They are crazy. We were Muslims for a thousand years before they came along . . . Their ideology is imposed from outside. It is not Wahhabism – it goes far beyond that. Everyone is upset with them, and so now they must be . . . disciplined.'

This last remark was accompanied by a barely concealed smirk. It was as though he regarded al-Shabaab almost as naughty children rather than al-Qaida-linked terrorists, and that all that was needed to bring them back into line was the smack of schoolmasterly authority.

It was, I supposed, hardly surprising that the difference between him and the extremists was so blurred. In 2010, after all, a Raskamboni splinter group had merged with al-Shabaab. The CIA, furthermore, had long ago identified Ras Kamboni town as an al-Qaida training base. The attacks on the US embassies in Nairobi and Dar es Salaam in 1998, and the bombing of the Paradise Hotel in Mombasa in 2002, were all thought to have been organized from Ras Kamboni.

As late as 2007, an American AC-130 gunship launched an attack near Ras Kamboni against 'al-Qaida suspects' thought to include the Mombasa-born Saleh Ali Nabhan, one of the alleged masterminds of the embassy bombings.*

For all the Sheikh's outward scorn for al-Shabaab's ideology, therefore, I suspected that he was not necessarily as resistant to foreign influence as he said he was. In answer to another question about how he thought southern Somalia should be governed in future, he replied, sensibly enough, that there would have to be a grand conference of all the relevant regional stakeholders, who could thrash out a mutually satisfactory political settlement. What struck me most about his answer was the phrase he used to describe this grand conference of the future: he called it a *loya jirga*, the Afghan Pashtun for a 'grand council'. The last loya jirga, at which the possibility of peace talks with the Taliban was discussed, was held in Kabul in 2010.

Sheikh Moalim and his fighters were likely to be the first Somali militia into Kismayo, and would therefore have a decisive say in how the port was administered in the future. Although they were allies of the KDF for now, I couldn't help wondering what would happen once Kismayo fell and the Kenyans were of less use. Would Nairobi really be able to maintain influence over these most mercurial of local partners? More to the point, what would al-Shabaab do once they were ousted from their stronghold – and how would Kenya deal with the response?

There were already many signs that an al-Shabaab terror campaign was spreading southwards – and signs, too, of

---

* Nabhan survived until 2009, when he was finally tracked down and killed in the al-Shabaab-controlled port of Baraawe by a helicopter-borne squad of US Navy SEALs.

how ill-prepared the Kenyans were to cope. The home front's counter-terrorism strategy, in so far as it existed at all, was criticized by the Kenyan *Daily Nation* as 'reactive, sluggish and uninspiring'.[5] Compared to American or British government efforts to mobilize community leaders to persuade young Muslims to shun extremism, Kenya was years behind.

Low-level shootings and grenade attacks at nightclubs and bus stops, all of them linked to al-Shabaab, became ever more frequent as 2012 wore on. No city was safe, but as predicted it was Mombasa, the capital of the Swahili coast, that soon emerged as the focal point of the attacks. Many Kenyans feared that the city was filled with al-Shabaab sympathizers and sleeper cells; it had already proved a rich source of recruits for the insurgency over the border.

'We've lost many young men who have been recruited [into al-Shabaab] and taken to Somalia,' said Sheikh Athman Mponda, chairman of the Association of Muslim Organizations in Kenya, perhaps appropriately known as AMOK. 'I know of nine young men who have been killed in Somalia.'[6]

On 24 June 2012, the US embassy issued a warning that another terrorist attack in Mombasa was imminent. The warning was immediately denounced by the chairman of the National Security Advisory Council, Francis Kimemia, as an act of 'economic sabotage' and a 'betrayal of trust'. The Tourism Minister, Dan Mwazo, similarly described it as 'in bad taste and malicious'. Like Larry Vaughan, the mayor of the Amity Island beach resort in the movie *Jaws*, they were worried that the warning would scare off the tourists. Hours later, however, a rocket-propelled grenade was fired into Mombasa's Jericho Beer Garden where customers had gathered to watch England play Italy in the European Football Championship. Three people were killed and scores injured in the attack, which was uncomfortably reminiscent of the al-Shabaab strike on football fans in Kampala during the 2010 World Cup.

'You are fighting al-Shabaab in Somalia where the head is, but the tail is here,' a Mombasa local identified as Yusuf told a reporter from the Kenyan *Standard*. 'These people live among us. You will regret.'[7]

Earlier in the week, Kenyan police had already arrested two Iranians suspected of planning bombings in Mombasa and Nairobi. Kimemia and Mwazo fell silent as the American travel warning was repeated by the embassies of several other nations, and the British Foreign Office formally advised its citizens not to travel even to Nairobi. The economic implications were serious, for Kenya could not afford to lose its tourists, particularly its British ones. In 2011, there were more British holiday-makers than from any other country in the world: 200,000 of them, comfortably more even than from America.*

Britain, thanks to a relationship rooted in the days of Empire, was also Kenya's biggest foreign investor, and its second biggest trading partner after Uganda. British imports of Kenyan tea, coffee, vegetables and flowers rose 9 per cent in 2011, and Anglo-Kenyan trade was worth over

---

* Some 1.25 million foreigners visited Kenya in 2011, bringing in a record $1.16bn in an industry that accounted for 11 per cent of the country's GDP – the second biggest source of foreign revenue after the export of tea, according to Bloomberg.com.

£1bn a year.[8] All of this was now under threat. As the British High Commission was at pains to point out, Operation Linda Nchi wasn't just about combating terrorism: its success or failure would have a considerable impact on important British business interests too.

The bad news did not let up for the Kenyan government. The Jericho Beer Garden attack in Mombasa was followed a week later by another atrocity, this time in Garissa, where the congregations of two churches were attacked during their Sunday sermon by what local police called 'balaclava-clad goons' armed with grenades and automatics.[9] Fifteen worshippers were killed, and forty wounded. For old soldiers, it must have felt like the Shifta War all over again; while for the younger generation, the fragility of the stasis between the country's Muslims and Christians was for the first time laid frighteningly bare.

At the end of August in Mombasa, Aboud 'Rogo' Mohammed, a radical cleric and an al-Shabaab supporter so well known that his name featured on both US and UN sanctions lists, was assassinated by unknown gunmen as he drove through the city with his wife and children. The ensuing riots lasted for two days. Tyre-burning mobs closed the road to the tourist town of Malindi, 70 miles to the north. Shops were burned, churches were looted, and five people, including three policemen, were killed. Muslim opinion in Mombasa was that the Kenyan government was behind Rogo's death, a view that was only strengthened a week later when a second al-Shabaab-supporting imam, Abubakr Ahmed, was charged with inciting the Rogo riots.

'We are certain that there is a hit squad targeting Muslim

clerics and other Muslims perceived to be extremists,' Ahmed told reporters.[10]

I never did get to witness the liberation of Kismayo. Sheikh Moalim's offer of a lift to Dhobley suddenly seemed much less attractive when, two days after my meeting with him, a combined KDF/Raskamboni convoy struck an IED on the road east of Garissa, killing three. Flying was the only sensible way of reaching the war from Nairobi. But the Kenyan colonels remained uncooperative to the last on this score, and in the end I reluctantly abandoned my attempt to persuade them.

In terms of the wider story, it probably didn't much matter. The fall of Kismayo was really a foregone conclusion; and al-Shabaab was surely finished in any case as an occupying military force, let alone as a viable alternative system of government for Somalia. The more important question was what would happen next, to which the unrest in Kenya in the summer of 2012 provided one chilling answer. As a rallying point for disaffected young Muslims, al-Shabaab was evidently as potent in Mombasa as it once was in Mogadishu. 'Their intention,' said the prime minister, Raila Odinga, 'is to divide the people of Mombasa into Christians and Muslims with the sole aim of creating an inter-religious conflict.'[11] The use of grenades, he added, proved that the riots had been planned, the work of a sinister (but unidentified) 'hidden hand'.

Was Odinga right? Whether or not the unrest was orchestrated, in 2012 the Swahili coast looked more and more like another new battleground in the long war between Islamists and infidels – the beginning by other means, perhaps, of al-Shabaab's breakout from the Horn of

Africa. Just as US forces failed to close the net on the Taliban and al-Qaida in Kandahar in 2001, allowing them to escape over the border to Pakistan to fight another day, so it was feared that the cream of al-Shabaab's foreign fighters had already abandoned Kismayo. News reports suggested that many had fled north across the Gulf of Aden, at night and by speedboat, to join the al-Qaida-linked separatists in south Yemen. Gandhi's sources had told him that al-Shabaab were in fact dispersing to all points of the compass. Some were said to have gone north, to Puntland's inaccessible Galgala Mountains, in order to join forces with Sheikh Atom, a pro-al-Shabaab separatist who had been harrying the Garowe government for years. Others had sought sanctuary in the Somali tribal areas of Ethiopia, or were hiding even further west in the impenetrable jungles of 'Zaire', the old Portuguese name for the Democratic Republic of the Congo. But most of all, according to Gandhi, they had come south to Kenya, filtering down the Swahili coast via Lamu, or along any of the inland routes across the long and porous border.

'There are many, many Kenyans fighting for al-Shabaab,' he said.

Local Somali fighters, meanwhile, naturally had an easier alternative than flight, which was to hide their guns, shed whatever scraps of uniform they possessed, and melt back into the population from which they came.

Kismayo's fall signalled the end of the conventional military campaign, but Mogadishu has barely begun the task of filling the enormous vacuum of governance the Islamists have left behind. The implications for the security of the East Africa region, and the world, are huge; and

Somalia, the wellspring of so much human misery and political instability, looks to be a contender once again for that unenviable title, *The World's Most Dangerous Place*.

Postscript to the Paperback edition

Gandhi was right to worry about al-Shabaab in Kenya. On 21 September 2013, almost exactly a year after I first submitted the manuscript of this book, a squad of keffiyeh-swathed gunmen attacked the Westgate shopping mall in Nairobi.

It was, perhaps, a disaster waiting to happen. The upmarket Westgate was the most conspicuous symbol of the 'new' Kenya, popular not just with Nairobi's prosperous middle classes but also with tourists and the city's elite. There had been warnings that it was a prime target for terrorists, yet security at the entrance never amounted to more than a couple of sleepy bag-checkers. At least 61 civilians were murdered, and over 200 injured, in the worst act of terrorism in Kenya since the US embassy bombings in 1998.

This outrage had more than a little resonance for me. I had shopped at the mall's Nakumatt supermarket on every one of my visits to Nairobi in 2011 and 2012. The mall's open-air ArtCaffé, with its free wi-fi and excellent coffee, virtually doubled as my office. The victims were mostly locals – they included President Kenyatta's nephew, Mbugua Mwangi, and his fiancée – but foreigners from eighteen different countries died, too: an architect from Tasmania, a doctor from Peru, a famous poet from Ghana. Up on the top floor, a party of schoolchildren who had gathered for a cookery competition were picked off one by one with an AK before final dispatch with a hand grenade.

Al-Shabaab linked the attack specifically to the KDF's continuing occupation of Kismayo. The spokesman Sheikh Rage warned that it was just 'a taste of what we will do' if Kenya did not withdraw from Somalia. The operation was, undoubtedly, a showcase of good organization. The attackers were thought to have stockpiled weapons and ammunition inside the mall ahead of time, and may even have rented an empty retail unit for the purpose. As a four-day siege unfolded, al-Shabaab boasted that they were in constant radio contact with their 'mujahideen', heightening a sense that this, too, was slickly choreographed, that they were in control, and that the KDF were merely bit-players in the drama.

The target was certainly well chosen if media attention was what they sought. The story dominated international headlines for almost a fortnight, pushing even the war in Syria from the front pages; for what Western shopper could fail to imagine themselves lying in the blood-slicked aisles of the Nakumatt, a supermarket virtually indistinguishable from any other in the developed world?

Somalia-watchers were divided over what it all signified. Prime Minister Odinga's warning that al-Shabaab were intent on sewing inter-religious discord seemed borne out at the Westgate, where some of the victims were executed because they were unable to name the Prophet's mother*.

---

*A news detail that sent me scurrying to Google for future reference. She was called Aminah bint Wahb.

And yet the attackers were not consistently callous. The motives of some of them seemed conflicted – as well they might, given the insane contradiction of killing children in the name of a religion called peace. In one extraordinary episode, a four-year-old British boy from Windsor, Elliott Prior, scolded one of the gunmen as a 'very bad man,' who replied: 'Please forgive me – we are not monsters,' and gave him and his sister a Mars Bar each before pointing them and their mother towards the exit.

Some analysts said the attack marked the beginning of a new and deadlier phase in the al-Shabaab campaign, an expression of Godane's determination to internationalize his struggle, and to establish his credentials as the staunchest African ally of al-Qaida. Others argued that the choice of such a soft target was not a sign of strength, but a mark of desperation. Al-Shabaab, they pointed out, had failed to regain control of Kismayo, and was everywhere under pressure from the ever-swelling ranks of AMISOM. Godane felt so insecure that he had ordered the recent assassinations of rival leaders, including the influential Abu Mansoor al-Amriki. According to this reading, the Westgate was an attempt to re-invigorate a movement that was struggling at home.

Either way, there is no longer any dispute that the threat of militant Islam has now over-spilled Somalia's borders. Few if any of the attack squad were drawn from al-Shabaab's domestic membership. The Kenyan Foreign Minister, Amina Mohamed, said during the siege that 'two or three Americans' were among the gunmen, which, she observed, 'goes to underline the global nature of the war that we're fighting.' She could produce no evidence of a

Somali-American connection, but she was right in the latter respect. One of the gunmen was identified as Abu Baara, a Sudani. Another, Abdi Dhuhulow, was a Somali who had spent half his life in the small Norwegian town of Larvik.

A fortnight after the mall attack, US Navy SEALs stormed the port of Baraawe, 110 miles south of Mogadishu, in an unsuccessful bid to capture a senior al-Shabaab leader known as Ikrima, a Kenyan-Somali who had also once lived in Norway. A Kenyan National Intelligence Service (NIS) report, leaked to Al Jazeera in late September,[1] revealed that Ikrima was the co-ordinator of a Mombasa-based terror cell that included the fugitive Briton Samantha Lewthwaite, the so-called 'White widow' of the 2005 London suicide bomber Germaine Lindsay. At the same time, in Tripoli, US Special Forces captured Abu Anas al Libi, wanted in connection with the Kenyan and Tanzanian embassy bombings of 1998.

Al-Shabaab, it seems, is morphing into a genuinely international organization, with cells said by the NIS to be operating everywhere from Mali to Pakistan. It is Kenya, however, that now sits at the centre of their international operations. The NIS report noted that fifteen al-Shabaab agents had recently been given Swahili language lessons along with false refugee documents that would allow them to slip into Kenya unnoticed; survivors of the mall attack reported that the gunmen had mostly communicated with each other in Swahili.

The KDF did not cover themselves with glory during the siege. Their senior officers bickered with each other over strategy, delaying a counter-assault that finally ended when the roof was brought down by RPG fire, burying an unknown number of survivors and corpses, along with potentially crucial forensic evidence. They also failed to cordon off the mall, an elementary oversight that may have allowed some attackers to escape. CCTV footage later emerged showing soldiers pillaging the mall's hastily abandoned shops. There were even reports that they had looted the bodies of the dead.

The NIS were plaintive in their report's recommendations to the Nairobi government. Kenya's counter-terrorism strategy needed 'urgent' review; the security sector lacked the necessary legal powers and resources; more public support for their efforts was required, as well as greater international support for the KDF in Somalia. Their final point, tacked on like an afterthought, was a recommendation to 'engage Muslim leaders, elders and Islamic scholars to counter radicalization by terrorist operatives.'

It all seems too little, too late. The Kenyans are choking on the blowback from Operation Linda Nchi. Their country, the economic kingpin of East and Central Africa, looks riper than ever for exploitation; and the world is now bracing for the consequences of an al-Shabaab breakout from the Horn.

Edinburgh, November 2013

Notes and Sources

Introduction

1 According to Reuters, whose source was 'a Western diplomat', quoted by Jerome Starkey in *The Times*, 11 September 2011

2 *The Times*, 8 October 2011

3 ICM/*Guardian*, 10 August 2012

4 Martin Fletcher, *The Times*, 6 August 2012

Chapter 1 An African Stalingrad: The war against al-Shabaab

1 'The Family House' in the Swiss-based European Graduate School's *Transition* magazine, no. 99, 2008, pp 6–15

Chapter 2 At the Bancroft Hotel: America's proxy war

1 http://www.bbc.co.uk/news/world-africa-11246394

2 See, for instance, Prof. Chester Crocker of Georgetown University, *Foreign Affairs Magazine*, vol. 73, no. 3, 1995, often reprinted, e.g. at www.pbs.org. Operation Restore Hope is often described as the first American troop deployment in Africa since the Barbary Wars of the early 1800s

3 http://www.state.gov/p/af/rls/rm/2010/138314.htm

4,5 Jeffrey Gettleman, *New York Times*, 10 August 2011, 'US

Relies on Contractors in Somalia Conflict'
6   Josh Kron, Associated Press, 12 July 2010; BBC, 12 July 2010
7   UPDF Brigadier Paul Lokech interviewed by Andrew M. Mwenda in the *Kampala Independent*, 25 August 2012
8   Tony Doyle, BBC News Africa, 26 June 2012
9   Gerald Hanley, *Warriors – Life and Death among the Somalis*, Hamish Hamilton 1971

Chapter 3 The field hospital: What bombs and bullets do to people
1   www.bbc.co.uk/news/world-africa-14985549, 20 September 2011
2   Richard Burton, *First Footsteps in East Africa*, 1856
3   Harald Swayne, *Seventeen Trips through Somaliland and a Visit to Abyssinia*, preface to the 3rd ed., Rowland Ward Ltd 1903
4   A declassified Memorandum of Conversation that took place between Acting Foreign Minister H.A. Kassim and Secretary of State Kissinger on 8 October 1976; PA/HO Department of State EO12958, as amended 4 May 2006

Chapter 4 Aden's story
1   http://www.sunatimes.com/view.php?id=564, May 2011
2,3,4 http://www.finalcall.com/artman/publish/World_News_3/article_2716.shtml
5   http://www.b.dk/danmark/en-terrorist-fra-roedovre
6   Xan Rice, *Guardian*, 20 October 2010
7   John Lee Anderson, *New Yorker*, 14 December 2009
8   For more detail on the Aweys story see: http://ashaacira.wordpress.com/taariikhda-shiikh-uweys-axmad-oo-looy-aqaano-sheekh-aweys-al-qaadirioo-somalida-intabada-diinta-gaarisiiyo-illaa-iyo-south-afrika/
9   http://www.irinnews.org/Report.aspx?ReportID=91267

Chapter 5 The failure of Somali politics

1   Alex Athure, *Daily Nation* (Kenya), 9 July 2012
2   *Suna Times*, 11 September 2011

Chapter 6 What makes al-Shabaab tick?

1   Telephone interview published in *Getting Somalia Wrong? Faith, War and Hope in a Shattered State* by Mary Harper, Zed Books 2012
2   http://www.bbc.co.uk/news/uk-16920643
3   http://www.guardian.co.uk/politics/2010/sep/17/mi5-chief-somalia-terro-threat
4   David Barret, *Sunday Telegraph*, 7 July 2012
5   Nelly Lahoud, CTC *Sentinel*, February 2012, vol. 5, issue 2
6   http://www.somaliareport.com/index.php/post/976/Fazulrsquos_Last_Moments
7   CIA *World Factbook* 2012
8   Hanley, *Warriors*, op. cit.
9   Reported by Mary Harper, *Getting Somalia Wrong?*, p91
10 *Daily Mail*, 15 May 2011
11 For an introduction to this topic, see the excellent collection of essays *Suicide Bombers: The Psychological, Religious and Other Imperatives*, IOS Press, Nato Science for Peace and Security Series, E: Human and Societal Dynamics, vol. 41, edited by Mary Sharpe
12 Harper, *Getting Somalia Wrong?*, op. cit.

Chapter 7 The Famine

1   http://news.xinhuanet.com/english2010/world/2011-07/22/c_131003043.htm
2   Author interview with Abdirizaq Mohedin, the Minister for Water Resources, citing the 2010 Assessment Report by the Somali NGO Green Hope
3   SomaliaReport, 27 July 2011

4 http://socialitelife.com/angelina-jolie-honored-by-unhcr-says-refugees-made-her-a-better-mother-photos-10-2011

5 http://www.wfp.org/videos/50cent-somalia-never-seen-any-thing-like-this

6 http://www.guardian.co.uk/commentisfree/2011/aug/01/liz-jones-somalia-famine

7 http://www.guardian.co.uk/global-development/2011/jul/20/un-declares-famine-somalia

8 http://www.bbc.co.uk/news/world-africa-14422427, 5 August 2011

9 UN Monitoring Group report, March 2010

10 *Daily Nation*, (Kenya) quoted by *UPI*, 26 July 2011

11 http://www.bbc.co.uk/news/world-africa-15166107?OCID=fbwin, 4 October 2011

Chapter 8 In the court of King Farole

1 CIA *World Factbook* 2012

2 *The Economics of Piracy*, Geopolicity (consultancy), 24 April 2011

3 Burton, *First Footsteps in East Africa*, op. cit.

4 Hanley, *Warriors*, op. cit.

5 I.M. Lewis, *A Pastoral Democracy*, OUP 1961, p12

6 International Chamber of Commerce, International Maritime Bureau

7 Holly Watt, *Telegraph Magazine*, 7 April 2012

8 *Myanmar Times*, 11 November 2011

Chapter 9 Galkacyo: Pirateville

1 Hanley, *Warriors*, op. cit.

2,3 *Somali Customary Law and Traditional Economy – Cross-sectional, pastoral, frankincense, and marine norms*, Puntland Development and Research Centre, Garowe 2003

4 the-numbers.com/movies

5 Allie Shah, *Star Tribune*, 4 November 2011

6 David Cameron speech at Witney, Oxfordshire, 15 August 2011

7 Jay Bahadur, *Deadly Waters – Inside the Hidden World of Somalia's Pirates*, Profile Books 2011, p100

8 *The Times*, 28 March 2011

9 Sucaad Mire, 'Women Flock to Pirates with Money', SomaliaReport, 24 September 2011

10 Jamestown Foundation, 'Was the Battle for Galkacyo a Clan Dispute or a Victory for Puntland Over al-Shabaab?', *Terrorism Monitor*, vol. 9, issue 35, 15 September 2011

11 FCO Communiqué, 23 February 2012

12 SomaliaReport, 31 March 2012

Chapter 10 Hargeisa Nights

1 Eric Lafforgue, medeshivalley.com, 2 May 2012

2 Capt Malcolm McNeill, DSO, & Lt A.C.H. Dixon, *In Pursuit of the 'Mad' Mullah: Service and Sport in the Somali Protectorate*, C. Arthur Pearson Ltd 1902, republished by Kessinger

3 Mark Tran, *Guardian*, 4 January 2012; CIA *World Factbook* 2012

4 Monty Munford, *The Kernel*, 18 May 2012

5 http://www.alunmichael.com/news/general-news/news.aspx? p=102554

6 *'Hostages to Peace': Threats to Human Rights and Democracy in Somaliland*, Human Rights Watch, July 2009

7 http://en.rsf.org/somalia-in-past-week-in-somaliland-25-16-01-2012,41685.html

Chapter 11 How to start a border war

1 Jeffrey Bartholet, 'It's a Mad, Mad, Mad, Mad World', *Newsweek*, 22 October 2009

2 Abridged version of translation by B.W. Andrzejewski, *Somali Poetry: An Introduction* (Oxford Library of African Literature), Clarendon 1964

3   Douglas Jardine, *The Mad Mullah of Somaliland*, Herbert Jenkins Ltd, 1923
4   Bartholet, *Newsweek*, 22 October 2009, op. cit.
5   Akiva J. Lorenz, 'Analyzing the *USS Cole* Bombing', MaritimeTerrorism.com, 27 December 2007
6   Translator's introduction to *Ignorance is the Enemy of Love* by Faarax M.J. Cawl, Zed Books 1982
7   The noted poet Hadraawi, quoted by Jeffrey Bartholet, op. cit.
8   http://www.qi.com/talk/viewtopic.php?t=7064&view=previous &sid=e65ee32112ce2a70f5a70914fc064485 and http://itre.cis.upenn.edu/~myl/languagelog/archives/000457.html
9   Peter Bridges, *Safirka: An American Envoy*, Kent State University Press 2000
10 Jardine, *The Mad Mullah of Somaliland*, op. cit.
11 http://www.somaliareport.com/index.php/post/3202/ Somaliland_ Arrest_Journalists_In_Las-Anod

Chapter 12 The Somali youth time-bomb

1   http://www.bbc.co.uk/news/uk-16296849
2   House of Commons Home Affairs Committee, *Roots of violent radicalisation*, Nineteenth Report of Session 2010–12, vol. 1, HC1446, 6 February 2012
3   Also reported by the *Sun* in August 2011: http://www.thesun.co.uk/ sol/homepage/news/3782328/A-third-of-youth-prisoners-are-foreign.html
4   Joseph Rowntree Foundation, *Young People and Territoriality in British Cities*, October 2008
5   Jason Lewis, *Daily Telegraph*, 13 August 2011
6   Ministry of Justice statistics quoted by Alan Travis, *Guardian*, 24 October 2011
7   http://www.bbc.co.uk/news/uk-england-london-13566526
8   http://www.spittoon.org/archives/10654

9   *New York Times*, 5 October 2011
10 Pew Research Centre; Sean Rayment and Colin Freeman, *Sunday Telegraph*, 18 February 2012
11 Richard Norton-Taylor, *Guardian*, 7 February 2012
12 House of Commons Home Affairs Committee, *Roots of violent radicalisation*, op. cit.

Chapter 13 The missing of Minneapolis

1   http://www.fbi.gov/minneapolis/press-releases/2011 minneapolis-man-pleads-guilty-to-terrorism-offense
2   Opening statement to the Third Committee on Homeland Security, US Congress, 27 July 2011
3   Andrea Elliott, *New York Times*, 11 July 2009
4   Osman Dagane, president of the All-Somali Community of Minnesota
5   Andrea Elliott, op. cit.
6   For more details see Laura Yuen, MPR, 15 April 2009 http://minnesota. publicradio.org/display/web/2009/04/14/friends_of_the_missing/
7   For more details see: http://www.nefafoundation.org/newsite/ file/US_v_AminaFarahAli_dojprguilty.pdf
8   Richard Meryhew, Allie Shah and James Walsh, 'The Making of a Minneapolis Suicide Bomber', *Star Tribune*, 6 May 2009
9   http://www.kfai.org/somalicommunitylink
10 For more detail see: http://pjmedia.com/blog/minneapolis-imam-decries-the-hell-of-living-in-america/
11 Mark Tran, *Guardian*, 4 January 2012, op. cit.
12 For more detail see: http://www.npr.org/2011/09/07/140234451/ under-suspicion-at-the-mall-of-america
13 http://www.startribune.com/local/minneapolis/128663938.html
14 Jim Adams, *Star Tribune*, and Jason Ryan, ABC News, 31 October 2011

Chapter 14 'Clanism is a disease like AIDS'

1   Haight-Ashbury Free Medical Clinic, *Journal of Psychoactive Drugs*, vol. 41, 2009
2   Somali militants target addicts in UK's 'khat cafés', CNN, 23 February 2012
3   See, for instance, Home Office Research Report no. 44, 'Perceptions of the social harms associated with khat use'
4   Burton, *First Footsteps*, op. cit.
5   Robert Young Pelton, SomaliaReport, 8 May 2011
6   Ian Black, *Guardian*, 26 February 2010; Mohammed Jamjoom and Gena Somra, CNN, 2 December 2010
7,8 Mark Lancaster MP, *Hansard*, 11 January 2012
9   Prof Abdulahi A. Osman, *Cultural Diversity and the Somali Conflict: Myth or Reality?*, African Studies Institute, University of Georgia 2007
10 Hanley, *Warriors*, op. cit.
11 David St George, *Camden New Journal*, 13 May 2004
12 Robert Verkaik, 'How MI5 blackmails British Muslims: "Work for us or we will say you are a terrorist"', *Independent*, 21 May 2009
13 FCO, 15 November 2011
14 London *Evening Standard*, 15 November 2010; and see: http://www.youtube.com/watch?v=eFsIaUj1NPo
15 The *Sun*, 23 November 2010 and 14 April 2011
16 Quoted in the Puntland Development Research Centre's booklet, *Somali Customary Law and Traditional Economy,* 2003
17 Jeffrey Gettleman, *New York Times*, 5 October 2011

Chapter 15 Operation Linda Nchi: The end for al-Shabaab?

1   See data.unher.org for updates of Dadaab's fluctuating population
2   *Daily Nation*, 21 June 2012/Sabahi.com (Kenya)
3   *Daily Nation*, 30 May 2011 (Kenya)

4   Knight Frank Prime International Residential Index, March 2012
5   Rashid Abdi, *Daily Nation* (Kenya), 25 June 2012
6,7 *Standard* (Kenya), 26 June 2012
8   UK High Commission, Nairobi; Allafrica.com
9   http://www.bbc.co.uk/news/world-18662975/, 1 July 2012
10 http://www.bbc.co.uk/news/world-africa-19466828, 3 September 2012
11 *Daily Nation* (Kenya), 29 August 2012

Postscript to the Paperback edition
1   http://publicintelligence.net/kenya-shabaab-file/

Bibliography

Awde, Nicholas, *Somali-English Dictionary & Phrasebook*, Hippocrene Books 2009

Bahadur, Jay, *Deadly Waters – Inside the Hidden World of Somalia's Pirates*, Profile Books 2011

Bowden, Mark, *Black Hawk Down*, Bantam Press 1999

Bridges, Peter, *Safirka: An American Envoy*, Kent State University Press 2000

Burton, Richard F., *First Footsteps in East Africa* (1856), Konemann Classics 2000

Cawl, Faarax M.J., *Ignorance is the Enemy of Love*, 1974, translated for Zed Books 1982

Chandler, Paul & Rachel, *Hostage – A Year at Gunpoint with Somali Gangsters*, Mainstream Publishing 2011

Cooper, Frederick, *Africa Since 1940 – The Past of the Present*, Cambridge University Press 2002

Dowden, Richard, *Africa – Altered States, Ordinary Miracles*, Portobello Books 2009

Drysdale, John, *Whatever Happened to Somalia?* Haan Publishing 1994

Farah, Nuruddin, *Crossbones*, Riverhead Books 2011

Farah, Nuruddin, *Links*, Duckworth 2005

Fazzina, Alixandra, *A Million Shillings – Escape from Somalia*, Trolley Books 2010

Freeman, Colin, *Kidnapped – Life as a Somali Pirate Hostage*, Monday Books 2011

Hanley, Gerald, *Warriors – Life and Death among the Somalis*, Hamish Hamilton 1971

Harper, Mary, *Getting Somalia Wrong? Faith, War and Hope in a Shattered State*, Zed Books 2012

Hartley, Aidan, *The Zanzibar Chest*, Harper Collins 2003

Hirsi Ali, Ayaan, *Infidel – My Life*, Pocket Books (Simon & Schuster) 2008

Hirsi Ali, Ayaan, *Nomad – A Personal Journey Through the Clash of Civilizations*, Simon & Schuster 2010

Jardine, Douglas, OBE, *The Mad Mullah of Somaliland*, Herbert Jenkins Ltd 1923

Laird, Elizabeth, *The Ogress and the Snake and Other Stories from Somalia*, Frances Lincoln Ltd 2009

Leonard, Elmore, *Djibouti – A Middle East Western on Water*, Weidenfeld & Nicolson 2011

Lewis I.M., *A Pastoral Democracy*, Oxford University Press 1961

Lewis I.M., *Understanding Somalia and Somaliland*, Hurst & Co 2009

McNeill, Capt Malcolm, DSO, & Lt A.C.H. Dixon, *In Pursuit of the 'Mad' Mullah: Service and Sport in the Somali Protectorate*, C. Arthur Pearson Ltd 1902, republished by Kessinger

Mohamed Abdi, Mohamed, *Anthropologie Somalienne*, Université de Besançon 1993

Mohamed Abdi, Mohamed, *Histoire des Croyances en Somalie*, Université de Besançon 1992

Mohamed Abdi, Mohamed, *Pour une Culture de la Paix en Somalie*, Association Européene des Etudes Somaliennes 1997

Murphy, Martin N., *Somalia: The New Barbary? Piracy and Islam in the Horn of Africa*, Hurst & Co 2011

Notten, Michael van, *The Law of the Somalis*, The Red Sea Press 2007

Osman, Abdurahman A. (Shuke), *Somali Customary Law and*

BIBLIOGRAPHY

Traditional Economy – Cross-sectional, pastoral, frankincense and marine norms, Puntland Development Research Centre 2003

Roble, Abdi & Doug Rutledge, *The Somali Diaspora – A Journey Away*, University of Minnesota Press 2008

Smith, Wilbur, *Those in Peril*, Macmillan 2011

Swayne, Harald G.C., *Seventeen Trips through Somaliland and a Visit to Abyssinia: With Supplementary Preface on the 'Mad Mullah' Risings*, Rowland Ward Ltd 1903

Waugh, Evelyn, *Black Mischief* (1932), republished Penguin Modern Classics 2000

James Fergusson is a freelance journalist and foreign correspondent who has written for many publications including the *Independent*, *The Times*, the *Daily Mail* and *The Economist*. A regular television and radio commentator on Afghanistan and the Taliban, he is the author of four previous books, including *A Million Bullets*, which was the British Army's Military Book of the Year. He is married with four children and lives in Edinburgh.

For more information on James Fergusson and his books, see his website at www.jamesfergusson.info

Acknowledgements

A great many people helped me with this book, but I am particularly indebted to the Airey Neave Trust, and its guardians Michael Bottenheim, Ed Butler, John Giffard and the late Paul Wilkinson, whose generous fellowship grant made an expensive research project financially viable. It was a privilege to have the confidence of so distinguished a body of people. My one regret is that the renowned Professor Wilkinson, who died suddenly in 2011 at the age of seventy-four, never saw the result of his kind support. Part of the Trust's objective is to promote research 'designed to make a discernible impact and to contribute in a practical way to the struggle against international terrorist activity'. I sincerely hope the trustees will feel that this book fulfils that brief.

Alongside a handful of people whose identities must remain undisclosed, I extend my especial thanks to Ahmed Abdullahi, Sahal Abdulle, Musa Duale Aden, Julian Alexander, Mohamed Ali (Wandsworth), Willy Athill, Richard Bailey, James Bays, Nick Beresford, John Bradshaw, Salih Brandt, Miles Bredin, Sophie Butler, Paul & Rachel Chandler, Charlie Courtauld, Osman Dagane,

Julian Davies, Kabir Dhanji, Chris Donnelly, Sarah Edworthy, Mohammed Ismail Elmi, Hassan Eymoy, Abdulhakim Mohamoud Haji Faqi, Mohamed Farah (Yare), Nuruddin Farah, Toby Fenwick-Wilson, Anders Folk, Per Gallestrup, Vivien Garrett, Patrick Gatara, Ngethe Gitungo, Nils Giversen, Kate Green, Cyprien Hakiza, Nick Hardwick, Stephen Harley, Simon Haselock, Mohamed H. Hassan (Gudbaaye), Mohamed-Rashid Sheikh Hassan, Carole Hillenbrand, Kate Holt, 'Hotzi', Fiona Houston, Buster Howes, David Stewart Howitt, Nick Hughes, Oliver Lee, Iman Nur Icar, Richard Jermy, Hugo Macpherson, Justin Marozzi, Herbert Mensah, Dick Meryhew, Will Milliken, Hassan Mohamed (Harlesden), Abdirizaq Mohedin, Rob Murphy, Mohamed Mustafa (Harlesden), Poly Muriithi, Jo Nickolls, William Noblett, Simona Opitz, Paddy O'Kennedy, Abdulrahman Abdurahman Osman (Shuke), David Orr, Andy Pring, David Ramsbotham, Dido Rasso, Alex Renton, Ruth Renton, Phil Rees, Hugh Riddell, Mari Roberts, Abdi Roble, Doug Rutledge, Hashi Shafi, Allie Shah, Mary Sharpe, William Snook, Jeremy Stampa-Orwin, Jon Stephenson, David Stirling, Jason Straziuso, Steve Turner, Henry Vines, Doug Young and Sabah Yusuf.

This list is not exhaustive: I have deliberately left out the names of several people who may find themselves mentioned in the main text. The most important name of all, however, is that of my wife Melissa. Without her love, patience, and encouragement – and exceptional proof-reading skills – I could not have written this book.

Picture and Map Acknowledgements

All images have been supplied courtesy of the author unless otherwise stated. Every effort has been made to trace copyright holders. We apologize for any omissions in this respect and will be pleased to make the appropriate acknowledgments in future editions.

Maps

Somalia clan demography map based upon a CIA estimate only, as of 2002.

Section One

Page 1: Paul Lokech briefing © AMISOM. Page 2: Mogadishu street scene © Tim Freccia. Page 4: street fighting © AFP/Getty Images; al-Shabaab troops © Farah Abdi Warsameh/AP/Press Association Images. Page 5: children learning to shoot © AFP/Getty Images; children playing with toy guns © Farah Abdi Warsameh/AP/Press Association Images. Page 6: panoramic shot of Badbaado refugee camp © Farah Abdi Warsameh/AP/Press Association Images. Page 8: qat trader and Hargeisa money changers, both © AFP/Getty Images; Mogadishu marketplace © Farah Abdi Warsameh/AP/ Press Association Images.

Section Two

Index

451

INDEX